A Course Guide
to Accompany

THE NORTON ANTHOLOGY OF
AMERICAN LITERATURE

Third Edition

PUBLISHER'S NOTE

This Course Guide has been revised for use with *The Norton Anthology of American Literature*, Third Edition, Volumes 1 and 2.

For the convenience of teachers who wish to use "The Declaration of Sentiments" of the Seneca Falls Woman's Rights Convention in their classrooms, as occasionally suggested in this Guide, we have provided the text of that document—not readily available except in libraries—as an appendix. It may be photocopied and distributed to your students.

A Course Guide
to Accompany

THE NORTON ANTHOLOGY OF
AMERICAN LITERATURE

Third Edition

Marjorie Pryse, Ph.D., M.S.W.

W. W. Norton & Company
New York   London

ISBN 0-393-95742-X

W. W. Norton & Company, Inc.
500 Fifth Avenue, New York, N.Y. 10110

W. W. Norton & Company Ltd.
37 Great Russell Street, London WC1B 3NU

1 2 3 4 5 6 7 8 9 0

CONTENTS

A DETAILED CONTENTS LIST FOR VOLUME 1

A DETAILED CONTENTS LIST FOR VOLUME 2

1

THINKING ABOUT PLANNING A COURSE

Whether you are preparing to teach the American literature course for the first time or consider yourself well seasoned, perhaps you share my own experience that writing a syllabus takes art, and that you can often predetermine success—even before you have met your students—by making certain choices rather than others in the list and order of readings, and in the overall rationale for your course organization. How do you create a course outline that will guide, but not dictate, your students' approach to American literature, that will allow you a sense of mastery without precluding digression and idiosyncrasy, that will make it possible to manifest for your students the pleasures you find in any given work? Such a task brings out in me an enormous sense of challenge and possibility, as well as an awareness of my own human limitations. Individual students, academic requirements, the size and quality of the physical classroom, the extent to which any of us has autonomy in creating a syllabus, and the scheduled hour of the day or the days of the week any given course meets will all affect any attempt to achieve coherence and clarity by design. Still, the moment of planning in the ideal becomes part of the process of making American literature realizable for students who will themselves, once the course begins, become inevitably—and delightfully—real.

Reading the course guide can help you clarify your objectives in teaching American literature before you enter the classroom. Beyond the concerns we all share that we introduce students to "great works" and help them learn to read with appreciation, enjoyment, and understanding, what other goals are possible to achieve, particularly if you are teaching the course at the sophomore level to students for whom it is required? Students with certain major areas of concentration may find studying literature of less apparent benefit to their projected careers than liberal-arts majors do. Are there ways of teaching American literature that can help them perceive themselves as members of a larger society with a culture that includes them, and to see that their engagement in understanding that culture as literature records it is, therefore, essential to their lives? Many students expect to be "taught" American literature as if it were a body of finite knowledge to be assimilated with the rational part of the mind. Is it possible to create a course guide that will help them see literature itself as a way of knowing the world, as well as something itself to know, and, in the process, to rediscover or to find for the first time the capacity to develop their nonrational and nonlinear sensors—in effect, to make the very process of learning a significant part of what they learn?

In my own planning I begin with one basic goal in mind: to encourage students to read, think, speak, and write from within their own perspective as they simultaneously learn to place that perspective within a larger context, for it allows students to test their own responses and interpretations among a diverse group that can come to feel safe. But literature classrooms can also feel threatening, in particular to students who have arrived in college without, in effect, having learned how to read. For the American literature course, especially at the sophomore level, where I am most likely to draw students satisfying general education requirements, I try to write a course outline that will help them balance needs that appear to be in conflict—to write about the loved and familiar author, and to explore new and possibly more difficult works; to enjoy literature, and at the same time to take it seriously; to express their own response, and yet not risk being "wrong" or "stupid."

Over the years, I have tried three different models of course organization, will use each of them again, and have become convinced of the value of choosing some model. I have found that stating my awareness of where I want to go in defining, conserving, or debating aspects of American literary history or cultural heritage helps me read individual works with my students' eyes, knowing that the model of course organization will eventually demystify for them what initially appears to be the "boggy, soggy, squitchy picture" of American literature. They benefit from being able to see how and why I have selected the authors and readings that appear on their syllabus and from understanding that there is no single best way to make that selection.

Choosing a model of course organization can help your students use the coherence of an organizing principle as a way of extending the security of the known to writers they might otherwise find alien—because they write in a different century, out of an ethnic background other than the students' own, from the point of view of another gender, or by means of experimenting with language or genre. Younger students and students with previous difficulty in high school English courses obviously need more assistance in making the bridge between recognizing their own response to or interpretation of a literary work and learning how to locate that response against a spectrum of cultural understanding. But students at any level can doubt their own reading and can look to others—peers, the instructor, secondary materials in the library—to tell them how to think. The specific practical problem for us as we design our own individual course guides involves making those choices from the enticing array available in the *NAAL* that will encourage developmental reading and thinking in our students. How do we get them to learn to trust the authenticity of their own experience with the text and, at the same time, to want to know enough about history, about the aesthetic and linguistic choices writers make, and about what other readers in different times and places have thought about the same authors they are reading?

In the chapters that follow, I will describe the models of course organization that I have used to help students develop a conceptual framework for the study of American literature: the historical approach, the "major authors" approach, and the literary-traditions approach. What are the various reasons for choosing a certain model of course organization? Does one model work particularly well in a certain kind of classroom situation, given the class level and/or background you anticipate your students will have? How does a model allow detours as well as central focus? What are the advantages and special features of various rationales for course organization? How can you use each one to help students learn to think for themselves? Chapters 2 through 4 begin with general remarks that address these questions in light of each model. I encourage you to think through general considerations before you decide how to present the material in the text. If you are a teaching assistant or if you are teaching in a department that prescribes a certain way to teach the course, you may have less autonomy in creating a syllabus. Chapter 5, which suggests ways to use genre and theme as organizing principles, may help you work toward coherence, even if you are using a departmental syllabus that appears to lack it. Then, following each discussion, I offer sample lists of readings from the *NAAL* that illustrate the particular model of course organization or that categorize works by genre or theme. In each list I have tried to illustrate the range of choices available in the *NAAL;* however, you will need to narrow each list further in order to write a manageable course guide.

Chapter 6 provides some readings of individual authors and works arranged according to the chronology of authors in the text. In this chapter, I provide teaching notes, questions to stimulate discussion (or student writing), and commentary on historical periods. I intend that all of my commentary will either supplement the excellent period and headnote introductions in the anthology or will adapt some of that material for specific use in the classroom. Chapter 7 extends the teaching notes to include suggested exam and essay topics, arranged as general questions followed by questions about individual authors and texts. Following my chronological lists of questions, I include a second set designed to help anyone interested in teaching the course as a study of literary traditions developed by white and black women and white and black men. This set complements my description of this model of course organization in Chapter 4.

The format and content of this course guide deviate considerably from what you might expect to find in the standard "instructor's manual." Throughout, I have tried to keep in mind that we who use this anthology are teaching students, not established critics, although the patterns of feeling and analysis that students develop in our classrooms ought to lead them to greater critical sophistication. If this course guide helps you in any way, or if you can offer suggestions for its future revision, please write to me c/o W. W. Norton and Company.

—Marjorie Pryse

A NOTE TO READERS

Just as *The Norton Anthology of American Literature,* Third Edition, includes much new material, so does this revision of the course guide. Readers already familiar with my discussions of models or approaches to teaching American literature in Chapters 2 through 5 will find new material in Chapter 6, "Teaching Notes for Individual Periods, Authors, and Works," and Chapter 7, "Exam Questions and Essay Topics." In reworking entire sections of this guide, I wrote specifically for individuals who sent comments to Norton or directly to me concerning ways in which you have found the guide helpful. From Maine and Michigan, South Carolina and Kansas, even from Puerto Rico and Nova Scotia, those of you who have commented on the guide confirmed my sense of a community of teachers who share my concerns for integrating American literature into the total intellectual and emotional development of students. I was particularly cheered by the response of one colleague who packed the guide in her bags to go teach American literature to students in China and who commented afterward, "I would have been sunk without it," even though she wished that some of the exam questions had been more straightforward. (Unlike some varieties of teaching aids, this one does not include the answers to questions.)

Some of you may be curious about the professional context within which I am currently working with American literature. In the previous version of the course guide, I addressed readers from my position as associate professor at the University of Tennessee. Since that time, I have added clinical social work to my professional credentials, and, as part of my work with individuals and families, both at Parsons Child and Family Center in Albany, New York, and at nearby community mental health clinics, I have used thematically appropriate poetry from *NAAL* to supplement more traditional forms of therapy. Perhaps some subsequent version of the course guide will include notes on using *NAAL* with treatment groups or in other kinds of community "classrooms" that extend the applicability of American literature beyond the domain of departments of English.

—M.P.

2

THE HISTORICAL APPROACH

PLANNING THE COURSE

The *NAAL* is organized according to the chronology of the authors' birth dates, and most of us probably write schedules of required reading that are more or less chronological and basically follow the order presented in the anthology. But mere chronology does not produce a perspective on literary history, and many teachers would argue that it is impossible to understand literature without placing it in its historical context. The historical approach to teaching American literature makes room for students to ask questions that interest them about the writers' lives; about the ethnic, literary, geographical, and political environments within which they wrote; about the ideologies or religious beliefs that influenced their readers. It also makes it possible for the instructor to combine the breadth of a survey with the coherence of a conceptual framework.

The specific framework that I adopt in teaching the historical approach examines the unfolding of ideas that dominate our literary history. In teaching from Volume 1, I choose works that have a connection to specific historical events, and the events themselves can generally inform the presentation of readings on the syllabus, can provide a focus for background discussion, and can give students the basis for asking questions in class or for selecting essay topics. One advantage to this approach for the Volume 1 readings is that it allows students to place literary works in the context of the American history course they may also be taking, or have taken, as part of their general education requirements. In Volume 2, where American literature proliferates with such a variety of voices, themes, and degrees of connection to actual events, I focus on the development of an American literature itself and both the individual writers and the aesthetic movements that produced it as events of historical significance.

Such an approach does not have to be proscriptive, although the catalogue of "-isms" in the list of suggested works that follows may seem so to some teachers. The model offers the coherence of parallelism; many writers both before and after 1865 were influenced by prevailing assumptions, and although initially it may seem arbitrary to write a syllabus that eventually sets up Puritanism and modernism as equivalent terms (because they form parallel sections in the course organization), doing so can produce ongoing discussion in the classroom. What connections can students find, as they read specific works, between ideologies such as Puritanism and deism that suggest a world view, and others such as transcendentalism or realism that are more philosophical and aesthetic in their focus? At the same time, to what extent do particular writers enhance, subvert, or simply ignore the assumptions of their age?

Class discussion and analysis of individual texts can usefully challenge the apparent subordination of writers and works to categories on a syllabus or course guide. The historical model helps students see each successive "-ism" not as inevitable but rather as evolutionary change in the way people choose to express themselves, as well as what that choice tells us about how they think. The framework of the course organization can provide a boundary or a container for the course as well as a series of abstract distinctions that students will probably be only too delighted to help you dismantle. Puritanism, for example, becomes a useful umbrella concept in discussing many of the writers in the 1620–1820 period in the *NAAL*. However, the anthology includes many writers who had no relation to Puritan thinking in that period—and others, with Hawthorne being the notable example, in later periods who continue to examine Puritan thinking in their works. How, then, can students learn to modify their understanding of Puritanism as a controlling idea in American literature? Similarly, coming to terms with the concept of modernism can help students understand a lot of the thematic and aesthetic choices writers make in the 1914–1945 period. But what happens to the concept if you ask students to consider the "modernism" of Whitman and Dickinson? or to try to explain the persistence of interest in traditional themes and lyric forms in many poets from the modern period?

The historical approach certainly requires that the teacher be a course guide—and yet one of the fascinations in presenting American literature this way is that it gives each of us the opportunity to ask questions about the development of American writing that we may not have thought about when we were students. Why *does* "The Declaration of Independence" have the power it has?— just because we were taught to hold it sacred? How might certain works thought to influence the course of history—such as Thomas Paine's *Common Sense*, Harriet Beecher Stowe's *Uncle Tom's Cabin*, or W. E. B. DuBois's *The Souls of Black Folk*—have influenced us had we been their contemporaries? And if, as the chronological development of American literature past or post-modernism may seem to imply to students, we should all have been exposed to modernist thinking and writing, why do some of us still think, write, or read as Puritans or eighteenth-century people? To what extent does our national literature speak for all of us, and to what extent does it record the evolution in thinking of a very few? Do any students sense that they are in the process of evolutionary change in the present moment? Does critical thinking promote such change? How do individual readers give themselves over to the pleasure of reading American texts and still maintain the philosophical and political distance they need in order to develop their own ways of thinking? Conversely, does the goal of developing a conceptual view work against the experience of reading for pleasure? (Is the notion of a conceptual framework, which implies rational abstraction, the ultimate form of "escapist" reading?) The historical approach leads to these and many other questions and, in my own experience, helps students become deeply engaged in American texts. This model of course organization helps undergraduate students explore the possibility that what they are reading may have essential significance. It helps them find their own place, at any given point in time, in the history of American expression as our literature reflects that history.

SUGGESTED READINGS

VOLUME 1

1620–1820

Puritan Writers

John Winthrop, "A Model of Christian Charity"
William Bradford, from *Of Plymouth Plantation*, esp. "The Mayflower Compact"
Anne Bradstreet, esp. "The Prologue," "Contemplations," "The Flesh and the Spirit," "The Author to Her Book," "Here Follows Some Verses upon the Burning of Our House," "As Weary Pilgrim," "Meditations Divine and Moral"
Michael Wigglesworth, "The Day of Doom"
Mary Rowlandson, "A Narrative of Captivity and Restoration of Mrs. Mary Rowlandson"
Edward Taylor, esp. "Psalm Two," "Prologue" and individual lyrics from *Preparatory Meditations*, "The Preface" from *God's Determinations*, "The Joy of Church Fellowship Rightly Attended," "Upon Wedlock, and Death of Children," "Huswifery," "A Fig for Thee, Oh! Death"
Samuel Sewall, "The Diary of Samuel Sewall"
Cotton Mather, from *The Wonders of the Invisible World*, "The Life of William Bradford" and "The Life of John Winthrop" from *Magnalia Christi Americana*, and "Bonifacius"

"Other" Colonial Writers

Thomas Morton, from "New English Canaan"

Robert Beverley, from *The History and Present State of Virginia*

William Byrd, "The Secret Diary of William Byrd of Westover"

Elizabeth Ashbridge, *Some Account of the Fore-Part of the Life of Elizabeth Ashbridge*

John Woolman, from *The Journal of John Woolman*

The Puritan Vision under Siege

Jonathan Edwards, "Personal Narrative," "A Divine and Supernatural Light," "Letter to Rev. Dr. Benjamin Colman," "Sinners in the Hands of an Angry God"

Federalism and the Deist Vision

Benjamin Franklin, "The Way to Wealth," "An Edict by the King of Prussia," "Information to Those Who Would Remove to America," "Remarks Concerning the Savages of North America," *The Autobiography*

John Adams and Abigail Adams, Letters

Thomas Paine, from *Common Sense*, "The Crisis, No. 1," from *The Age of Reason*

Thomas Jefferson, "The Declaration of Independence," from "Notes on the State of Virginia," letters to Peter Carr (concerning "A Young Man's Education") and Nathaniel Burwell (concerning "Women's Education")

Philip Freneau, "On the Emigration to America and Peopling the Western Country," "The Wild Honey Suckle," "The Indian Burying Ground," "On the Religion of Nature"

Royall Tyler, *The Contrast*

The Issue of Slavery

William Byrd, from "The Secret Diary of William Byrd of Westover"

John Woolman, from *The Journal of John Woolman*

St. Jean de Crèvecoeur, "Letter IX" from *Letters from an American Farmer*

Thomas Jefferson, "The Declaration of Independence"

Olaudah Equiano, *The Interesting Narrative of the Life of Olaudah Equiano, or, Gustavus Vassa, the African, Written by Himself*

Philip Freneau, "To Sir Toby"

Phillis Wheatley, "On Being Brought from Africa to America," "To the University of Cambridge, in New England," "Thoughts on the Works of Providence, "To S.M., a Young African Painter, on Seeing His Works"

1820–1865

The New Americanness of American Literature

Washington Irving, "Rip Van Winkle"
James Fenimore Cooper, from "Notions of the Americans"
William Cullen Bryant, "Thanatopsis," "The Prairies," "The Poet"
Ralph Waldo Emerson, "The American Scholar," "The Divinity School Address," "Self-Reliance," "The Poet"
Nathaniel Hawthorne, "Young Goodman Brown," "The May-Pole of Merry Mount," "The Minister's Black Veil," *The Scarlet Letter*
Edgar Allan Poe, poems, esp. "The Raven" and "Annabel Lee," and "Ligeia," "The Fall of the House of Usher," "The Philosophy of Composition"
Herman Melville, "Hawthorne and His Mosses," "The Town-Ho's Story" from *Moby-Dick*, "Bartleby, the Scrivener," *Billy Budd, Sailor*

American Transcendentalism

Ralph Waldo Emerson, *Nature*
Henry David Thoreau, *Walden*

Literature of the House Divided

Abraham Lincoln, "A House Divided," "Address Delivered at the Dedication of the Cemetery at Gettysburg"
Margaret Fuller, from "The Great Lawsuit"
Harriet Beecher Stowe, "The Mother's Struggle" from *Uncle Tom's Cabin*
Henry David Thoreau, "Resistance to Civil Government," "Slavery in Massachusetts," "A Plea for Captain John Brown"
Frederick Douglass, *Narrative of the Life of Frederick Douglass, an American Slave*
Walt Whitman, poems from *Drum-Taps*
Herman Melville, "The Paradise of Bachelors and The Tartarus of Maids," poems from *Battle-Pieces*
Elizabeth Drew Stoddard, "Lemorne *versus* Huell"
Emily Dickinson, esp. the poems about being starved, silenced, constricted, or alienated: 49, 125, 185, 187, 241, 258, 303, 305, 348, 435, 441, 510, 536, 547, 640, 709, 754, 824, 1099, 1129, 1138, 1400, 1545, 1575
Rebecca Harding Davis, "Life in the Iron-Mills"

Democratic Vistas

Abraham Lincoln, "Second Inaugural Address"
Walt Whitman, "Preface to *Leaves of Grass*," "Song of Myself," "Letter to Ralph Waldo Emerson," "From Pent-up Aching Rivers," "Facing West from California's Shores," "Scented Herbage of My Breast" from *Calamus,* "Crossing Brooklyn Ferry," "Out of the Cradle Endlessly Rocking" and "As I Ebb'd with the Ocean of Life" from *Sea-Drift,* "When Lilacs Last in the Dooryard Bloom'd" and "The Sleepers," "A Noiseless Patient Spider" from *Whispers of Heavenly Death,* from *Democratic Vistas*
Emily Dickinson, esp. the poems about struggle, triumph, and vision: 67, 214, 249, 280, 303, 315, 322, 328, 341, 448, 465, 501, 505, 528, 632, 712, 822, 1540, 1593, 1651, 1670, 1732

VOLUME 2

1865–1914

Regionalism and "Local Color" Writing

Bret Harte, "The Outcasts of Poker Flat"
Joel Chandler Harris, "The Wonderful Tar-Baby Story," "Mr. Rabbit Grossly Deceives Mr. Fox," "Free Joe and the Rest of the World"
Sarah Orne Jewett, "A White Heron," "The Foreigner"
Mary E. Wilkins Freeman, "A New England Nun," "The Revolt of Mother"
Charles W. Chesnutt, "The Goophered Grapevine"
Hamlin Garland, "Under the Lion's Paw"
Gertrude Simmons Bonnin (Zitkala-Sä), "Impressions of an Indian Childhood," "The School Days of an Indian Girl," "An Indian Teacher among Indians"

Realism

Samuel Clemens, *Adventures of Huckleberry Finn,* "The War Prayer," "Letter IV"
W. D. Howells, "Novel-Writing and Novel Reading," "Editha"
Ambrose Bierce, "Chickamauga"
Henry James, "Daisy Miller, *The Turn of the Screw,* "The Beast in the Jungle," "The Art of Fiction"
Edith Wharton, *Ethan Frome,* "The Other Two"

Naturalism

Samuel Clemens, "The Man That Corrupted Hadleyburg"
Kate Chopin, *The Awakening*

Booker T. Washington, from *Up from Slavery*
Charlotte Perkins Gilman, "The Yellow Wallpaper"
Jane Addams, from *Twenty Years at Hull-House*
W.E.B. DuBois, from *The Souls of Black Folk*
Frank Norris, "Suggestions," "[Truth and Accuracy]," "Vandover and the Brute"
Stephen Crane, "An Experiment in Misery," "The Open Boat," "The Blue Hotel," "An Episode of War"
Theodore Dreiser, "The Strike" from *Sister Carrie*, "Old Rogaum and His Theresa"
Jack London, "The Law of Life"
Henry Adams, from *The Education of Henry Adams*

1914–1945

Thematic Modernism

I have found certain writers and works more teachable than others in presenting the 1914–1945 period historically, and choose these as focal points for our reading and discussion. At the sophomore level in particular, I emphasize thematic links between these writers in order to convey how it feels to write with a modernist sensibility.

Willa Cather, "My Mortal Enemy," "Neighbour Rosicky"
Gertrude Stein, *The Good Anna*
Robert Frost, poems, esp. "Mending Wall," "The Death of the Hired Man," "After Apple-Picking," "An Old Man's Winter Night," "The Oven Bird," "Birches," "'Out, Out—,'" "Nothing Gold Can Stay," "Stopping by Woods on a Snowy Evening," "Two Tramps in Mud Time," "Desert Places," "Design," "Neither out Far nor in Deep," "The Gift Outright," "Directive," "The Figure a Poem Makes"
Sherwood Anderson, from *Winesburg, Ohio*, "The Egg"
Wallace Stevens, esp. "Sunday Morning," "Anecdote of the Jar," "A High-toned Old Christian Woman," "The Snow Man," "The Emperor of Ice-Cream," "Thirteen Ways of Looking at a Blackbird," "The Idea of Order at Key West," "Of Modern Poetry"
William Carlos Williams, "Portrait of a Lady," "The Widow's Lament in Springtime," "Spring and All," "To Elsie," "The Red Wheelbarrow," "The Wind Increases," "Death," "This Is Just to Say," "The Dead Baby," "Classic Scene," "The Term," "A Sort of a Song," "The Dance," "Lear," "Landscape with the Fall of Icarus"
Robinson Jeffers, "Boats in a Fog," "Shine, Perishing Republic," "Hurt Hawks," "November Surf," "Carmel Point"
T. S. Eliot, "The Love Song of J. Alfred Prufrock," "Tradition and the Individual Talent," "The Hollow Men"

Eugene O'Neill, *Long Day's Journey into Night*

Katherine Anne Porter, *Old Mortality*

E. E. Cummings, poems, esp. "Buffalo Bill's," "the Cambridge ladies who live in furnished souls," "Poem, or Beauty Hurts Mr. Vinal," "nobody loses all the time," "'next to of course america i,'" "i sing of Olaf glad and big," "anyone lived in a pretty how town," "pity this busy monster, manunkind"

Jean Toomer, from *Cane*

F. Scott Fitzgerald, "Winter Dreams"

William Faulkner, *As I Lay Dying*, "Barn Burning"

Ernest Hemingway, "The Snows of Kilimanjaro"

Langston Hughes, poems, esp. "The Negro Speaks of Rivers," "Mother to Son," "Dream Variations," "Young Gal's Blues," "Morning After," "Trumpet Player"

Formal and Technical Aspects of Modernism

In an upper-division class or with a particularly motivated group of sophomores, I also include selections from the following list of works that illustrate formal and technical aspects of modernism.

Gertrude Stein, from *The Making of Americans*

Ezra Pound, poems, esp. "A Pact," "In a Station of the Metro," "Villanelle: The Psychological Hour," and from *The Cantos*

H.D., "Oread," "Leda," "At Baia," "Helen," "Fragment 113," from *The Walls Do Not Fall*

Marianne Moore, "The Past Is the Present," "To a Snail," "New York," "Poetry," "The Fish" "The Student," "Bird-Witted," "The Mind Is an Enchanting Thing"

T. S. Eliot, "The Waste Land," "Burnt Norton"

John Dos Passos, from *The Big Money*

Hart Crane, poems, esp. "Chaplinesque," "At Melville's Tomb," *The Bridge*

Traditional Poetry, Other Perspectives, and Humor

At both the sophomore and upper-division levels, I examine other writers who deal with more traditional themes and forms, whose work illustrates perspectives other than the modernist one, or who choose humor as a way of dealing with modern life. In any given course, I choose a few writers from the following list:

Black Elk
Edgar Lee Masters
Ellen Glasgow
Carl Sandburg
Elinor Wylie

John Crowe Ransom
Zora Neale Hurston
Edna St. Vincent Millay
Dorothy Parker
James Thurber
E. B. White
Allen Tate
Thomas Wolfe

AMERICAN PROSE SINCE 1945

Each of you will have your own reasons for making the choices you do in the post-1945 period. Rather than apply historical labels to contemporary writers, I choose a few who suggest the various traditions representative of twentieth-century literature. For a discussion of how to organize the entire course as a study of literary traditions, see Chapter 4. In any given course, I choose from among the following:

Black Writers

Ralph Ellison, from *Invisible Man*
James Baldwin, from *The Fire Next Time*
Adrienne Kennedy, *A Movie Star Has to Star in Black and White*
Alice Walker, "Everyday Use"

Southern Writers

Eudora Welty, "Petrified Man"
Peter Taylor, "What You Hear from 'Em?"
Flannery O'Connor, "The Life You Save May Be Your Own," "Good Country People"
Bobbie Ann Mason, "Drawing Names"
Alice Walker, "Everyday Use"

Jewish Writers

Bernard Malamud, "The Magic Barrel"
Saul Bellow, *Seize the Day*
Philip Roth, "Defender of the Faith"

Dramatists

Tennessee Williams, *A Streetcar Named Desire*
Arthur Miller, *Death of a Salesman*

Adrienne Kennedy, *A Movie Star Has to Star in Black and White*

Sam Shepard, *True West*

New Yorker Writers

John Cheever, "The Country Husband"
John Updike, "The Happiest I've Been," "Separating"
Robert Stone, "Helping"
Bobbie Ann Mason, "Drawing Names"
Ann Beattie, "Weekend"

Experimental or "Postmodernist" Writers

Vladimir Nabokov, from *Pnin*
Jack Kerouac, from *On the Road*
Norman Mailer, "The Man Who Studied Yoga," from *The Armies of the Night*
John Barth, "Life-Story"
Thomas Pynchon, from *The Crying of Lot 49*

Native American Writers

Leslie Marmon Silko, "Lullaby"
Louise Erdrich, "Lulu's Boys"

AMERICAN POETRY SINCE 1945

Grouping Individual Poets

In presenting the contemporary poetry included in the *NAAL*, I have sometimes chosen a few poets who offer a variety of themes, techniques, and traditions and asked students to read all of the included selections. Two possible groupings include:

(1) Robert Penn Warren
Elizabeth Bishop
Robert Lowell
Adrienne Rich
Imamu Amiri Baraka

(2) Theodore Roethke
John Berryman
Gwendolyn Brooks
James Wright
Sylvia Plath

<u>Presenting Individual Poems</u>

More often, I choose an array of individual poems, some of which we analyze closely in class; others become the basis for student writing. I know that the following poems engage students in detailed discussion because I have taught them; no doubt you have successfully used others as the basis for extended analysis.

Theodore Roethke, "My Papa's Waltz"
Elizabeth Bishop, "In the Waiting Room," "The Moose," "One Art"
Randall Jarrell, "The Death of the Ball Turret Gunner," "Well Water"
John Berryman, *Dream Songs*, esp. 1, 14, 40
Robert Lowell, "Memories of West Street and Lepke," "Skunk Hour," "For the Union Dead"
Gwendolyn Brooks, "Kitchenette Building," "A Song in the Front Yard
Allen Ginsberg, "Howl"
James Wright, "Autumn Begins in Martin's Ferry, Ohio," "A Blessing," "A Finch Sitting out a Windstorm"
Anne Sexton, "Sylvia's Death"
Adrienne Rich, "A Valediction Forbidding Mourning," "Diving into the Wreck," from "Twenty-One Love Poems," esp. XI, XIX, and "The Floating Poem"
Sylvia Plath, "Lady Lazarus," "Daddy"
Imamu Amiri Baraka, "An Agony. As Now."
Rita Dove, from *Thomas and Beulah*

3

THE "MAJOR AUTHORS" APPROACH

PLANNING THE COURSE

Presenting the American literature course as a study of single figures or "major authors" makes it possible to read more of each writer's work, to spend more class time discussing each writer, and to encourage in the students more sustained rumination, contemplation, and appreciation of each writer. This approach does not have to eliminate the historical context or the literary history within which any given writer wrote—although the course design does emphasize the development of each writer's individual career and relegates historical and cultural context to the background. The *NAAL* does provide excellent period introductions and headnotes for each writer in the anthology, and requiring students in the "major authors" course to read these can supply much of the contextual information they will need without requiring you to schedule class time for it.

The "major authors" model of course organization works particularly well as the middle course in a three-tiered curriculum, where first-year students may have already taken an "Introduction to Literature" course and where upper-division students will be required to study several literary periods in detail. The "major authors" course can allow students to read more of writers they have become acquainted with, either in high school or in the first-year course, and, at the same time, can increase their desire to read other writers who were contemporaries of major figures or who wrote in the same genre or literary tradition. If the American literature course is likely to be the last literature course many of your students will take, then your choice of the "major authors" model may be more complicated. Among my own colleagues who have debated the question, in a university where many of our students will probably not go on to take upper-division courses in literature, some advocate giving students more exposure to fewer writers in the hope that they will discover a love for reading. Others argue that students are more likely to do so if they read a wider variety of authors and understand the way literature is connected to history.

As part of writing a course guide for a "major authors" course, you might find it useful to think through some of your own criteria for "major." Some of the works we might casually use to explain our choices of certain writers over others—"great," "universal," "enduring," the word "major" itself—can actually obscure the process of literary evaluation. The "major authors" course highlights this process. How does an author become "major"? Who decides? Is the question open to debate? Is there a "dictionary" of "major authors" that establishes the criteria for inclusion, or does the inclusion of any particular author reflect the opinions of readers over time, and, if so, which readers? Why do there appear to be so many "major authors" in one period (such as 1820–1865), and so few in others (such as 1620–1820)? Where are the authors not included in the anthology? Can we be certain that we would not consider any of them major? One of the ways of opening up the question of literary evaluation implied in the design of the "major authors" model is to allow students to choose any of their favorite authors not already on the syllabus— and perhaps not included in the anthology—and to write an essay in which they struggle with the author's literary value. Does a student's literary taste reflect on his or her own value? And what is literary taste? Are some people born with it? Can it be learned? Asking questions like these throughout the course can help dispel one disadvantage to teaching by means of the "major authors" model: that the course design can have the effect of predetermining student taste and limiting students' ability to ask evaluative questions on their own.

In choosing selections for my own "major authors" course, I have tried to examine what the concept means. I have defined writers as "major" if they satisfy more than one of the following conditions:

(1) appeal to a wide variety of readers

(2) wrote works that influenced more than one other major author

(3) contributed an acknowledged "masterpiece" to American literature

(4) sustained a literary career beyond a single tour de force

(5) were pioneers or innovators in subject matter, literary tradition, technique, or genre

(6) have been recognized as major literary critics or historians.

Applying these criteria to the writers in the *NAAL* can help with a preliminary list of possible "major authors" to include in the American literature course, and being selective in the number or length of works you assign by any given author will make room for more figures. The list that follows offers my own suggestions for a "major authors" syllabus. I have included a second list of authors who might be considered "major minor" writers, if we add at least the following criterion, that the writers have:

(7) found literary expression for a particularly unique perception or experience.

The language of "major authors" and "major minor authors" itself contributes to confusion for students. We need to distinguish between "major" as it implies "significant" and as it is often used to mean "mainstream." If the space allotted to black male writers and black and white women writers in the *NAAL* can be used as a yardstick here, those particular literary historians and critics who edited the *NAAL* have identified several black and female authors as "major." And the list of "major minor" writers includes several white men. Perhaps one of the ultimate challenges in teaching the "major authors" course is helping students break down any associations they may have that "major" always equals "white" or "male" and that women or black writers, because they appear as a numerical minority in the *NAAL*, are always "minor" writers.

A related semantic problem is the hierarchy implied by the terms "major" and "minor." While it might make sense to argue that certain writers "dominated" particular literary centers or circles, the language of dominance ceases to have meaning when we apply it to literary works themselves. Does "The Raven" dominate over *Uncle Tom's Cabin*? In teaching by means of the "major authors" model, I find myself continually working to correct the impression students have that literary evaluation resembles an athletic contest. Wherever possible, given the representation of works in the anthology, I try to design the course as a series of single authors, and I include some of my favorite noncanonical writers. Nothing tests the concept of "major authors" like the inclusion of a few good literary works that appear to satisfy none of the criteria for "greatness." In a third list, I suggest a few of these.

SUGGESTED READINGS

VOLUME 1

1620–1820

> Anne Bradstreet
> Edward Taylor
> Jonathan Edwards
> Benjamin Franklin, including *The Autobiography*

1820–1865

> Ralph Waldo Emerson, including *Nature*
> Nathaniel Hawthorne, including *The Scarlet Letter*

Henry David Thoreau, including *Walden*
Frederick Douglass, including *Narrative of the Life of Frederick Douglass, an American Slave*
Walt Whitman
Herman Melville, including *Billy Budd, Sailor*
Emily Dickinson

VOLUME 2

1865–1914

Samuel Clemens, including *Adventures of Huckleberry Finn*
Henry James
Edith Wharton

1914–1945

Robert Frost
Wallace Stevens
T. S. Eliot
Eugene O'Neill
William Faulkner
Langston Hughes

AMERICAN PROSE SINCE 1945

Tennessee Williams
Bernard Malamud
Ralph Ellison
Saul Bellow
Arthur Miller
Flannery O'Connor
Sam Shepard
Alice Walker
Ann Beattie

AMERICAN POETRY SINCE 1945

Robert Lowell
Robert Penn Warren
Gwendolyn Brooks
James Wright
Adrienne Rich

SOME "MAJOR MINOR" WRITERS

VOLUME 1

1620–1820

> William Bradford
> Thomas Jefferson

1820–1865

> Washington Irving
> Edgar Allan Poe
> Harriet Beecher Stowe

VOLUME 2

1865–1914

> W. D. Howells
> Sarah Orne Jewett
> Kate Chopin
> Mary E. Wilkins Freeman
> Charles W. Chesnutt
> Stephen Crane
> Theodore Dreiser
> Henry Adams

1914–1945

> Willa Cather
> Gertrude Stein
> Sherwood Anderson
> William Carlos Williams
> Ezra Pound
> H.D.
> Marianne Moore
> Katherine Anne Porter
> Zora Neale Hurston
> F. Scott Fitzgerald
> Ernest Hemingway
> Hart Crane
> Richard Wright

AMERICAN PROSE SINCE 1945

Eudora Welty
Norman Mailer
Alice Walker

AMERICAN POETRY SINCE 1945

Theodore Roethke
Charles Olson
Robert Hayden
Elizabeth Bishop
John Berryman
Denise Levertov
A. R. Ammons
James Merrill
John Ashbery
Anne Sexton
Sylvia Plath
Audre Lorde
Imamu Amiri Baraka

WORKS BY NONCANONICAL WRITERS WORTH EVALUAT-ING IN A "MAJOR AUTHORS" COURSE

VOLUME 1

1620–1820

Michael Wigglesworth, "The Day of Doom"
Mary Rowlandson, "A Narrative of the Captivity and Restoration of Mrs. Mary Rowlandson"
Thomas Paine, from *Common Sense* or "The Crisis, No. 1"
Phillis Wheatley, poems
Royall Tyler, *The Contrast*

1820–1865

William Cullen Bryant, "The Prairies"
Margaret Fuller, from "The Great Lawsuit"
Harriet Beecher Stowe, "The Minister's Housekeeper"
Rebecca Harding Davis, "Life in the Iron-Mills"

VOLUME 2

1865–1914

Bret Harte, "The Outcasts of Poker Flat"
Ambrose Bierce, "Chickamauga"
Joel Chandler Harris, tales
Booker T. Washington, "The Atlanta Exposition Address"
Hamlin Garland, "Under the Lion's Paw"
Charlotte Perkins Gilman, "The Yellow Wallpaper"
W. E. B. DuBois, from *The Souls of Black Folk*
Frank Norris, from *Vandover and the Brute*

1914–1945

Black Elk
Edgar Lee Masters, poems
Zora Neale Hurston
Dorothy Parker, essays
E. E. Cummings, poems
Jean Toomer, from *Cane*
Thomas Wolfe, "The Lost Boy"

AMERICAN PROSE SINCE 1945

John Cheever, "The Country Husband"
Jack Kerouac, from *On the Road*
James Baldwin, from *The Fire Next Time*
John Updike, "The Happiest I've Been" or "Separating"
Philip Roth, "Defender of the Faith"
Thomas Pynchon, from *The Crying of Lot 49*
Robert Stone, "Helping"
Leslie Marmon Silko, "Lullaby"

AMERICAN POETRY SINCE 1945

Randall Jarrell, poems
Richard Wilbur, poems
Richard Hugo, poems
Robert Creeley, poems
Gary Snyder, poems

4

THE LITERARY-TRADITIONS APPROACH

PLANNING THE COURSE

Implicit in the framework of the literary-traditions approach is a certain plurality: students will study more than one tradition, because American literature as we know it in the twentieth century combines several. The format of the course requires evaluative choice, but in a different way than either the historical or the "major authors" approach. Instead of initially dealing with writers either as part of a historical period or as single figures, you must decide instead which literary traditions you want to include, and which authors best represent those traditions. In doing so each of us engages in the process of defining which literary traditions are more "major" than others; and, at the same time, in presenting the development of various traditions, we will be locating that development historically.

The *NAAL* offers the central figures and at least a representative selection from major works in each of the following literary traditions: white male (and predominantly eastern); black male; white female; and southern. Also represented in the *NAAL* are works that might be used to begin a discussion of black-female and the twentieth-century–immigrant or Jewish traditions, and a tradition that we might describe as labor, protest, or populist literature. In effect, the text is a statement that certain literary traditions are more "major" than others. If you wish to supplement the text in order to expand the offerings in the black- and white-female literary traditions, and if your course budget allows it, you might consider using the *NALW* (*The Norton Anthology of Literature by Women*, edited by Sandra M. Gilbert and Susan Gubar) along with the *NAAL*. Among the lists that follow this discussion, I will include some suggestions from the *NALW*.

The literary-traditions approach raises the very questions of literary tradition: How does any given tradition begin? What other writers influence the tradition? How do historical or social events contribute to or inhibit the formation and development of the tradition? Is the tradition imitative or self-defined? What are its distinctive genres? Who are its major figures? What are its central themes? What is its contribution to the concept of American literature itself? What is its relation to oral or folk traditions? What formal or cultural or thematic connections exist between any two literary traditions? And how do we define the boundaries of single traditions in American literature? To what extent does any given American writer express a self-conscious sense of inclusion within or exclusion from a particular literary tradition? Is the concept of literary tradition (and the concept of a plurality of literary traditions) invented by the writer or by the student- or teacher-critic? And to what extent is the concept of literary tradition useful as a way of providing the context for either writing or studying American literature? In my own brief listing of various literary traditions included in the *NAAL*, I have implied that racial or ethnic origin, regional identity, gender, and class experience define boundaries or categories of authors and works. Are there some writers who defy categorization—either by their own disclaimers or by their thematic concerns? (Frequently, for example, minority writers will ask not to be considered "minority" at all, but simply "writers.") Are there some writers who belong to more than one literary tradition in such a way as to call into question the usefulness of the very concept of literary tradition? (Black women writers, in particular, may belong to several literary traditions at once.) And after we have examined the disparate parts that form the whole of American literature, does it still make any sense at all to talk about an American literary tradition?

The pedagogical method I employ in teaching the course by means of the literary-traditions approach expresses a general faith in the usefulness of analysis: that after dividing and examining the parts of American literature, and spending class time discussing them, we will then be in a position to view American literature as a complex interweaving and unfolding of disparate threads and literary voices, and that the result of the separate analysis will be an integrated vision for students. Including a discussion of contemporary literature—and the question of whether contemporary works also form a literary tradition is an interesting one—is crucial to helping students achieve this integrated vision. The *NAAL* offers a wide variety of contemporary authors and works that demonstrate the influence of various literary traditions on each other. Here you can also ask students to think about how the contemporary writers and works they know from leisure reading (whether or not these are represented in the *NAAL*) are also the products of an American literature that is increasingly pluralistic. Some students also write creatively. Do these students view themselves as part of a literary tradition? Are they conscious of writing, say, as southerners or as white women? And do other aspects of their lives carry such an influence on personal voice in their writing as to seem yet other categories that might define literary traditions? (Are they conscious, for example, of writing as students, or as lesbians, or as Vietnam veterans?)

The approach raises the fundamental question of the universal. Without denying the existence of human commonalities that cross boundaries of ethnic, gender, or regional perspectives, the implied pluralism of the literary-traditions approach may challenge the existence of any given central point of view by which many of your students define their own value and identity. Without question, such an approach shifts the center of classroom discourse away from the white male tradition, challenges the concept of "mainstream," and invites new questions. The experience of reading as central and integral to a literary tradition what literary historians may have referred to as "minor" or "minority" writers may be initially disconcerting to students who identify themselves as members of a cultural "mainstream," who value "universals" in literature, or who insist that "humanism" ought to erase boundaries of ethnic, gender, regional, or class identity. Perhaps it is particularly difficult for white students in the eighteen-to-twenty-two age group to participate in an intellectual process that will require them to view from a "minority" perspective at a time in their lives when they are trying to achieve their own intellectual and emotional maturity (their "majority").

But even white male authors in American literature have written some of their best work from within the perspective of marginality. In *The Mark and the Knowledge: Social Stigma in Classic American Fiction* (Ohio State University Press, 1979), I examined works by Hawthorne, Melville, Faulkner, and Ellison to show how American writers often achieve their capacity for vision through the experience of feeling marked, alienated, or stigmatized. In the 1980s, when relatively few undergraduates in the general American-literature classroom will be planning to choose English or any other field in the humanities as a college major (viewing their own creative writing, if they do any, as a hobby), anyone who commits herself or himself to writing will already seem to your students, by that choice, to be marginal. In the white male tradition, writers such as Hawthorne, Thoreau, Whitman, Clemens, and many others suggest that beginning in the nineteenth century, being a writer was itself enough to marginalize an American white man. (Among the lists that follow, I will include writers and works that develop themes of marginality among white male writers.)

You might want to discuss the differences between, for example, Thoreau's choice to write from the isolation of Walden Pond and to embrace eccentricity, and Douglass's imposed position and perspective as slave and, later in his *Narrative*, as heroic fugitive. For white men, choosing marginality often helps them focus their individual vision. But they begin with a sense of their literary authority that minority writers do not share. Minority writers, on the other hand, must somehow transcend the apparent limitations of marginality—that they do not see themselves as possessing literary authority, and that, instead, they feel silenced by white male culture—in order to write at all. Who knows what individual writers within minority literary traditions might have accomplished in American literary history without the burden of social stigma? In the literary traditions of black male and female writers, Charles Chesnutt and Zora Neale Hurston are extremely significant figures, for both of these writers were able to locate some other source than the Christian god for their own creativity. For both Chesnutt and Hurston, writing out of the perspective of black folk life allowed them to imagine a source for storytelling authority that was accessible to them—in particular, through the traditional figure of the storytelling conjure woman or conjure man in the black community—and thereby to disengage the silencing function of Puritan and patriarchal typology. As the white writer Joel Chandler Harris recorded, in the Uncle Remus tales of the 1880s and 1890s (represented in the *NAAL*), black people on the southern plantation well before Emancipation were prolific oral storytellers and kept alive the traditions of African folklore.

Engaging your students in a comparative discussion of the sources of literary authority available to white male writers and to writers from other traditions represented by American literature can help them break pervasive associations inherited from the Puritans that only white males have the authority to speak—for others, as well as for themselves. It can also lead them to think in new ways about their own nascent authority—as thinkers, speakers, and writers in the classroom. When they see black and white female authors finding the power to speak, they find the models they may need to break down their own passivity. Instructors often find themselves perplexed by the lack of interest their students express toward the literature they are "forced" to read because the American-literature course may be satisfying one of their graduation requirements. The classroom discussion that results when students consider the struggle for expression in others can ease the isolation and alienation white women and minority students often feel, and it can dissolve for all of your students their indifference to literary study. Students—whatever their gender or ethnic origin—learn to see cultural power as something they may not necessarily inherit, but may discover in themselves.

In the lists that follow, I have chosen writers and works that illustrate the development of several literary traditions. Within each tradition, I have evaluated writers only against each other. This process eliminates the necessity of weighing the relative significance of, say, Zora Neale Hurston and Ernest Hemingway. You may need to choose among Faulkner, Fitzgerald, and Hemingway because of the limitations of classroom time, but you can reserve the question of Hurston's influence for that part of your course set aside for studying the black female tradition. Within the tradition of literature by white males, you may want to discuss different choices of genre, perhaps even dividing the reading into subtraditions (I will offer some notes on teaching genre in Chapter 5).

You may also need to decide in what order to present the traditions on the syllabus. If you choose to begin with the white male tradition, will that have the effect of once again setting up white male experience as the norm, all others as marginal? White women and black men and women have written in full awareness of the literary standards established by white men, and one way to organize the course is to remain roughly chronological, then to discuss literary traditions that emerge as significant. This allows you to make specific connections between writers from different traditions who wrote at about the same time, as well as to create a literary context within each tradition that will help students avoid setting minority writers against white male writers.

Another way to organize the syllabus is to group writers for periodic discussion. Early readings can introduce students to those writers who establish origins or are early figures in several literary traditions: William Bradford or Edward Taylor, Anne Bradstreet, Phillis Wheatley, and Frederick Douglass. Later, you may group polemical or political writers from several traditions: Jonathan Edwards and Thomas Jefferson, Margaret Fuller, Booker T. Washington, and W. E. B. DuBois. (If you have decided to supplement with the *NALW*, you may also include Elizabeth Cady Stanton and Sojourner Truth here.) At any point in the course, you may group writers from several traditions according to theme (see my lists in Chapter 5).

One specific grouping that I have used on the first day of class to set the tone of the course involves the following lyric poems: Robert Frost, "The Gift Outright," in which Frost writes ostensibly as an American poet but clearly, also, from the perspective of the white male writer (in the way he feminizes the land and makes it the task of the writer to "surrender" himself to her and to correct her "unstoried, artless, unenhanced" condition); Gwendolyn Brooks, "Kitchenette Building," in which she suggests that being poor in Bronzeville, the fictional black neighborhood of the collection of poems in which "Kitchenette Building" first appeared, makes it difficult to "send up" a dream "through onion fumes" and "yesterday's garbage ripening in the hall"; Langston Hughes, "Dream Variations," in which Hughes expresses the black poet's desire to "whirl and to dance," and "to fling my arms wide / In the face of the sun," as a way of making art out of his experience. Such a grouping allows you to combine some analysis of specific poems with a general discussion of the goals of the literary-traditions approach beginning with the first day of class.

Supplementing the *NAAL* with recent novels not included in the text can allow you to develop the pluralism of contemporary fiction. In the view of William Pritchard, the *NAAL* anthologist for the period, "The major American novelists of the post–World War II decades are Saul Bellow, Norman Mailer, and John Updike," although he adds that there are easily "fifty or so American novelists and story writers . . . of real distinction." I have taught the following novels and story collections as part of the American-literature course; each has engaged students in discussion and in out-of-class essays:

James Baldwin, *Go Tell It on the Mountain*
Ann Beattie, *The Burning House*
Ralph Ellison, *The Invisible Man* (excerpted in the *NAAL*)
John Gardner, *Grendel* or *The Sunlight Dialogues*
Lillian Hellman, *Pentimento* (autobiographical prose)
Norman Mailer, *An American Dream*
Bernard Malamud, *The Assistant* or *God's Grace*
Toni Morrison, *The Bluest Eye* (included in the *NALW*) or *Sula*
May Sarton, *Plant Dreaming Deep* (a journal) or *Mrs. Stevens Hears the Mermaids Singing*
Alice Walker, *In Love and Trouble* or *The Color Purple*
Eudora Welty, *The Optimist's Daughter*
Richard Wright, *Uncle Tom's Children*

CHARTING THE TRADITIONS: WHITE, BLACK, MALE, FEMALE

However you decide to present the literary traditions in your own course—chronologically or by means of groupings—it may help your students to visualize individual writers within their historical period. Pages 30–31 chart major figures in white and black, male and female literary traditions, by tradition and according to chronology. I have marked with an asterisk those writers available only in the *NALW*, if you have chosen to supplement with that anthology.

SUGGESTED READINGS: WHITE, BLACK, MALE, FEMALE

VOLUME 1

1620–1820

White Male

William Bradford, from *Of Plymouth Plantation* or Edward Taylor, "Psalm Two," "Prologue" and "Meditations 8, 16, 38, 42, from *Preparatory Meditations*, "The Preface" from *God's Determinations*, "Upon Wedlock, and Death of Children," "Huswifery," "A Fig for Thee, Oh! Death"
Jonathan Edwards, "Personal Narrative," "[Sarah Pierrepont]," "A Divine and Supernatural Light," "Letter to Rev. Dr. Benjamin Colman," "Sinners in the Hands of an Angry God"

VOLUME 1

	1620–1820	*1820–1865*
White *male*	Bradford *or* Taylor Edwards Franklin John Adams Jefferson	Irving Emerson Hawthorne Thoreau Whitman Melville
White *female*	Bradstreet Ashbridge Abigail Adams	Fuller *Elizabeth Cady Stanton Stowe Dickinson Davis
Black *female*	Wheatley	*Sojourner Truth *"Linda Brent" (Harriet Jacobs)
Black *male*	Equiano	Douglass

	1865–1914	*1914–1945*	*Since 1945*	
			Prose	*Poetry*
White *male*	Clemens Howells *or* Adams James Crane	Frost Stevens Williams *or* Eliot O'Neill Faulkner	Williams Malamud Bellow Miller Shepard	Warren Lowell Ashbery *or* Wright
White *female*	Jewett Chopin Freeman *or* Gilman Wharton	Cather Stein *Susan Glaspell Porter	Welty O'Connor *Grace Paley Beattie	Bishop Levertov Rich Plath
Black *female*	*Frances E. W. Harper	Hurston	Kennedy *Toni Morrison *Toni Cade Bambara Walker	Brooks Lorde Dove
Black *male*	Washington Chesnutt DuBois	Toomer Hughes Wright	Ellison Baldwin	Hayden Baraka Harper

Benjamin Franklin, "The Way to Wealth," "Information to Those Who Would Remove to America," Remarks Concerning the Savages of North America," *The Autobiography*

John Adams, Letters to Abigail Adams

Thomas Jefferson, "The Declaration of Independence," Query VI and XVII from *Notes on the State of Virginia*, Letters to Peter Carr and Nathaniel Burwell

White Female

Anne Bradstreet, "The Prologue," "To the Memory of My Dear and Ever Honored Father, Thomas Dudley Esq.," "To Her Father with Some Verses," "Contemplations," "The Author to Her Book," "Before the Birth of One of Her Children," "To My Dear and Loving Husband," "A Letter to Her Husband, Absent upon Public Employment," "In Memory of My Dear Grandchild Anne Bradstreet," "Here Follows Some Verses upon the Burning of Our House"

Elizabeth Ashbridge, *Some Account of the Fore-Part of the Life of Elizabeth Ashbridge*

Abigail Adams, Letters to John Adams

Black Female

Phillis Wheatley, "On Being Brought from Africa to America," "To the University of Cambridge, in New England," "Thoughts on the Works of Providence," "To S.M., a Young African Painter, on Seeing His Works"

Black Male

Olaudah Equiano, *The Interesting Narrative of the Life of Olaudah Equiano, or, Gustavus Vassa, the African, Written by Himself*

1820–1865

White Male

Washington Irving, "Rip Van Winkle"

Ralph Waldo Emerson, "The American Scholar," "Self-Reliance," "The Poet," "Experience," Journals and Letters: "Myself," "[Protest; Writing; America]," "[The Business of Education]," "[Dead Sentences vs. Man-Making Words]," "[The Lyceum Should Exclude Nobody]," "[The London Literati on Male Chastity]," "[Negro Slavery vs. Quite Other Slaves to Free]"

Nathaniel Hawthorne, "Young Goodman Brown," "The Minister's Black Veil," "Rappaccini's Daughter," *The Scarlet Letter*

Henry David Thoreau, "Resistance to Civil Government," "Slavery in Massachusetts," "A Plea for Captain John Brown," and from *Walden*: "Economy," "Where I Lived and What I Lived For," "Former Inhabitants; and Winter Visitors," "Conclusion"

Walt Whitman, "Preface to *Leaves of Grass*," "Song of Myself," the *Calamus* poems, "The Sleepers"

Herman Melville, "Bartleby, the Scrivener," *Benito Cereno* or *Billy Budd, Sailor*

White Female

Margaret Fuller, from "The Great Lawsuit"

Harriet Beecher Stowe, "The Mother's Struggle" from *Uncle Tom's Cabin*, "The Minister's Housekeeper"

Emily Dickinson, esp. 49, 67, 125, 185, 187, 214, 241, 249, 258, 280, 303, 305, 322, 348, 435, 441, 448, 465, 501, 505, 510, 520, 528, 536, 640, 709, 744, 754, 986, 1099, 1100, 1129, 1138, 1400, 1545, 1575, 1670, Letters to Thomas Wentworth Higginson

Rebecca Harding Davis, "Life in the Iron-Mills"

Black Male

Frederick Douglass, *Narrative of the Life of Frederick Douglass, an American Slave*

VOLUME 2

1865–1914

White Male

Samuel Clemens, Letter to Will Bowen, *Adventures of Huckleberry Finn*, "The Man that Corrupted Hadleyburg"

W. D. Howells, "Novel-Writing and Novel-Reading" or Henry Adams, from *The Education of Henry Adams*

Henry James, "Daisy Miller," *The Turn of the Screw*, "The Beast in the Jungle"

Stephen Crane, "The Open Boat," "The Bride Comes to Yellow Sky"

White Female

Sarah Orne Jewett, "A White Heron," "The Foreigner"

Kate Chopin, *The Awakening*

Mary E. Wilkins Freeman, "The Revolt of 'Mother'," "A New England Nun" or Charlotte Perkins Gilman, "The Yellow Wallpaper"
Edith Wharton, *Ethan Frome*

Black Male

Booker T. Washington, from *Up from Slavery*
Charles W. Chesnutt, "The Goophered Grapevine"
W. E. B. DuBois, from *The Souls of Black Folk*

Native American Female

Gertrude Simmons Bonnin (Zitkala-Sä), "Impressions of an Indian Childhood," "The School Days of an Indian Girl," "An Indian Teacher among Indians"

1914–1945

White Male

Robert Frost, "The Death of the Hired Man," "Home Burial," "A Servant to Servants," "The Road Not Taken," "An Old Man's Winter Night," "The Oven Bird," "Birches," " 'Out, Out—,' " "Stopping by Woods on a Snowy Evening," "Two Tramps in Mud Time," "Desert Places," "Design," "The Gift Outright," "Directive"
Wallace Stevens, "Sunday Morning," "A High-toned Old Christian Woman," "Thirteen Ways of Looking at a Blackbird," "The Idea of Order at Key West," "Of Modern Poetry"
William Carlos Williams, "The Young Housewife," "Portrait of a Lady," "The Widow's Lament in Springtime," "Spring and All," "To Elsie," "The Dead Baby," "This Is Just to Say," "A Sort of a Song" or T. S. Eliot, "The Love Song of J. Alfred Prufrock"
Eugene O'Neill, *Long Day's Journey into Night*
William Faulkner, *As I Lay Dying*

White Female

Willa Cather, "My Mortal Enemy," "Neighbour Rosicky"
Gertrude Stein, *The Good Thing*
Katherine Anne Porter, *Old Mortality*

Black Female

Zora Neale Hurston, "The Eatonville Anthology," from *Their Eyes Were Watching God*

Black Male

Jean Toomer, from *Cane*
Langston Hughes, "The Negro Speaks of Rivers," "Mother to Son," "Dream Variations," "Mulatto," "Song for a Dark Girl," "Trumpet Player," "Dear Dr. Butts"
Richard Wright, "The Man Who Was Almost a Man"

Native American Male

Black Elk, from *Black Elk Speaks*

AMERICAN PROSE SINCE 1945

White Male

Tennessee Williams, *A Streetcar Named Desire*
Bernard Malamud, "The Magic Barrel"
Saul Bellow, *Seize the Day*
Arthur Miller, *Death of a Salesman*
Sam Shepard, *True West*

White Female

Eudora Welty, "Petrified Man"
Flannery O'Connor, "The Life You Save May Be Your Own," "Good Country People"
Ann Beattie, "Weekend"

Black Female

Adrienne Kennedy, *A Movie Star Has to Star in Black and White*
Alice Walker, "Everyday Use"

Black Male

Ralph Ellison, from *Invisible Man*
James Baldwin, from *The Fire Next Time*

Native American Female

Leslie Marmon Silko, "Lullaby"
Louise Erdrich, "Lulu's Boys"

Chicana

Denise Chávez, "The Last of the Menu Girls"

AMERICAN POETRY SINCE 1945
White Male

Robert Penn Warren, selections from *Audubon*
Robert Lowell, "My Last Afternoon with Uncle Devereux Winslow," "Memories of West Street and Lepke," "Skunk Hour," "Night Sweat," "For the Union Dead"
John Ashbery, "Illustration," "Soonest Mended," "Self-Portrait in a Convex Mirror" or James Wright, "Autumn Begins in Martins Ferry, Ohio," "A Blessing," "A Finch Sitting out a Windstorm"

White Female

Elizabeth Bishop, "The Fish," "The Bight," "At the Fish-houses," "Questions of Travel," "The Armadillo," "In the Waiting Room," "One Art"
Denise Levertov, "To the Snake," "In Mind"
Adrienne Rich, "Snapshots of a Daughter-in-Law," "Orion," "A Valediction Forbidding Mourning," " 'I Am in Danger—Sir—,' " "Diving into the Wreck," from "Twenty-One Love Poems"
Sylvia Plath, "Morning Song," "Lady Lazarus," "Daddy"

Black Female

Gwendolyn Brooks, "Kitchenette Building," "A Song in the Front Yard," "The Vacant Lot," "The Lovers of the Poor"
Audre Lorde, "Coal," "The Woman Thing," "Black Mother Woman," "Chain"

Black Male

Robert Hayden, "Middle Passage," "Homage to the Empress of the Blues," "Elegies for Paradise Valley"
Imamu Amiri Baraka, "An Agony. As Now.," "A Poem for Willie Best," "Will They Cry When You've Gone, You Bet"
Michael Harper, "American History," "Martin's Blues," "Tongue-Tied in Black and White," "The Militance of a Photograph in the Passbook of a Bantu under Detention"

<u>Native American Male</u>

Simon J. Ortiz, all the selections

<u>Chicano</u>

Alberto Ríos, all the selections

<u>Chicana</u>

Lorna Dee Cervantes, "For Virginia Chavez," "Visions of Mexico While at a Writing Symposium in Port Townsend, Washington," "Emplumada"

<u>Asian-American Female</u>

Cathy Song, "Beauty and Sadness," "Lost Sister," "Chinatown," "Heaven"

USING *THE NORTON ANTHOLOGY OF LITERATURE BY WOMEN* WITH *NAAL*

The following writers and works included in the *NALW* may be used to expand students' awareness of black and white female literary traditions:

<u>White Female</u>

Elizabeth Cady Stanton, "Address to the New York State Legislature, 1860"
Susan Glaspell, *Trifles*
Grace Paley, "Enormous Changes at the Last Minute"

<u>Black Female</u>

Sojourner Truth, "Ain't I a Woman," "What Time of Night It Is," "Keeping the Thing Going While Things Are Stirring"
"Linda Brent" [Harriet Jacobs], from *Incidents in the Life of a Slave Girl*
Francis E. W. Harper, "Vashti," "Aunt Chloe's Politics," "Learning to Read"
Toni Morrison, *The Bluest Eye*
Toni Cade Bambara, "My Man Bovanne"

In addition, the following selections from the *NALW* may expand your presentation of some writers included in the *NAAL*:

<u>White Female</u>

Anne Bradstreet, "In Honour of That High and Mighty Princess Queen Elizabeth of Happy Memory," "To Her Father with Some Verses"
Margaret Fuller, from *Woman in the Nineteenth Century*
Emily Dickinson, esp. 24, 271, 288, 312, 365, 385, 392, 401, 425, 462, 508, 512, 569, 579, 593, 613, 642, 657, 669, 670, 722, 732, 959, 1072, 1445, 1657, 1705, 1737
Mary E. Wilkins Freeman, "Old Woman Magoun"
Edith Wharton, "The Angel at the Grave"
Willa Cather, "Coming, Aphrodite!"
Eudora Welty, "The Wide Net"
Marianne Moore, "Sojourn in the Whale," "Sea Unicorns and Land Unicorns," "Silence," "Marriage," "The Paper Nautilus," "His Shield," "O to Be a Dragon"
Denise Levertov, "The Goddess," "Song for Ishtar," "Hypocrite Women," "The Ache of Marriage," "The Crack," "Eros at Temple Stream," "About Marriage," "The Wings," "Abel's Bride," "The Son," "Stepping Westward," "The Mutes"
Adrienne Rich, " 'I Am in Danger—Sir—,' " "I Dream I'm the Death of Orpheus," "Power," from "Twenty-One Love Poems," "Phantasia for Elvira Shatayev," "Culture and Anarchy," "When We Dead Awaken: Writing as Re-Vision"

<u>Black Female</u>

Zora Neale Hurston, "Sweat"
Alice Walker, "In Search of Our Mothers' Gardens"
Gwendolyn Brooks, "The Womanhood," "We Real Cool," "Jessie Mitchell's Mother," "The Crazy Woman," "Bronzeville Woman in a Red Hat," "Queen of the Blues," "Riot"
Audre Lorde, "On a Night of the Full Moon," "Now That I Am Forever with Child"

THE SOUTHERN TRADITION

The Southern tradition is well represented in the *NAAL* by the following authors:

VOLUME 1

1620–1820

John Smith
Robert Beverley
William Byrd
Thomas Jefferson

1820–1865

Augustus Baldwin Longstreet
George Washington Harris
T. B. Thorpe
Johnson Jones Hooper
Frederick Douglass

VOLUME 2

1865–1914

Joel Chandler Harris
Kate Chopin

1914–1945

Ellen Glasgow
John Crowe Ransom
Katherine Anne Porter
Zora Neale Hurston
William Faulkner
Allen Tate
Thomas Wolfe

SINCE 1945

Eudora Welty
Tennessee Williams
Peter Taylor
Flannery O'Connor
Tom Wolfe
Bobbie Ann Mason
Alice Walker
Robert Penn Warren
James Dickey

THE PROTEST TRADITION

The tradition of protest literature begins early among the writers represented in the *NAAL* and includes the following:

VOLUME 1

Henry David Thoreau
Margaret Fuller
Frederick Douglass
Rebecca Harding Davis

VOLUME 2

Charlotte Perkins Gilman
W. E. B. DuBois
Allen Ginsberg
Jack Kerouac
Norman Mailer

If you are using the *NALW* with the *NAAL*, selections by Lillian Hellman, Tillie Olsen, and Judy Grahn expand the protest tradition.

MARGINALITY IN THE WHITE-MALE TRADITION

The following list presents a few works by white male writers that illustrate the relationship between marginality and vision, in effect suggesting that many white male American authors have been members of a self-defined minority.

VOLUME 1

1620–1820

Roger Williams, from *A Key into the Language of America*, from "The Bloody Tenet of Persecution," "A Letter to the Town of Providence"
John Woolman, from "The Journal of John Woolman"

1820–1865

Washington Irving, "Rip Van Winkle"
Nathaniel Hawthorne, "The Custom-House" and *The Scarlet Letter*
Henry David Thoreau, *Walden*

Walt Whitman, "Song of Myself"
Herman Melville, "Bartleby, the Scrivener," *Billy Budd, Sailor*

VOLUME 2

1865–1914

Samuel Clemens, *Adventures of Huckleberry Finn*
Henry James, "The Beast in the Jungle"

1914–1945

Sherwood Anderson, from *Winesburg, Ohio,* "The Egg"
Robinson Jeffers, "Shine, Perishing Republic"
Eugene O'Neill, *Long Day's Journey into Night*
F. Scott Fitzgerald, "Winter Dreams"
William Faulkner, *As I Lay Dying,* "Barn Burning"

SINCE 1945

Jack Kerouac, from *On the Road*

5

DISCUSSIONS OF GENRE AND THEME

GENRE

Genre raises one of the central questions in the study of American literature, namely, the dialectic between imitative and indigenous voices and forms. Our own teachers taught us that those writers who imitated British poets and adapted English genres were thereby flawed, and we may find ourselves apologizing for the lack of originality throughout the entire 1620–1820 period of American literature until we can finally point to Walt Whitman as the first "American" poet. Yet, focusing on the awareness of form in our earliest writers can help students begin to consider American literature itself as a process rather than a product. And the continual metamorphosis of American literature often accompanies changes in the theological, political, or cultural "forms of being" that writers express and address. Unlike British literature, in which readers may compare ballads, sonnets, villanelles, and epic poems written in different centuries, American literature has produced a history of genre marked by idiosyncrasy and discontinuity between periods. The perennial change in the forms of American literature from its colonial origins to the present day provides the instructor with a rich source of questions for consideration in the classroom:

How do the major genres of a particular literary period reflect the thinking of the time? In what ways does experimentation with literary form produce change in social or political thinking? How does any given literary work both adhere to and work against its apparent form? What is the thematic or ideological "content" of certain genres in American literature? Do some genres (such as the Puritan sermon) actually contain elements of forms they appear to reject (such as drama)? In a literature marked by a proliferation of genres, what constitutes originality or experimentation? In his general introduction to the 1820–1865 period in the *NAAL*, Hershel Parker talks about what he calls "the new Americanness of American literature" and the difficulty critics have had then and ever since trying to define that "special quality" that makes a writer or a work American. What characterizes the "special quality" of American genres in that or any other period? Are some genres more "American" than others? Does indigenous vision, per se, help define the "Americanness of American literature," and, if so, does it produce indigenous genres? If not, what does explain the invention of the Indian captivity narrative or the slave narrative? How does a work written in a traditional genre, such as the picaresque *Adventures of Huckleberry Finn*, achieve its originality? While autobiography, itself, was not an American invention, Benjamin Franklin invented his own *Autobiography*; what makes it unique? Are American writers such as William Cullen Bryant or Robert Frost less "American" when they choose traditional poetic forms? The genres some writers choose are difficult to categorize. Is *The Scarlet Letter* a novel or a romance, and, if so, what is the distinction? Is *Moby-Dick* a novel at all? Is *The Education of Henry Adams* a work of fiction or history? Should we worry that American literature has not yet produced an epic poet?

And what of those writers and works that really do create continuity of form that crosses literary periods? Despite the array of writers (especially in the nineteenth century) who appeared to invent their own forms and who produced texts that are "classic" partly because of their uniqueness, American writers also worked together in genres that would accumulate the force of tradition. Elements of Puritan literature continue to influence American forms long after the decline of Puritanism. The regionalism of late nineteenth-century writers such as Sarah Orne Jewett and Mary Wilkins Freeman appears to undergo simultaneous metamorphosis and rebirth in the southern Renaissance writers of the twentieth century. Despite the modernists' rejection of tradition and Ezra Pound's call to "make it new," late nineteenth-century literary realism provides the narrative design for our most experimental modernist fiction writer, William Faulkner. How does the presence of literary influence contribute to the development of an "American" literature? Despite the individualism of American myth, each literary period has produced writers who worked closely together and commented on each others' work. How do the forms of, for example, "The Declaration of Independence" or *The Waste Land* reflect the collaborative process of their composition? The authors of slave narratives often quite literally worked in collaboration with Northern abolitionist presses and editors. Writers as different as Edward Taylor and Harriet Beecher Stowe claimed to owe their inspiration and even their works to God. How does a writer's understanding of his or her source of literary authority affect genre? How do related questions of audience and literary convention affect the American writer's choice of form?

In the lists that follow, I have summarized the multiplicity of American literary genres and identified writers by the forms in which they primarily worked. Whatever model you choose to guide your course organization, uncovering the peculiar facts about American genres that any attempt to categorize them reveals will enhance your ability to present the large picture of American literature for your students.

SUGGESTED READINGS

VOLUME 1
1620–1820

Major genres: lyric (primarily religious poetry), nonfiction writing, sermon
Indigenous genre: Indian captivity narrative

Writers Organized by Genre

Historical writing: John Smith, Thomas Morton, William Bradford, Robert Beverley, Cotton Mather
Indian captivity narrative: Mary Rowlandson
Journal: John Winthrop, Samuel Sewall, William Byrd, John Woolman
Lyric poetry: Anne Bradstreet, Edward Taylor, Philip Freneau, and Phillis Wheatley; Michael Wigglesworth and Jonathan Edwards wrote theological poetry
Mock epic: Joel Barlow
Public/Political writing: William Bradford ("The Mayflower Compact"), Roger Williams, Benjamin Franklin, St. Jean de Crèvecoeur, Thomas Paine, Thomas Jefferson (the letters as well as "The Declaration of Independence"), Alexander Hamilton and James Madison (as "The Federalist" papers); some of Joel Barlow's poetry may also be considered political writing
Sermon: John Winthrop, Edward Taylor (from "Sermon VI"), Cotton Mather (from "Bonifacius"), Jonathan Edwards
Travel literature: Sarah Kemble Knight, St. Jean de Crèvecoeur, William Bartram
Conversion narrative: Elizabeth Ashbridge
Slave narrative: Oloudah Equiano
Drama: Royall Tyler

1820–1865

Major genres: fiction, journals and letters, literary statement, lyric poetry, philosophical essay
Indigenous genres: early regionalism, "Southwest Humor," slave narrative

Writers Organized by Genre

Early regionalism: Harriet Beecher Stowe
Fiction: Washington Irving, James Fenimore Cooper, Au-

gustus Baldwin Longstreet, Nathaniel Hawthorne, Edgar Allan Poe, Harriet Beecher Stowe, George Washington Harris, T. B. Thorpe, Johnson Jones Hooper, Herman Melville, Elizabeth Drew Stoddard, Rebecca Harding Davis

Literary statement: James Fenimore Cooper, Ralph Waldo Emerson, Nathaniel Hawthorne, Edgar Allan Poe, Walt Whitman, Herman Melville

Lyric poetry: William Cullen Bryant, Ralph Waldo Emerson, Henry Wadsworth Longfellow, John Greenleaf Whittier, Edgar Allan Poe, Oliver Wendell Holmes, James Russell Lowell, Walt Whitman, Herman Melville, Emily Dickinson

Philosophical essay: Ralph Waldo Emerson, Henry David Thoreau

Political writing: Abraham Lincoln, Margaret Fuller, Henry David Thoreau

Slave narrative: Frederick Douglass

"Southwest Humor": Augustus Baldwin Longstreet, George Washington Harris, T. B. Thorpe, Johnson Jones Hooper

VOLUME 2

1865–1914

Major genres: naturalism, realism, regionalism
Indigenous genres: folk literature, "local color," regionalism

<u>Writers Organized by Genre</u>

Feminist writing: Charlotte Perkins Gilman, Jane Addams
Folk literature: Joel Chandler Harris, Charles W. Chesnutt
Historical writing: Henry Adams, Jane Addams
Humor: Samuel Clemens
Literary statement: Samuel Clemens, W. D. Howells, Henry James
"Local color" writing: Samuel Clemens, Bret Harte, Joel Chandler Harris, Hamlin Garland, Stephen Crane
Lyric poetry: Stephen Crane
Naturalism: Samuel Clemens, Kate Chopin, Charlotte Perkins Gilman, Frank Norris, Stephen Crane, Theodore Dreiser, Jack London
Public/Political writing: Booker T. Washington, W.E.B. DuBois
Realism: Samuel Clemens, W. D. Howells, Ambrose Bierce, Henry James, Edith Wharton
Regionalism: Sarah Orne Jewett, Kate Chopin, Mary E.

Wilkins Freeman, Charles W. Chesnutt, Gertrude Simmons Bonnin (Zitkala-Sä)

1914–1945

Major genres: lyric poetry, realism in drama, fiction
Indigenous genres: black fiction and poetry, southern regionalism

Writers Organized by Genre

Black fiction: Zora Neale Hurston, Jean Toomer, Richard Wright
Realistic drama: Eugene O'Neill
Experimental prose: Gertrude Stein, William Faulkner
Humor: Dorothy Parker, James Thurber, E. B. White
Lyric poetry:
 Black poetry: Langston Hughes, Countee Cullen
 Dramatic lyric: Edgar Lee Masters
 Folk lyric: Carl Sandburg
 Longer modernist poem: William Carlos Williams, Ezra Pound, H. D., T. S. Eliot, Hart Crane
 Modernist lyric: Gertrude Stein (represented in the *NAAL* by prose), Robert Frost, Wallace Stevens, William Carlos Williams, Ezra Pound, H. D., Robinson Jeffers, Marianne Moore, T. S. Eliot, E. E. Cummings, Hart Crane
 New-critical lyric: John Crowe Ransom, Allen Tate
 Traditional lyric: Edwin Arlington Robinson, Elinor Wylie, Edna St. Vincent Millay, Louise Bogan
Realistic fiction: Ellen Glasgow, Willa Cather, Sherwood Anderson, Katherine Anne Porter, John Dos Passos, F. Scott Fitzgerald, William Faulkner, Ernest Hemingway, John Steinbeck
Southern regionalism: Katherine Anne Porter, Thomas Wolfe

AMERICAN PROSE SINCE 1945

Writers Organized by Genre

Black fiction: Ralph Ellison, Alice Walker
Drama: Tennessee Williams, Arthur Miller, Adrienne Kennedy, Sam Shepard
Fantasy fiction: Vladimir Nabokov, John Barth, Thomas Pynchon
Jewish fiction: Bernard Malamud, Saul Bellow, Philip Roth
"New York" fiction: John Cheever, Bernard Malamud, Ralph Ellison, Saul Bellow, Norman Mailer, Tom Wolfe, John Updike,

Robert Stone, Ann Beattie

Nonfiction: Edmund Wilson, Norman Mailer, James Baldwin

Southern fiction: Eudora Welty, Peter Taylor, Flannery O'Connor, Bobbie Ann Mason, Alice Walker

Regional fiction: Leslie Marmon Silko, Denise Chávez, Louise Erdrich

AMERICAN POETRY SINCE 1945

<u>Writers Organized by Genre</u>

Autobiographical poetry: Theodore Roethke, Elizabeth Bishop, John Berryman, Robert Lowell, Denise Levertov, Allen Ginsberg, James Merrill, Anne Sexton, Adrienne Rich, Sylvia Plath

"Beat" poetry: Allen Ginsberg, Gary Snyder

Black poetry: Gwendolyn Brooks, Robert Hayden, Imamu Amiri Baraka, Audre Lorde, Michael Harper, Rita Dove

Dramatic lyric: Randall Jarrell, John Berryman, Adrienne Rich

Feminist poetry: Adrienne Rich, Audre Lorde

The long poem: James Merrill

Love poetry: Theodore Roethke, Adrienne Rich

Nature and landscape poetry: Lorine Niedecker, Robert Penn Warren, Theodore Roethke, Elizabeth Bishop, Richard Hugo, A. R. Ammons, James Merrill, James Wright, Gary Snyder, Sylvia Plath

New York School: Frank O'Hara, John Ashbery, Imamu Amiri Baraka

Poetry of private vision: Robert Penn Warren, Elizabeth Bishop, John Berryman, James Dickey, A. R. Ammons, James Merrill, John Ashbery, James Wright, W. S. Merwin

"Projective verse": Charles Olson, Denise Levertov

"Protest" and political poetry: Robert Lowell, Denise Levertov, Allen Ginsberg, Adrienne Rich, Imamu Amiri Baraka

Regional poetry: Richard Hugo

Short lyric meditation: Richard Wilbur, A. R. Ammons, W. S. Merwin, James Wright

War poetry: Randall Jarrell

THEME

Given the vast array of poems, essays, stories, plays, and literature in other genres included in the *NAAL*, and considering that writers work out in each literary text themes that in a certain sense are individual and idiosyncratic, a listing of categories of themes and the American works in which they appear will necessarily be reductive. In the lists that follow, I have chosen some of the themes that recur throughout American literature and may, therefore, integrate discussion in the classroom however you choose to organize your syllabus, and I suggest some of the texts that directly address the themes. Instead of categorizing those themes that are often termed "universal," I have limited myself to certain themes that are characteristic of, though not necessarily exclusive to, American experience, and that includes the following: the problem of American identity; the individual and the community; the problem/expression of literary authority; the American Dream; the American landscape; the immigrant experience; family relationships and attitudes toward children; race, segregation, and slavery; gender issues of women's lives, work, and vision; and politics and war.

The Problem of American Identity

American literature becomes an epistemology, a way of knowing, for many American writers. This theme so pervades American literature that it might usefully serve as the basis for an entire course organization, one focused on an American Studies approach that would work particularly well for students who are simultaneously enrolled in courses in American history and culture. Here are some of the works and the issues they raise in the texts included in the *NAAL*:

VOLUME 1

1620–1820

The New World and Its Nature

William Bradford, from *Of Plymouth Plantation*
Roger Williams, from *A Key into the Language of America*
Mary Rowlandson, *A Narrative of the Captivity and Restoration of Mrs. Mary Rowlandson*
Robert Beverley, from *The History and Present State of Virginia*, Olaudah Equiano, *The Interesting Narrative of the Life of Olaudah Equiano, or Gustavus Vassa, the African, Written by Himself*
Philip Freneau, especially "On the Emigration to America and Peopling the Western Country," "The Indian Burying Ground," "On Mr. Paine's Rights of Man"
Phillis Wheatley, "On Being Brought from Africa to America"

How to Locate Personal Voice in a Theological Society

Anne Bradstreet, especially "The Prologue," "The Author to Her Book," "Here Follows Some Verses upon the Burning of Our

House," and those addressed to or in memory of family members; see also the essay "To My Dear Children"

Edward Taylor, "Upon Wedlock, and Death of Children," "Huswifery"

Elizabeth Ashbridge, *Some Account of the Fore-Part of the Life of Elizabeth Ashbridge*

Private Papers as a Way of Knowing

Samuel Sewall, from *The Diary of Samuel Sewall*
Sarah Kemble Knight, "The Private Journal of a Journey from Boston to New York"
William Byrd, "The Secret Diary of William Byrd of Westover 1709–1712"
John and Abigail Adams, letters

Knowledge as Revealed by God

Anne Bradstreet, "Contemplations," "To My Dear Children"
Edward Taylor, poems
Michael Wigglesworth, "The Day of Doom"
Cotton Mather, from *The Wonders of the Invisible World*
Jonathan Edwards, "Personal Narrative," "A Divine and Supernatural Light," "Images or Shadows of Divine Things"
Elizabeth Ashbridge, *Some Account of the Fore-Part of the Life of Elizabeth Ashbridge*
John Woolman, from "The Journal of John Woolman"
Phillis Wheatley, "Thoughts on the Works of Providence"

Inventing the Pre-Romantic Self

Benjamin Franklin, "The Way to Wealth" and *The Autobiography*
Royall Tyler, *The Contrast*

Public and Political Writing as Ways for a Nation to Know Itself

St. Jean de Crèvecoeur, from *Letters from an American Farmer*
Thomas Paine, from *Common Sense, The Crisis,* and *The Age of Reason*
Thomas Jefferson, "The Declaration of Independence," from *Notes on the State of Virginia*, and the letters
Joel Barlow, "The Hasty Pudding"

Fictionalizing the Problem of American Identity

Washington Irving, "Rip Van Winkle"

Defining American Intellectual Thought

Ralph Waldo Emerson, essays, especially "The American Scholar," "The Divinity School Address," "Self-Reliance," "The Poet," "Fate"
Henry David Thoreau, "Thomas Carlyle and His Works"

Evading Self-Knowledge

Nathaniel Hawthorne, "Young Goodman Brown," "The Minister's Black Veil," "Wakefield," "The Custom-House," and *The Scarlet Letter*

The Literature of the Dream World

Edgar Allan Poe, poems and tales

Personal Scripture as a Way of Knowing

Henry David Thoreau, *Walden, or Life in the Woods*

Slave Narrative as Ontology

Frederick Douglass, *Narrative of the Life of Frederick Douglass, an American Slave*

Self-Invention in New Forms

Walt Whitman, poems from *Leaves of Grass,* especially "Song of Myself"

The Limitations of Vision

Herman Melville, the June 1(?), 1851 letter to Hawthorne, "Bartleby, the Scrivener," *Billy Budd, Sailor*

<u>Self-Revelation as Vision</u>

Emily Dickinson, poems, especially 125, 185, 214, 241, 258, 280, 303, 305, 341, 348, 435, 441, 448, 465, 505, 510, 520, 547, 632, 664, 754, 822, 986, 1099, 1129, 1400, 1581, 1651, 1670, 1732

VOLUME 2

In the works by writers included in the second volume of the *NAAL*, the question of American identity becomes one among many that interest late nineteenth-century and early twentieth-century writers. Although citing the entire table of contents for Volume 2 makes sense here, a brief representative list of works that can organize a thematic syllabus on American identity includes the following:

1865–1914

Samuel Clemens, *Adventures of Huckleberry Finn*
Henry James, "Daisy Miller"
Kate Chopin, *The Awakening*
Booker T. Washington, from *Up from Slavery*
Edith Wharton, *Ethan Frome*
W. E. B. DuBois, from *The Souls of Black Folk*
Gertrude Simmons Bonnin (Zitkala-Sä)
Henry Adams, from *The Education of Henry Adams*

1914–1945

Black Elk, *Black Elk Speaks*
Edgar Lee Masters, poems
Edwin Arlington Robinson, poems
Robert Frost, poems, especially "Once by the Pacific," "The Gift Outright," "Directive"
Carl Sandburg, "Chicago"
William Carlos Williams, from *Paterson*
Robinson Jeffers, "Shine, Perishing Republic"
Marianne Moore, "New York," "The Student"
E. E. Cummings, "Buffalo Bill's," "Poem, or Beauty Hurts Mr. Vinal," "next to of course god america i," "i sing of Olaf glad and big"
James Thurber, "The Secret Life of Walter Mitty"
Jean Toomer, from *Cane*
John Dos Passos, from *U.S.A.*
F. Scott Fitzgerald, "Winter Dreams"
E. B. White, "Walden"
Hart Crane, *The Bridge*

Zora Neale Hurston, "How It Feels to Be Colored Me"
John Steinbeck, "The Leader of the People"

AMERICAN PROSE SINCE 1945

Saul Bellow, *Seize the Day*
Arthur Miller, *Death of a Salesman*
Jack Kerouac, from *On the Road*
Norman Mailer, from *The Armies of the Night*
Thomas Pynchon, from *The Crying of Lot 49*
Sam Shepard, *True West*

AMERICAN POETRY SINCE 1945

Robert Lowell, "For the Union Dead"
Allen Ginsberg, "Howl," "A Supermarket in California," "Sunflower Sutra"
Adrienne Rich, "Diving into the Wreck"

The Individual and the Community

VOLUME 1

William Bradford, from *Of Plymouth Plantation*
Cotton Mather, from *The Wonders of the Invisible World*
Elizabeth Ashbridge, *Some Account of the Fore-Part of the Life of Elizabeth Ashbridge*
Thomas Jefferson, "The Declaration of Independence"
Nathaniel Hawthorne, "Young Goodman Brown," "The May-Pole of Merry Mount," "The Minister's Black Veil," "Wakefield," *The Scarlet Letter*
Henry David Thoreau, "Resistance to Civil Government," *Walden*, "A Plea for Captain John Brown"
Frederick Douglass, *Narrative of the Life of Frederick Douglass, an American Slave*
Walt Whitman, "Song of Myself"
Herman Melville, "Bartleby, the Scrivener"

VOLUME 2

Samuel Clemens, *Adventures of Huckleberry Finn*, "The Man That Corrupted Hadleyburg"
Henry James, "Daisy Miller," "The Turn of the Screw," "The Beast in the Jungle"
Sarah Orne Jewett, "A White Heron," "The Foreigner"
Kate Chopin, *The Awakening*

Mary E. Wilkins Freeman, "A New England Nun," "The Revolt of 'Mother'"

Edith Wharton, *Ethan Frome*

Jane Addams, from *Twenty Years at Hull-House*

Stephen Crane, "The Bride Comes to Yellow Sky," "The Blue Hotel"

Theodore Dreiser, "The Strike" from *Sister Carrie*

Henry Adams, "Preface," Chapters I and XIX from *The Education of Henry Adams*

Gertrude Simmons Bonnin (Zitkala-Sä), autobiographical essays

Edgar Lee Masters, poems

Edwin Arlington Robinson, poems

Willa Cather, "Neighbour Rosicky"

Robert Frost, "The Tuft of Flowers," "Mending Wall," "The Death of the Hired Man," "A Servant to Servants," "Departmental," "Neither out Far Nor in Deep"

Sherwood Anderson, from *Winesburg, Ohio*

T. S. Eliot, "The Love Song of J. Alfred Prufrock," "Tradition and the Individual Talent"

E. E. Cummings, "the Cambridge ladies who live in furnished souls," "nobody loses all the time," "anyone lived in a pretty how town," "pity this busy monster, manunkind"

William Faulkner, *As I Lay Dying*, "Barn Burning"

Ralph Ellison, from *Invisible Man*

Jack Kerouac, from *On the Road*

The Problem of Expression of Literary Authority

VOLUME 1

Anne Bradstreet, "The Prologue," "The Author to Her Book"

Edward Taylor, "Prologue," "Meditation 22," "Upon a Wasp Chilled with Cold," "Huswifery"

Jonathan Edwards, "Personal Narrative," "Sinners in the Hands of an Angry God"

Benjamin Franklin, "The Way to Wealth"

Elizabeth Ashbridge, *Some Account of the Fore-Part of the Life of Elizabeth Ashbridge*

Phillis Wheatley, "To S.M., A Young African Painter, on Seeing His Works"

Ralph Waldo Emerson, "The American Scholar," "The Poet," "Merlin"

Nathaniel Hawthorne, "The Custom-House"

Henry David Thoreau, "Thomas Carlyle and His Works," *Walden*, "September 2, 1851," "September 4, 1851," "November 12,

1851," "July 13, 1852," "July 14, 1852," "April 8, 1854," "To Daniel
Ricketson," "January 2, 1859"

Frederick Douglass, *Narrative of the Life of Frederick Douglass, an American Slave*

Walt Whitman, especially "Preface to *Leaves of Grass*," "Song of Myself," "Letter to Ralph Waldo Emerson," "Trickle Drops," "Here the Frailest Leaves of Me," "As I Ebb'd with the Ocean of Life," from *Second Annex: Good-bye My Fancy*

Herman Melville, "Hawthorne and His Mosses," letters to Hawthorne, especially June 1(?), 1851, "The Town-Ho's Story" from *Moby-Dick*

Emily Dickinson, especially 125, 185, 441, 448, 505, 528, 754, 1129, 1545, 1575, 1651, letters to Thomas Wentworth Higginson

VOLUME 2

Samuel Clemens, "[The Art of Authorship]"
W. D. Howells, "Novel-Writing and Novel-Reading"
Henry James, "The Turn of the Screw"
Charles W. Chesnutt, "The Goophered Grapevine"
Charlotte Perkins Gilman, "The Yellow Wallpaper"
Edith Wharton, *Ethan Frome*
Henry Adams, "Preface" and Chapter 1 from *The Education of Henry Adams*
Black Elk, *Black Elk Speaks*
Gertrude Stein, from *The Making of Americans*
Wallace Stevens, "A High-toned Old Christian Woman," "Thirteen Ways of Looking at a Blackbird," "Of Modern Poetry"
William Carlos Williams, "Portrait of a Lady," "The Red Wheelbarrow," "The Term," "A Sort of a Song," "The Dance ('In Brueghel's great picture, The Kermess')"
Marianne Moore, "Poetry"
T. S. Eliot, "The Love Song of J. Alfred Prufrock," "Tradition and the Individual Talent"
Katherine Anne Porter, *Old Mortality*
Ralph Ellison, "Prologue" to *Invisible Man*
Norman Mailer, "The Man Who Studied Yoga," from *The Armies of the Night*
John Barth, "Life-Story"

The American Dream

VOLUME 1

Benjamin Franklin, "The Way to Wealth"
Royall Tyler, *The Contrast*
Washington Irving, "Rip Van Winkle"

Nathaniel Hawthorne, "Young Goodman Brown"
Edgar Allan Poe, poems and tales
Frederick Douglass, *Narrative of the Life of Frederick Douglass, an American Slave*
Walt Whitman, "The Sleepers"
Elizabeth Drew Stoddard, "Lemorne *versus* Huell"

VOLUME 2

Samuel Clemens, *Adventures of Huckleberry Finn*, "The Man That Corrupted Hadleyburg"
Henry James, "The Turn of the Screw"
Sarah Orne Jewett, "A White Heron"
Kate Chopin, *The Awakening*
Hamlin Garland, "Under the Lion's Paw"
Edith Wharton, *Ethan Frome*
Theodore Dreiser, "The Strike" from *Sister Carrie*
Henry Adams, from *The Education of Henry Adams*
Edgar Lee Masters, poems
Willa Cather, "My Mortal Enemy," "Neighbour Rosicky"
Sherwood Anderson, from *Winesburg, Ohio* and "The Egg"
James Thurber, "The Secret Life of Walter Mitty"
John Dos Passos, from *U.S.A.*
F. Scott Fitzgerald, "Winter Dreams"
E. B. White, "Walden"
John Steinbeck, "The Leader of the People"
Ralph Ellison, Chapter 1 from *Invisible Man*
Arthur Miller, *Death of a Salesman*
Jack Kerouac, from *On the Road*
Adrienne Kennedy, *A Movie Star Has to Star in Black and White*
Thomas Pynchon, from *The Crying of Lot 49*
Sam Shepard, *True West*

The American Landscape

VOLUME 1

Thomas Morton, "The General Survey of the Country" from *New English Canaan*
William Bradford, from *Of Plymouth Plantation*, especially Book I, Chapters IX and X
Sarah Kemble Knight, "The Private Journal of a Journey from Boston to New York"
Robert Beverley, from *The History and Present State of Virginia*
William Byrd, from *History of the Dividing Line*

St. Jean de Crèvecoeur, from *Letters from an American Farmer*

William Bartram, from *The Travels of William Bartram*

Thomas Jefferson, from *Notes on the State of Virginia*

Philip Freneau, "On the Emigration to America and Peopling the Western Country"

Washington Irving, "The Legend of Sleepy Hollow"

James Fenimore Cooper, from *The Pioneers*

William Cullen Bryant, "The Prairies"

Henry David Thoreau, *Walden*

Walt Whitman, especially "Song of Myself" (section 33), "Crossing Brooklyn Ferry"

VOLUME 2

Samuel Clemens, *Adventures of Huckleberry Finn*

Sarah Orne Jewett, "A White Heron"

Hamlin Garland, "Under the Lion's Paw"

Edith Wharton, *Ethan Frome*

Willa Cather, "Neighbour Rosicky"

Robert Frost, especially "The Wood-Pile," "Birches," "'Out, Out—,'" "Design," "Directive"

Robinson Jeffers, "Boats in a Fog," "November Surf," "Carmel Point"

Hart Crane, *The Bridge*

Edmund Wilson, "The Old Stone House"

Jack Kerouac, from *On the Road*

James Wright, "A Blessing"

Gary Snyder, "Milton by Firelight," "August on Sourdough," "Blue Sky"

The Immigrant Experience

VOLUME 1

William Bradford, from *Of Plymouth Plantation*

Robert Beverley, from *The History and Present State of Virginia*

Benjamin Franklin, "Information to Those Who Would Remove to America"

Elizabeth Ashbridge, *Some Account of the Fore-Part of the Life of Elizabeth Ashbridge*

St. Jean de Crèvecoeur, Letter III, "What Is an American"

Olaudah Equiano, *The Interesting Narrative of the Life of Olaudah Equiano, or Gustavus Vassa, the African, Written by Himself*

Philip Freneau, "On the Emigration to America and Peopling the Western Country"

Phillis Wheatley, "On Being Brought from Africa to America"
Walt Whitman, "Song of Myself," "Crossing Brooklyn Ferry"
Rebecca Harding Davis, "Life in the Iron-Mills"

VOLUME 2

Sarah Orne Jewett, "The Foreigner"
Hamlin Garland, "Under the Lion's Paw"
Theodore Dreiser, "Old Rogaum and His Theresa"
Willa Cather, "Neighbour Rosicky"
Vladimir Nabokov, from *Pnin*
Bernard Malamud, "The Magic Barrel"
Saul Bellow, *Seize the Day*
Philip Roth, "Defender of the Faith"
Denise Levertov, "Illustrious Ancestors"
Sylvia Plath, "Daddy"

Family Relationships and Attitudes toward Children

VOLUME 1

Anne Bradstreet, "To the Memory of My Dear and Ever Honored Father Thomas Dudley, Esq.," "To Her Father with Some Verses," "Before the Birth of One of Her Children," "To My Dear and Loving Husband," "A Letter to Her Husband, Absent upon Public Employment," "Another [Letter to Her Husband, Absent upon Public Employment]," "In Reference to Her Children, 23 June, 1659," "In Memory of My Dear Grandchild Elizabeth Bradstreet," "In Memory of My Dear Grandchild Anne Bradstreet," "On My Dear Grandchild Simon Bradstreet"
Michael Wigglesworth, "The Day of Doom"
Edward Taylor, "Upon Wedlock, and Death of Children"
Samuel Sewall, "The Diary of Samuel Sewall"
Cotton Mather, "Bonifacius"
William Byrd, "The Secret Diary of William Byrd of Westover 1709–1712"
John and Abigail Adams, letters
Washington Irving, "Rip Van Winkle"
Augustus Baldwin Longstreet, "The Horse Swap"
Nathaniel Hawthorne, "Young Goodman Brown," "Wakefield," "Rappaccini's Daughter," *The Scarlet Letter*
Margaret Fuller, from "The Great Lawsuit"
Harriet Beecher Stowe, "The Mother's Struggle" from *Uncle Tom's Cabin*
Elizabeth Drew Stoddard, "Lemorne *versus* Huell"

Samuel Clemens, *Adventures of Huckleberry Finn*
Henry James, "Daisy Miller"
Sarah Orne Jewett, "A White Heron," "The Foreigner"
Kate Chopin, *The Awakening*
Mary E. Wilkins Freeman, "The Revolt of 'Mother' "
Charlotte Perkins Gilman, "The Yellow Wallpaper"
Edith Wharton, *Ethan Frome*
Henry Adams, Chapter I from *The Education of Henry Adams*
Edgar Lee Masters, poems
Ellen Glasgow, "The Difference"
Willa Cather, "My Mortal Enemy," "Neighbour Rosicky"
Robert Frost, "The Death of the Hired Man," "Home Burial," "Birches," "'Out, Out—'"
Sherwood Anderson, from *Winesburg, Ohio,* especially "Mother," "The Egg"
Eugene O'Neill, *Long Day's Journey into Night*
Katherine Anne Porter, *Old Mortality*
E. E. Cummings, "if there are any heavens my mother will (all by herself) have," "my father moved through dooms of love"
James Thurber, "The Night the Bed Fell"
William Faulkner, *As I Lay Dying*
Thomas Wolfe, "The Lost Boy"
John Steinbeck, "The Leader of the People"
Eudora Welty, "Petrified Man"
John Cheever, "The Country Husband"
Bernard Malamud, "The Magic Barrel"
Saul Bellow, *Seize the Day*
Flannery O'Connor, "The Life You Save May Be Your Own," "Good Country People"
John Updike, "Separating"
Robert Stone, "Helping"
Bobbie Ann Mason, "Drawing Names"
Sam Shepard, *True West*
Alice Walker, "Everyday Use"
Ann Beattie, "Weekend"
Leslie Marmon Silko, "Lullaby"
Louise Erdrich, "Lulu's Boys"
Theodore Roethke, "My Papa's Waltz"
Robert Lowell, "My Last Afternoon with Uncle Devereux Winslow"
Gwendolyn Brooks, "A Song in the Front Yard"
Denise Levertov, from "Olga Poems"
Allen Ginsberg, "To Aunt Rose"
W. S. Merwin, "To My Brother Hanson"

Adrienne Rich, "Snapshots of a Daughter-in-Law"
Sylvia Plath, "Daddy"

Race, Segregation, and Slavery

VOLUME 1

John Smith, from "The General History of Virginia, New England, and the Summer Isles"

William Bradford, from *Of Plymouth Plantation*, Book I, Chapters IX, X; Book II, Chapter XIX

Roger Williams, from *A Key into the Language of America*

Mary Rowlandson, *A Narrative of the Captivity and Restoration of Mrs. Mary Rowlandson*

William Byrd, "The Secret Diary of William Byrd of Westover 1709–1712"

John Woolman, "Early Life and Vocation" from *The Journal of John Woolman*

St. Jean de Crèvecoeur, Letter IX, "Description of Charles-Town; Thoughts on Slavery; on Physical Evil; A Melancholy Scene"

Thomas Jefferson, "The Declaration of Independence"

Olaudah Equiano, *The Interesting Narrative of the Life of Olaudah Equiano, or, Gustavas Vassa, the African, Written by Himself*

Philip Freneau, "The Indian Burying Ground," "To Sir Toby"

Phillis Wheatley, "On Being Brought from Africa to America," "To S.M., a Young African Painter, on Seeing His Works"

Ralph Waldo Emerson, "To W. J. Rotch," [August 1, 1852, Concord] "Negro Slavery vs. Quite Other Slaves to Free"

Henry Wadsworth Longfellow, "The Slave's Dream"

Abraham Lincoln, "A House Divided," "Second Inaugural Address"

Margaret Fuller, from "The Great Lawsuit," "Two Kinds of Slavery: Miranda: No Man Is Willingly Ungenerous"

Harriet Beecher Stowe, "The Mother's Struggle" from *Uncle Tom's Cabin*

Henry David Thoreau, "Resistance to Civil Government," "Slavery in Massachusetts," "A Plea for Captain John Brown," October 1, 1851

Frederick Douglass, *Narrative of the Life of Frederick Douglass, an American Slave*

Walt Whitman, from "Song of Myself," "The Sleepers"

Herman Melville, *Benito Cereno*

VOLUME 2

Samuel Clemens, *Adventures of Huckleberry Finn*

Joel Chandler Harris, "The Wonderful Tar-Baby Story," "Mr. Rabbit Grossly Deceives Mr. Fox," "Free Joe and the Rest of the World"

Kate Chopin, *The Awakening*

Booker T. Washington, from *Up from Slavery*

Charles W. Chesnutt, "The Goophered Grapevine"

W.E.B. DuBois, from *The Souls of Black Folk*

Zora Neale Hurston, "The Eatonville Anthology," "How It Feels to Be Colored Me"

Jean Toomer, from *Cane*

Langston Hughes, poems

Countee Cullen, poems

Richard Wright, "The Man Who Was Almost a Man"

Ralph Ellison, from *Invisible Man*

James Baldwin, from *The Fire Next Time*

Alice Walker, "Everyday Use"

Robert Hayden, poems

Robert Lowell, "For the Union Dead"

Gwendolyn Brooks, poems

Audre Lorde, poems

Imamu Amiri Baraka, poems

Gender Issues of Women's Lives, Work, and Vision

VOLUME 1

John Winthrop, from "The Journal of John Winthrop"

Anne Bradstreet, poems, especially "The Prologue," "The Flesh and the Spirit," "The Author to Her Book," "Before the Birth of One of Her Children," "To My Dear and Loving Husband," "A Letter to Her Husband, Absent upon Public Employment," "Here Follows Some Verses upon the Burning of Our House"

Samuel Sewall, "The Diary of Samuel Sewall"

Cotton Mather, "The Trial of Martha Carrier"

William Byrd, from "The Secret Diary of William Byrd of Westover 1709–1712"

Elizabeth Ashbridge, *Some Account of the Fore-Part of the Life of Elizabeth Ashbridge*

John and Abigail Adams, letters

Thomas Jefferson, "The Declaration of Independence," Letter to Nathaniel Burwell, Esq.

Washington Irving, "Rip Van Winkle"

Ralph Waldo Emerson, [June 24, 1840, Concord]

Nathaniel Hawthorne, "Wakefield," "Rappaccini's Daughter," *The Scarlet Letter*

Edgar Allan Poe, "The Sleeper," "The Raven," "To ——— ——— ———. Ulalume: A Ballad," "Annabel Lee," "Ligeia," "Fall of the House of Usher," "The Philosophy of Composition," Letters to Maria Clemm and Annie L. Richmond

Margaret Fuller, from "The Great Lawsuit"

Harriet Beecher Stowe, "The Mother's Struggle" from *Uncle Tom's Cabin*

George Washington Harris, "Mrs. Yardley's Quilting"

Walt Whitman, Preface to *Leaves of Grass,* "Song of Myself," "Letter to Ralph Waldo Emerson"

Herman Melville, "The Paradise of Bachelors and the Tartarus of Maids"

Elizabeth Drew Stoddard, "Lemorne *versus* Huell"

Emily Dickinson, poems, especially 67, 187, 214, 249, 303, 322, 348, 435, 441, 505, 510, 520, 528, 640, 754, 1099, 1100, 1129, 1545

Rebecca Harding Davis, "Life in the Iron-Mills"

VOLUME 2

Samuel Clemens, *Adventures of Huckleberry Finn*

Bret Harte, "The Outcasts of Poker Flat"

W. D. Howells, "Novel-Writing and Novel-Reading," "Editha"

Henry James, "Daisy Miller," "The Real Thing," "The Turn of the Screw," "The Beast in the Jungle"

Sarah Orne Jewett, "A White Heron," "The Foreigner"

Kate Chopin, *The Awakening*

Mary E. Wilkins Freeman, "A New England Nun," "The Revolt of 'Mother' "

Charlotte Perkins Gilman, "The Yellow Wallpaper"

Jane Addams, from *Twenty Years at Hull-House*

Edith Wharton, *Ethan Frome*

Stephen Crane, "The Bride Comes to Yellow Sky"

Theodore Dreiser, "Old Rogaum and His Theresa"

Gertrude Simmons Bonnin (Zitkala-Sä), autobiographical essays

Henry Adams, Chapter XXV, "The Dynamo and the Virgin (1900)" from *The Education of Henry Adams*

Edgar Lee Masters, "Serepta Mason," "Margaret Fuller Slack," "Lucinda Matlock"

Ellen Glasgow, "The Difference"

Willa Cather, "My Mortal Enemy," "Neighbour Rosicky"

Gertrude Stein, *The Good Anna*

Robert Frost, "The Death of the Hired Man," "Home Burial"

Sherwood Anderson, "Mother" from *Winesburg, Ohio*

William Carlos Williams, "The Young Housewife," "The Widow's Lament in Springtime"

H. D., "Leda," "At Baia," "Helen," from *The Walls Do Not Fall*

Eugene O'Neill, *Long Day's Journey into Night*

Katherine Anne Porter, *Old Mortality*

Zora Neale Hurston, from *Their Eyes were Watching God*
Edna St. Vincent Millay, poems
Dorothy Parker, "De Profundis," "Résumé," "General Review of the Sex Situation," "Experience," "The Waltz"
Jean Toomer, "Fern" from *Cane*
John Dos Passos, "Mary French" from *The Big Money*
F. Scott Fitzgerald, "Winter Dreams"
William Faulkner, *As I Lay Dying*
Langston Hughes, "Mother to Son," "Young Gal's Blues"
Eudora Welty, "Petrified Man"
Tennessee Williams, *A Streetcar Named Desire*
John Cheever, "The Country Husband"
Bernard Malamud, "The Magic Barrel"
Ralph Ellison, Chapter 1 from *Invisible Man*
Flannery O'Connor, "The Life You Save May Be Your Own," "Good Country People"
Bobbie Ann Mason, "Drawing Names"
Alice Walker, "Everyday Use"
Denise Chávez, "The Last of the Menu Girls"
Louise Erdrich, "Lulu's Boys"
Theodore Roethke, "Frau Bauman, Frau Schmidt, and Frau Schwartze"
Elizabeth Bishop, "In the Waiting Room," "The Moose," "One Art"
Gwendolyn Brooks, poems
Denise Levertov, poems, especially from "Olga Poems"
Allen Ginsberg, "To Aunt Rose"
Anne Sexton, poems
Adrienne Rich, poems
Sylvia Plath, poems
Audre Lorde, poems

Politics and War

VOLUME 1

William Bradford, from *Of Plymouth Plantation*
Mary Rowlandson, *A Narrative of the Captivity and Restoration of Mrs. Mary Rowlandson*
Benjamin Franklin, "An Edict by the King of Prussia," "The Sale of the Hessians," *The Autobiography* (especially Part Three)
Thomas Paine, works
Thomas Jefferson, "The Declaration of Independence"
The Federalist, papers No. 1 and No. 10
Philip Freneau, "On Mr. Paine's Rights of Man"
Phillis Wheatley, "To His Excellency General Washington"
Joel Barlow, "Advice to a Raven in Russia"

Washington Irving, "Rip Van Winkle"

William Cullen Bryant, "Abraham Lincoln"

Ralph Waldo Emerson, "Hymn Sung at the Completion of the Concord Monument, April 19, 1836"

Nathaniel Hawthorne, "My Kinsman, Major Molineux," "[Abraham Lincoln]"

Abraham Lincoln, speeches and addresses

Oliver Wendell Holmes, "Old Ironsides," "The Last Leaf"

Henry David Thoreau, "Resistance to Civil Government"

Walt Whitman, poems from *Drum-Taps*, "When Lilacs Last in the Dooryard Bloom'd," from *Specimen Days*, letters to Thomas Jefferson Whitman, Nathaniel Bloom, and John F. S. Gray

Herman Melville, from *Battle-Pieces*

VOLUME 2

Ambrose Bierce, "Chickamauga"

Stephen Crane, "An Episode of War," poems from *War Is Kind*

Black Elk, from *Black Elk Speaks*

Allen Tate, "Ode to the Confederate Dead"

Norman Mailer, from *The Armies of the Night*

Philip Roth, "Defender of the Faith"

Robert Stone, "Helping"

Randall Jarrell, "The Death of the Ball Turret Gunner," "Second Air Force"

Robert Lowell, "For the Union Dead"

6

TEACHING NOTES FOR INDIVIDUAL PERIODS,

AUTHORS, AND WORKS

The *NAAL* contains excellent period introductions, headnotes on each author, and, at the end of the volume, selected bibliographies. My intention in the discussions that follow is not to duplicate this material, but rather to offer additional suggestions for teaching that emerge from my own personal readings of individual works. In some cases, I have chosen to write at length about works or concepts that students find difficult to read or understand at the sophomore or lower-division level. In others, I suggest connections that may stimulate students to compare authors and works, to think across periods or genres, or to assess the development of literary traditions at a given historical moment. I have included some general teaching notes for each historical period and have organized specific readings chronologically according to the placement of authors in the *NAAL* for easy referral; further suggestions on these and other writers and works in the anthology appear in Chapter 7, "Exam Questions and Essay Topics."

VOLUME 1

1620–1820

I often begin by asking students to imagine what they would have felt, had they been citizens of the most civilized country in the world in the seventeenth century, to leave England behind and to take one-way passage to the New World (no Holiday Inns at Plymouth, no jet service back home for those who survived the initial voyage, etc.). How did their view of home town, family, or high-school friends change by the first Thanksgiving of their freshman year in college? Ask them to describe what happened to their consciousness of self or identity as a result of leaving home. The 1620–1820 segment of the course traces the general trajectory by which the colonials evolved from being British, to possessing a consciousness of inhabiting a new world, to inventing themselves as Americans by means of the Revolution.

As English separatists, they were primarily, though not exclusively, Puritan in ideology, which meant that most believed in the literal authority of the Bible. They saw the Bible as a typological model for their own lives (Puritan writers use biblical metaphors to explain the Puritan condition; they often refer to themselves, for example, as Israelites, and the new world becomes Canaan). You will probably need to outline several basic tenets of Puritan thought: original depravity (we are all born sinners); limited atonement (there is little or nothing we can do to change that fact); irresistible grace (if God chooses us as members of his elect, there is nothing we can do about that either); and predestination (God has chosen his elect before we were born). Students are quick to see some of the contradictions in basic Puritan thinking. Why bother to live a good life, for example, if good works neither confer election nor alter damnation? But here you can point out that, by Cotton Mather's time, Puritan theologians devised a series of corollary ideas to resolve logical inconsistencies in their theology. Covenant theology was one of these. Puritans viewed the Bible as God's covenant to them, and in reading the Bible they discovered that God, though arbitrary in his power, was not malicious or capricious. The evildoers in the Old Testament die in the Flood; when God chooses someone to survive, he picks Noah, a good man. So covenant theology taught that although individual Puritans could never know for certain whether or not they were saved, the chances were excellent that members of the elect were the good people, those who would behave accordingly.

Still, students can see that not even covenant theology could definitively ease the anxieties of individual Puritan men. If no one can know his fate for certain (although outward actions might give him a clue), the question of individual salvation remains of major significance throughout a man's life, and Puritans engaged in personal meditation—a process of lengthy closeted soul-searching—to discover whether they might have on their souls any black spots or marks. Students can understand the combination of self-confrontation and self-evasion that such a process might entail—and that Hawthorne, later, explores in his fiction. Ask them to consider what might happen if a Puritan minister engaged in meditation should discover that he had such a black mark. The possibility must have made the act of self-confrontation extremely difficult.

JOHN WINTHROP

"A Model of Christian Charity" (1630) gives students the earliest example of a Puritan sermon delivered in the New World (or en route to the New World, since Winthrop delivered it on board the *Arbella*). Ask students to trace the image patterns by which

Winthrop characterizes the community he envisions; find allusions to biblical passages and persons and consider the application to the Puritans; discuss the discursive form of the sermon, pointing out to them that the sermon was one of the literary genres in Puritan culture.

"The Journal of John Winthrop" offers examples of typology and evidence of the principle of exclusion by which the Puritans founded their New World government. Ask students to assess Winthrop's comments on Roger Williams (possibly asking them to read the selections from Williams) and Anne Hutchinson. What were the Puritans' attitudes toward women, as reflected in Winthrop? Who could speak with divine authority in Puritan society? What might the "devout women" who attended services with Williams and Hutchinson have found in their teachings that severely distressed Puritan theologians?

WILLIAM BRADFORD

Of Plymouth Plantation is an excellent foundation text for the study of colonial American literature. Writing more than a century before the colonists would begin to imagine independence, William Bradford seems to have envisioned what a new country would need and to have supplied it, both in his public service and in his written legacy. I begin by asking students what Bradford's text created that would provide the foundation both for a new country and a nascent New World identity. Like John Smith and the journal writers of the period, Bradford records details of early obstacles and colonial life; even more than other historians, however, Bradford develops in *Of Plymouth Plantation* a larger sense of the meaning and importance of colonial history. Creating an awareness of history while the colonists were yet engaged in the process of establishing their society gave colonial America a cultural foundation. In addition, he offers the colonists a written document ("The Mayflower Compact") as a cornerstone of government, and he associates their origins with sacred rebirth, typologically interprets events as signs of connection with a higher authority, and, in the later chapters of Book II, conveys a sense of prophecy that serves to link his own historical text with the colonists' future.

The early selections from *Of Plymouth Plantation* help students to visualize the combined practical and spiritual concerns of the earliest colonials. In trying to find a harbor (Book I, Chapter X), the "lusty seaman" on board the shallop reminds the pilot to row, "or else they were all cast away." Bradford's account reveals the necessity for self-reliance among the first Puritan settlers; only after they reach "the lee of a small island" can they afford to give thanks to God "for his mercies in their manifold deliverances." Students are surprised to discover how secular and pragmatic the Puritans had to be in the process of creating their spiritual New World. In Book I, Chapter IV, Bradford cites physical hardships, premature aging, lack of control over their children, and, only last (if not least), their hope of "propagating and advancing the gospel of the kingdom of Christ" as the Puritans' reasons for "removing" to the "vast and unpeopled countries of America." How does Bradford's text challenge undergraduate students' preconceptions of the Puritans and their literature?

Among the excerpts from *Of Plymouth Plantation*, "The Mayflower Compact" (Book II, Chapter XI) deserves close analysis for classroom discussion. Bradford writes that the document was "occasioned partly by the discontented and mutinous speeches that some of the strangers [non-Puritans aboard the Mayflower] amongst them had let fall from them in the ship." How does what Bradford calls "the first foundation of their government in this place" establish a Puritan community from the beginning as one that excludes "strangers"? Locate evidence in the "Compact" that even before landing the Puritans defined themselves as an elect group in the secular as well as the spiritual sphere. And what implicit effect does writing and signing "The Mayflower Compact" have? Putting their first agreement into written form was an act of major significance for the Puritans—who believed in the Bible's literal truth and authority. Written words, from the beginning of American culture, carry the associative power of God's word. What does the writing of "The Mayflower Compact" indicate about the Puritans' need for divine authority? From the point of landing in the New World, the Puritans were already setting into motion the necessity of inventing for themselves solutions to material concerns that the Bible does not address. In "The Mayflower Compact," we see them trying to create other documents that would, like the Bible of their covenant theology, possess the power to compel respect and obedience.

I ask students to read later segments as if Bradford's own text were a prefiguring: In what ways do the anthologized excerpts from *Of Plymouth Plantation* recall for students later moments or patterns of thought in American history, even in our own time? Compare Book I, Chapter IV, with Book II, Chapter XXXII (A Horrible Case of Bestiality): both demonstrate early attempts to rationalize colonial life, but in Book II, Chapter XXXII, Bradford's own logic breaks down. In his "endeavor to give some answer hereunto," he ends by raising an unanswerable and prophetic question: "And thus, by one means or other, in 20 years' time it is a question whether the greater part be not grown the worser?" As Bradford records successive years in his history, he continues to convey a pattern of rise and fall, of end prefigured in the beginning. In Book II, Chapter XXXIV (Proposal to Remove to Nauset), he describes the split in the church that resulted from the "removal" to Nauset and characterizes the "poor church" as "an ancient mother grown old and forsaken of her children." Do the selections from Book II in particular suggest a less-than-optimistic view of our colonial origins? Social problems existed from the beginning—corruption, dissent, falling away from the "ancient mother," abandonment, lack of fidelity.

ANNE BRADSTREET

Bradstreet's poetry further illustrates the conflict the Puritans experienced between secular and spiritual life. She tries to humanize her religion—an attempt that the learned ministry of Puritan fathers would have opposed on the ground that Puritan election could not be earned or "felt." Poems that students respond to in line-by-line analysis in class include "The Prologue," "The Author to Her Book," "To My Dear and Loving Husband," and "Here Follows Some Verses upon the Burning of Our House." Students respond to the personal voice and the element of self-disclosure in Bradstreet that make for moving lyrics and can lead into a discussion of the constraints on individual expression in Puritan society. Ask students to find explicit evidence of Puritanism in Anne Bradstreet's poems of domestic life. Does her typological way of thinking affect her choice of metaphor in "The Author to Her Book" or increase her distress in " . . . upon the Burning of Our House"? Although some poems ("Contemplations" and "As Weary Pilgrim") reveal Bradstreet as a Puritan of strong faith, others demonstrate her doubts and the limitations she feels in trying to write poetry as a woman in her culture. What does "The Prologue" reveal about Bradstreet's struggle to locate literary authority within herself? Is she really as self-deprecating as a quick first reading of the poem might suggest? How does she assert her own achievement despite the poem's apparent apologetic tone? What are the several meanings of the line "It is but vain unjustly to wage war" in the context of Bradstreet's self-assertion?

Other selections in NAAL's Third Edition underscore Bradstreet's self-disclosure and search for personal voice in her work. The contrast between form and feeling in "Another [Letter to Her Husband Absent upon Public Employment]" emphasizes the radical nature of Bradstreet's writing. Although she builds her verse on a series of closely connected conceits and the conventional forms of iambic pentameter and end rhymes, she writes a deeply personal, rather than conventional, love poem. And in "To My Dear Children," she further explores her own doubts and perplexities "that I have not found that constant joy in my pilgrimage . . . which I supposed most of the servants of God have."

Even more striking and apparent in "In Reference to Her Children, 23 June, 1659" and in "To My Dear Children," Bradstreet conveys her sense of God as a mother. She writes in "To My Dear

Children" that when she has been troubled "concerning the verity of the Scriptures," she has found comfort in the order of things, "the daily providing for this great household upon the earth, the preserving and directing of all to its proper end." How does the language of "providing" help her view herself in God's image? She, too, has preserved and directed a household and speaks a language of provisions. Here, too, Bradstreet's vision expresses a departure from conventional Puritan thinking. In Puritan typology, it was the father, not the mother, who figured divine authority and power, and the literature of the colonial period noticeably omits references to mothers. Bradstreet clearly had a close relationship with her father (see "To the Memory of My Dear and Ever Honored Father Thomas Dudley Esq." and "To Her Father with Some Verses"), but she must also have learned her pattern of devoted and nurturing motherhood from her relationship with her own mother. In "In Reference to Her Children," she writes lovingly of her children and gives central importance, at the end of the poem, to the relationship between mother and children: "You had a dam that loved you well, / That did what could be done for young." What students may initially pass over as commonplace in this imagery (as a result of nineteenth- and twentieth-century institutionalization of motherhood) in effect was Bradstreet's attempt to repair the invisibility of mothers in Puritan society and Puritan theology. Bradstreet knows she will survive her death in the memory of her own children: "Thus gone, amongst you I may live / And dead, yet speak, and counsel give."

MICHAEL WIGGLESWORTH

"The Day of Doom" presents difficulties for students unless you tell them what to look for as they read. Point out that the poem became a best seller, and ask if they can figure out why. Ask them to find specific evidence of the tenets of Puritan theology; to characterize the contrast between Wigglesworth's sheep and goats; to summarize the portrait of hell in the poem; and to locate passages that suggest the nature of family relationships in Puritan society. In discussion, ask them to contrast Wigglesworth's descriptions of place (heaven and hell) with Bradford's in *Of Plymouth Plantation*; and to re-read Bradstreet's " . . . upon the Burning of Our House" (1666) in light of Wigglesworth's 1662 poem.

MARY ROWLANDSON

"A Narrative of the Captivity and Restoration of Mrs. Mary Rowlandson" will fascinate students at the same time as it helps them make thematic connections between several Puritan writers. Ask students to describe the plot or design of the Indian captivity narrative. Does Rowlandson have a literary or a didactic purpose? How does the narrative compare with other Puritan works that show triumph or redemption after suffering? Suggest that they think specifically about Bradford's portraits of the Indians in *Of Plymouth Plantation* or the form of salvation for the elect at the end of "The Day of Doom." What do the poems of Anne Bradstreet and the "Narrative" of Mary Rowlandson together reveal about the fears, anxieties, and accommodations that comprised ordinary life for women in Puritan society?

EDWARD TAYLOR

The success by which Taylor works through his extended metaphors to imagery of salvation demonstrates the energy that must have been required for the Puritan to engage in spiritual introspection. Help students focus their attention on Taylor's use of poetic form. Ask them to describe the stanzaic pattern of any of the *Preparatory Meditations*, to locate and examine his use of the extended metaphor, and to discuss the imagery of the poem. "Prologue" works well to analyze with them line by line and, especially by way of contrast with Bradstreet's poem of the same title, shows Taylor's awareness that his spiritual salvation and his poetic imagination are dependent on each other. Taylor's problem as a Puritan is to demonstrate to himself over and over again that he is one of the elect, and he does this by using the metaphysical conceit as a focus for literal as well as poetic meditation. If he can turn the mark or spot—the poem's central metaphor—into an image of salvation, then he will have proven his election both spiritually and aesthetically. How does Taylor resolve the problem of literary authority? Does he have difficulty seeing himself as God's pen? What does his struggle for poetic inspiration suggest about those who wrote poetry in Puritan society? Examine "The Preface" from *God's Determinations* to elicit Taylor's Puritan vision. What is the relationship between "nothing man" and "Might Almighty"? Ask students to trace the formal as well as thematic cohesion Taylor achieves through repetition of "nothing" and "might," "all might," and "almighty" throughout the poem. Trace Taylor's references to children in some of his poems; analyze his use of erotic and scatalogical imagery; or trace the triumph over death in "A Fig for Thee, Oh! Death," possibly asking students to compare the poem with John Donne's "Death Be Not Proud."

Discussing Bradstreet's "To My Dear and Loving Husband" side by side with Taylor's "Huswifery" can demonstrate the contrast between the two poets. Bradstreet is interested in physical life, is aware of love as a physical tie, views heaven as a consequence of human faithfulness, and chooses imagery from daily life and classical mythology; Taylor depicts spiritual rebirth, his dependence on God, love as a spiritual tie, and depends on the poetic conceit and biblical imagery to carry the power of his poems. Bradstreet gives us the sense of the individual; Taylor's poetry stifles or subordinates the individual to the spiritual type. Bradstreet's poetry allows her to express her doubts; Taylor tries to contain his within the tight form of the extended metaphor.

SAMUEL SEWALL

Discuss the *Diary* as Puritan introspection in practice. Contrast the form of the diary with Taylor's poetic forms in *Preparatory Meditations*. Weigh Sewall's expressed commitment to "great exercise of mind" in approaching his "Spiritual Estate" with his interest in daily life, "outward causes" of conflict, and public events. Summarize what Sewall's *Diary* reveals about personal life and human relationships in Puritan society.

COTTON MATHER

The headnote to Mather points out that the *Magnalia Christi Americana* "remains Mather's most impressive work" for its portraits of Bradford and Winthrop. Students will find the excerpts from *The Wonders of the Invisible World*, Mather's history of the Salem witch trials, and "Bonifacius," his discussion of family and community life and child rearing, equally interesting. "Bonifacius" can serve as the thematic culmination for a discussion of what it was like to have been a Puritan child. Ask students to re-read Bradford, Bradstreet, and Taylor for references to children and child rearing. It's clear that (1) God's will is more important than the love between parents and children; (2) children are born sinners and must be taught obedience, submission, and fear; and (3) children have the capacity to destroy Puritanism by becoming degenerate and following false teachers. Emory Elliott has written an account of the life of the young Puritan, and how life was different for second- and third-generation children (like Mather himself) in *Power and the Pulpit in Puritan New England.*

ROBERT BEVERLEY

Contrast Beverley's *History . . . of Virginia* with Bradford's *Of Plymouth Plantation*. Note the Virginians' dependence on provisions from England and the sequence of failed settlements that chronologically preceded the settlement at Plymouth. The headnote suggests that Beverley was more interested in place than in the destiny of a people; trace some of the features of his interest in place, including his interest in topography in Book II, and consider consequences for the development of Southern identity. In particular, examine Beverley's concern for "bounds" or boundaries that the English learn from early encounters with the Indians, that become redefined as the name "Virginia" comes to refer to a smaller tract of land than designated in the original grant, and that the early governor of Virginia, Francis Nicholson, transgresses in his attempts to "set the People at Variance as much as possible."

WILLIAM BYRD

Students need continual reminding that by no means all who settled the New World were Puritans and that we emphasize them as founders by choice, not historical necessity. Ask them to compare Sewall's *Diary* with Byrd's "Secret Diary." How does the Virginian Byrd's view of life differ from his New England Puritan counterpart? In form and apparent intention, Byrd's regular writing in his "secret diary" resembles the Puritan practice of introspection and meditation. But students will find it a refreshing contrast. Is Byrd's repetition of his prayers for "good health, good thoughts, and good humor" a cynical response to religion or an expression of well-being that we should take at face value? And what *does* he mean by doing his "dance"?

JONATHAN EDWARDS

A reading of "Personal Narrative" will set up a contrast between the Puritan Edwards and the Quaker John Woolman; it also shows Edwards's interest in science—linking him with Enlightenment thinking—despite the fact that we read him for his sermons and his narrative of his religious conversion. Students ought to read all of the Edwards selections, but I have found it most useful to them to analyze closely "Sinners in the Hands of an Angry God." In my own classroom, I discuss the earlier sermon, "A Divine and Supernatural Light," after we have analyzed "Sinners," and we focus on the contrast between the two.

In analyzing "Sinners in the Hands of an Angry God" in the classroom, it's useful to trace the evolution of semantic meaning in the sermon. Edwards takes a verse from Deuteronomy as his apparent text—"Their foot shall slide in due time"—but as a result of applying what I call a process of "literary interpretation" to the verse, he manages to convince his audience that he is justified in replacing God's words with his own: "There is nothing that keeps wicked men at any one moment out of hell, but the mere pleasure of God." He then dissects every word, idea, and element of syntax from his own statement and performs that same process of "logical" interpretation and extrapolation on it, just as he did on the verse from Deuteronomy. The following ten numbered points in the sermon may be shown to correlate with each of these. For example, in point 4 ("They are now the objects . . . "), students can see Edwards focusing on the present tense of his own restatement of Deuteronomy (clearly a revision, since the verse uses future tense); and point 6 expands on the implications of the word "wicked," and so on. The significance of tracing through this process, which culminates in the famous passage at the end of the first part of the sermon, "So that, thus it is that natural men are held in the hand of God," is that Edwards has managed to reconstruct a kind of scripture, but the language he interprets is his own. In the "Application" section of the sermon, he then chooses imagery that allows his audience to visualize their plight—here using biblical language to reinforce his own—and comes close to equating death of the individual with the day of judgment. If you take students through the sermon slowly enough, you can expect them to discover for themselves what is required for a Great Awakening that is also a reawakening, a revitalization of a theology. Edwards's sermon uses visual imagery as a means of spiritual revival; it provides the possibility of seeing damnation clearly and as if for the first time. "Sinners" is also a performance; Edwards's audience is clearly in the hands of an angry minister as well as an angry God.

"A Divine and Supernatural Light" defines religious conversion; "Sinners in the Hands of an Angry God" instills fear in the unconverted—a subject that students may feel has more varied and interesting literary possibilities than the subject of the earlier sermon. In "A Divine and Supernatural Light," Edwards tried to find words for his feeling of the infusion of the Holy Spirit, to express an ineffable experience; "Sinners" creates an experience for its listeners, as if Edwards believes that sinners don't have the equivalent sense of being damned that the elect have of being filled with grace. It's also interesting to note that Edwards, like Taylor, seems to equate complying with form (whether of religious poetry or of the sermon) with adhering to theology; that is, it allows him to contain his experience within a prescribed form. However, students can see that "Divine Light" is tighter in form than "Sinners"; it is also more straightforward and requires fewer turns in logic. Does this possibly suggest that the experience of feeling damned is more difficult to contain, and even somehow more human? And is the chaos of human life relatively more simple and comprehensible than the complexity and abstractness of "divine and supernatural" life?

Undergraduates may find the excerpt from Chapter I of *The Nature of True Virtue* daunting for Edwards's abstraction and his ability to discourse on virtue, benevolence, beings, love, and beauty without conveying that these qualities belong to living, flesh-and-blood persons. Suggest that, as in the contrast between "Sinners" and "A Divine and Supernatural Light"—where students may find Edwards's portrait of the damned more interesting than his description of salvation—Chapter III will, by contrast, redeem the value of *The Nature of True Virtue* and make Chapter I worth considering. For in Chapter III, Edwards takes up the question of the relation between spiritual beauty and "another, inferior, secondary beauty," which he views as a fixed "law of nature" and which will elicit challenges from students. The very simplicity and harmony of Edwards's values—"uniformity and mutual correspondence," "agreement and union," "consent or concord," all parts "sweetly united in a benevolent agreement of heart"—reduce society to a "beauty of order," in which all persons keep their "appointed office, place and station" and leave no room for dissent. From the retrospective view of our own mid-century's history, does Edwards's sense of order as a "law of nature" exclude social progress that may result from challenging the "natural" order of things? In preparation for their reading of Emerson later in the study of American literature, allow students to challenge Edwards's eighteenth-century conception of "nature."

BENJAMIN FRANKLIN

From William Bradford on, the requirements of the actual wilderness and the Puritans' expectations for their spiritual Promised Land decidedly contradict each other—so much so that in order for a Great Awakening audience to be able to visualize themselves in hell, Edwards must write as if his listeners are not in Enfield, Massachusetts, at all. The radical split between actual place and spiritual "place" creates an anxiety that Benjamin Franklin and his "theology" of economic "salvation" can address. By contrast with Edwards, Franklin, the paradigmatic eighteenth-century man—scientist, inventor, deist—yet pontificates in various modes (humor, in "The Way to Wealth"; fatherly piety, in *The Autobiography*) as if he, too, were a minister. For Franklin—despite his move to Quaker Philadelphia at the age of seventeen—retains many of the forms of Puritan thinking and simply alters its content in addressing his readers.

The transition to Franklin is an easy one after Edwards, partly because students find him more pleasurable to read and partly because, if you begin with "The Way to Wealth," almost all of them will have the feeling that they have read him before. I like to ask students how many have heard some of Poor Richard's maxims. Almost all of them will, even those who don't remember ever reading Franklin in high school. How, then, did they hear these maxims, and what does that say about the transmission, by means of an oral tradition, of American values and language? We choose a few of the maxims to analyze closely, focusing in particular on the way Franklin exploits the religious metaphors his audience, like Edwards's, would have already been familiar with—for example, "God helps them that help themselves," or "Those have a short Lent who owe money to be paid at Easter." Here students can see Franklin keeping the language of Puritan theology but changing its meaning—reversing Edwards's transformation of Deuteronomy in "Sinners in the Hands of an Angry God" (see previous discussion). For "The Way to Wealth" is an anti-sermon—ironically in the tradition of Jonathan Edwards, even though Franklin's "salvation" is financial prosperity. His language crosses religious metaphors and images from home industry, and his advice becomes the religious "practice" by which common people may increase their worldly (not spiritual) effects and position. He even associates his "old Gentleman" in the piece with a minister, concluding that Poor Richard's advice has as little effect "as if it had been a common Sermon."

The Autobiography introduces students to their first long work of significance, and no brief discussion can do more than suggest a few general ways to organize class analysis. One point I try to make is that in The Autobiography, as in Poor Richard's Almanack, Franklin offers practical solutions for the material concerns of the common people, in effect exchanging the spiritual goal of their religious practice for one of secular and economic salvation. The Autobiography gives us our earliest example of "business literature." In detail after detail that Franklin chooses to relate (and the book is a highly selective account of his life—ask students to compare it with Sewall's Diary or Byrd's "Secret Diary"), it's possible to show students that the development of the embryonic individual for Franklin takes precedence over any interest a man of his time might have had in received theology. Still, it's fascinating to see how Franklin takes the forms of that theology and turns them to his own use. Ask students how Franklin's "Project of arriving at moral Perfection" is similar in form to Puritan introspection and meditation. (He writes that "daily examination would be necessary," and he uses a "little Book" duly lined, "on which Line and in its proper Column I might mark by a little black Spot every Fault I found upon Examination to have been committed respecting that Virtue upon that Day." Yet Franklin is attempting to alter his own moral character, not to find evidence of his soul's salvation. Franklin's life and his "instruction" through his Autobiography transform the daily routine into a religious practice. Practical life itself becomes a "religion," governed by more precepts, self-discipline, introspection, and, above all, the desire for self-improvement, so that Franklin's work both derives from Puritan religious method and is a reaction against it.

How does The Autobiography reveal Franklin as an eighteenth-century man? Discuss Franklin's fascination with invention, scientific discoveries, and social institutions. In what ways does he adapt what he calls the "Age of Experiments" to political as well as personal life? Describe his plan for the "union of all the colonies," and suggest that it is as much a practical solution to a problem—another "invention"—as any of the more tangible projects he writes about. Final discussion of *The Autobiography* can prepare the way for "The Declaration of Independence," for which Franklin offered some revisions and directly influenced Jefferson's conceptual thinking. The title of Garry Wills's book on the Constitution, *Inventing America*, can help students think about what both Franklin and Jefferson are trying to do in their political writings. Franklin is motivated by the advice he receives to "invite all wise men to become like yourself," and students can get a clear picture of Franklin as both a self-made man and a "self-invented" one. Franklin offers his life as a blueprint, a repeatable experiment, evidence that an American man can resolve the confusion involved in being a colonial by "inventing" himself as a new kind of person.

Franklin's other prose both confirms and enlarges upon his self-portrait as a rational man. Discuss Franklin's use of satire, especially in "Rules by Which a Great Empire May Be Reduced to a Small One," as an eighteenth-century rhetorical device. Compare the form of "Rules" with the numbered, discursive, rational forms that William Bradford attempts (see *Of Plymouth Plantation*, Book I, Chapter IV) and Jonathan Edwards perfects (see especially "Sinners in the Hands of an Angry God"), and evaluate the power of Franklin's work. Recast each satirical point into a direct statement, and examine the quality of Franklin's logic. See also his letter to Joseph Priestley, in which Franklin describes his method of thinking through difficult cases. Contrast Franklin's self-presentation in *The Autobiography* with moments in the letters in which he reveals more of himself. See in particular his letter to his father Josiah, written when Franklin was in his early thirties, in which he gives us a rare glimpse of family dynamics; his letter to his sister Mrs. Jane Mecom, in which he assumes a didactic stance but also expresses filial concern; and his letters to Miss Georgiana Shipley and Madame Brillon, which suggest Franklin's fondness for relationships with women other than his wife (a well-known fact of his biography which he does not mention in his autobiography).

ELIZABETH ASHBRIDGE

After the absence of self-disclosure in Edwards and Franklin's guarded self-presentation, students may welcome Ashbridge's *Some Account*. Although Ashbridge expresses her intent to write a spiritual autobiography, and although her conversion to the Quaker faith substantially enhances John Woolman's self-portrait in his *Journal* (note that although both Quakers published their narratives in England in the same year, 1774, Ashbridge wrote hers much earlier), Ashbridge's account portrays much more than spiritual conversion. More than any other selection in the 1620–1820 period, Ashbridge conveys in detail the quality of her relationship with her mother, patterns of early-eighteenth-century family life and the inflexibility of the father's role, and her own particular form of what twentieth-century readers may call adolescent rebellion. Here, it may be interesting to take another look at Franklin's 1738 letter to his father. Franklin expresses a certain amount of rebellious independence in that letter, at an age well past what we would consider adolescence; and Ashbridge was about the same age as Franklin was in 1738 when she wrote her 1744 *Account* and gave us the portrait of her life's "fore-part." Might we speculate, with students, that our early identity as colonials replicated stages in human growth and development—the mid-eighteenth century, culminating in our collective *Declaration of Independence*, epitomizing cultural adolescence and the transition to adulthood? In Ashbridge's development, adolescent rebellion seems all the more striking because she was a girl; and our students may delight when she reports that she "sometimes grieved at . . . not being a boy."

Her youthful independence may reflect the antics of the tomboy; but in the context within which she makes her statement—that she had a high regard for ministers and grieved that she could not be one because she was not a boy—she is also identifying the compelling theme that unites the secular and spiritual aspects of her conversion narrative. In effect, she describes the process by which she began her New World life in servitude (she uses the word "sold" to describe her indenturing) and silence, and, through a long process containing much forward and backward movement, achieved freedom and speech, as well as sufficient literary authority to write her *Account*. In class discussion, trace the various stages of Ashbridge's development, focusing on those moments in which she keeps or breaks silence (see, for example, the incident with the whipper, the scene in the tavern when her husband tries to make her dance, and her determination to attend Quaker Meeting) and in which she discovers, to her surprise, that Quaker women become preachers.

Ashbridge uses silence as a defense against her husband's abuse; her silence may lead students to ask for whom Ashbridge wrote her story. The headnote describes *Some Account* as resembling an eighteenth-century popular novel; further, Ashbridge's language is colloquial, and she explicitly states her concerns for her reader. Did she see herself writing for women? In a useful digression, you might, in conjunction with Ashbridge, assign Thomas Jefferson's 1818 letter to Nathaniel Burwell on the subject of women's education in which he complains that women have an "inordinate passion" for novels, which poisons their minds. Although Ashbridge does not explicitly state that she writes her *Account* for a female audience, in stating that "it was required of me in a more public manner to confess to the world what I was," she is clearly referring to her social position as woman as well as Quaker. Does she decide to write her story of life as a woman who becomes a Quaker in part to demonstrate that such a story is not "poison" at all, but moral edification? A related aspect of *Some Account* is Ashbridge's description of interaction between husband and wife. She is particularly likely to report her husband's actual words when he criticizes her speech. It appears that for her husband, her "clack"—her speaking—is itself sufficient poison.

Ashbridge's description of her indenturing and passage to the colonies invites comparison with Olaudah Equiano's *Narrative*, in which he portrays life aboard the slave ships. While Ashbridge describes herself as "pretty well" treated, she also states that her master forced her to go barefoot in snowy weather "and to be employed in the meanest drudgery, wherein I suffered the utmost hardships that my body was able to bear."

JOHN WOOLMAN

The Journal of John Woolman is well taught in conjunction with Jonathan Edwards, for it allows students to see that Puritanism didn't simply disappear when deism walked in the door, but, rather, that the writings by colonial writers (both Puritans and non-Puritans, such as Woolman) reveal stresses on Puritanism from the beginning that foreshadow its own eventual decline as the dominant theology. The Puritan practice of inner scrutiny, the use of the poetic conceit in Edward Taylor's poetry, and the social ritual of executing witches all serve an analogous function: to allow the Puritans to externalize their own inner doubts and confusion and to create a false sense of security concerning their own salvation or election. In reading Woolman's *Journal,* students may wonder what was so terrible about the Quakers that the Puritans felt such a need to pass laws against them and to persecute them. The excerpt will also give students a different view of religion than the one they find in the selections from Puritan writers. Ask them to think about what Woolman means when he writes that "true religion consisted in an inward life." His consciousness of that inward life or the "inner light" of the Quakers may seem more closely akin to the development of individual voice in the poetry of Anne Bradstreet than the didactic poetry of Taylor or Wigglesworth. Woolman's *Journal* suggests that one of the schisms within Puritanism resulted from the discovery, by some colonials, of religious faith that was connected more to feeling than to the purely intellectual "delight" Edwards's work reveals. Are there other ways in which the *Journal* illustrates an increasingly deep split within colonial consciousness? Ask students to think about connections between expressions of self-reliance as early as Bradford's *Of Plymouth Plantation*, Woolman's "inward life," and the popular climate that led to Franklin's great popularity in Quaker Pennsylvania.

JOHN ADAMS AND ABIGAIL ADAMS

In the letters of John and Abigail Adams, students can see the rare intersection of public and personal life in colonial America, as well as evidence of intimate human relationship between two people. Organize class discussion of the letters by asking students to list the various conflicts that each of these writers reveals in his or her letters: Abigail is concerned with smallpox, lack of pins and other domestic equipment, encroachments of war with England, fear that others might read her letters, and pride in her connection with John's work; John is concerned about keeping his private identity alive, about affairs of the Continental Congress, about shaping the new country's independence, and about fear that others will intercept his letters. Both are capable of praising and chiding in the same letter, and of complaining about the other's lack of attention or expression of feeling. John's letter of July 20, 1776 (less than three weeks after the signing of *The Declaration of Independence*) opens, "This has been a dull day to me," because a letter he had expected to receive from Abigail did not arrive. John Adams is writing from the absolute center of political action, yet he worries that his friends at home may think he has forgotten his wife and children.

Ask students to compare the letters of John and Abigail Adams with those of Ashbridge, Franklin, and Jefferson. Like Ashbridge, John and Abigail Adams use language to communicate with a reader whom they know to be a real person; in contrast, Franklin and Jefferson produce letters that seem written for a general audience. John and Abigail transcend the formal requirements of eighteenth-century letter writing and allow feeling to interrupt form. John can write, in his letter of October 9, 1774, that "the Business of the Congress is tedious, beyond Expression," a sentiment that he clearly reserves for the private sphere of his relationship with Abigail, and the following year, in his letter of October 29, 1775, can recite the virtues of New England as if he were delivering a public speech. Abigail prefers those letters in which John transgresses conventional form, writing about one of his letters, in hers of July 21, 1776, that "I think it is a choice one in the Literary Way, . . . yet it Lacked some essential ingredients to make it complete." She wants from John more personal discourse and more words "respecting yourself, your Health or your present Situation." These letters exist within the dual contexts of personal relationship and political change, and the rapid shifts in the discourse reflect the way attention to audience changes the use of language, even in the late eighteenth century.

ST. JEAN DE CRÈVECOEUR; THOMAS PAINE; THOMAS JEFFERSON; THE FEDERALIST

Throughout the 1620–1820 period, I trace the way each subsequent shift in thinking retains old forms. The need the Mayflower Puritans felt for a document that would put their authority into writing is the earliest example of the pattern; the way Edwards uses biblical language and Franklin retains the forms—but alters the content—of Puritan thinking are eighteenth-century examples. In the writings of the federalist period, the pattern continues to hold. James Madison, in Federalist Paper No. 10, argues that one of the advantages of Union is "its tendency to break and control the violence of faction." By 1787, when Madison wrote his paper, Puritanism had long disappeared as an apparent force, and yet Madison's concern that factions be controlled by means of a Union that possesses a written document—the Constitution—establishes him as a distant cousin to his Puritan predecessors in the way that he views the power of the written text.

Many instructors find the federal period difficult to teach in a literature course. Thomas Paine and Thomas Jefferson can seem more like figures from the historical record than recorders of individual aesthetic vision. Yet if we focus on the ways the American Revolution and the "Declaration of Independence" address—like Franklin's work—the wide gap the Puritans experienced between the dictates of their theology and the pressing material concerns of their daily lives, the significant documents of the American Revolution can appear as a collective fiction. For "The Declaration of Independence," in particular, manages to create the illusion of identity that seems to have been required before early nineteenth-century writers could begin to give us an imaginative literature.

"THE DECLARATION OF INDEPENDENCE"

Like *The Autobiography*, "The Declaration of Independence" is a blueprint, an experiment that the French would repeat, and another invention. Yet many students won't do more than skim it out of class—believing that they don't need to, either because they read it in high school or because they are somehow "living" it. It has the aura of sacred text, and I've found it necessary to break down their assumption that the "Declaration" is like the Bible, another divinely authored text, in order to show them that it has motive, intention, character, and plot—as if it were a work of fiction. Ask your students to consider the way it "makes" history the same way Franklin "invents" his own life in *The Autobiography*. Do they see any resemblance between the "Declaration" and the sermon form, especially in "Sinners in the Hands of an Angry God"? And what level of diction does Jefferson use? Compare the language with Franklin's in "The Way to Wealth"; compare it with Edwards's as well. Show Jefferson trying to imbue secular and political concerns with the semantic aura of spiritual salvation. I suggest that the "art of virtue" that Franklin recalls in *The Autobiography* but never actually wrote finds its "text" in "The Declaration," democracy's "bible." Whatever else you choose to teach from Jefferson and the Federalist era, "The Declaration of Independence" becomes the central work to read closely with students. I have often moved outside of chronology at this point and circulated copies of the brief "Declaration of Sentiments," modeled on "The Declaration," that Elizabeth Cady Stanton wrote and women at the Woman's Rights Convention in Seneca Falls in 1848 signed (see Appendix). Examining the two documents together stimulates as much discussion as you want to allow time for.

EXPLORING THE ISSUE OF SLAVERY

An approach to teaching American literature that neglects the evidence of dissenting voices within apparent union makes it difficult for the classroom teacher to explain why anything ever changed—why writers in any historical period began to think differently, and why they experimented with different genres. Given the principle of exclusion that is our heritage from the Puritans (however far back and from whatever origin we are able to trace our personal lineage) and looking ahead to the Civil War of the 1860s, how our founding fathers saw fit to deal with factions, with social difference, and, in particular, with the issue of slavery can help us describe the tensions that have always been, and still remain, a part of American life (and that become part of our teaching whenever we make decisions based on the "major" or "minor" significance of particular texts or authors). In the literature of the federal period, then, in addition to discussing major figures and ideas of the Enlightenment, I also focus on the ways various writers and works address the issue of slavery.

Long before the early nineteenth century, slavery was a national issue, and in failing to resolve it, Jefferson, James Madison, and the Continental Congress created another "new world" with its own stresses—like those on Puritan government—that involve students of American literature in a discussion of the relationship between liberty and literary authority. The language of liberty that makes Thomas Paine's writing and "The Declaration of Independence" particularly effective suggests that it is the very articulation of the "United States of America" that makes revolution possible and thereby brings the country into being. The documents of American Revolution achieve their power in the same way that William Bradford does in "The Mayflower Compact": they focus the nebulous thinking of a larger group, and they offer the familiar form of written covenant. The writers of the federal period put language in the service of human liberty—for some but not all. And it seems important to point out to students that the unspoken omissions from the language of "all men are created equal" will require other internal revolutions—for the abolition of slavery and the fight for women's suffrage—before the liberty that makes possible the literary achievements of the 1820–1865 period will also support the literary authority of black men, white women, and black women.

Students can find discussions of slavery in several writers whose works may otherwise seem difficult to connect. John Woolman, in his *Journal*, records refusing to write a bill of sale for a Negro woman as early as the 1740s. William Byrd of Virginia writes casually of whipping Negro houseservants in his "Secret Diary." St. Jean de Crèvecoeur, in "Letter IX," describes the miserable condition of the slaves in Charles-Town. Jefferson, in "Notes on the State of Virginia," objects to slavery as much for what it does to the masters as for what it does to the slaves, fears "supernatural interference" and even the "extirpation" of the masters—yet makes no concrete proposal for ending slavery (and himself owned many slaves). "The Declaration of Independence," in its original version (the *NAAL* includes the original document Jefferson submitted to the Continental Congress, with the changes as adopted noted in the margins), clearly shows Jefferson's abhorrence of the institution of slavery. The passage in the "Declaration" that begins, "He has waged cruel war against human nature itself . . . " and that was completely excised from the document based on objections from representatives from South Carolina, Georgia, and some northern colonies engaged in profit from the slave trade, helps students understand the inherent contradiction in the document's reference to "all men." The textual revisions show them that the Continental Congress addressed the issue of slavery, then decided to eliminate it from consideration in "The Declaration." One essay that I have found extremely useful in preparing to teach the "Declaration" is Edwin Gittleman's article, "Jefferson's 'Slave Narrative': *The Declaration of Independence* as a Literary Text" (*Early American Literature* 8: 239–256).

OLAUDAH EQUIANO

Equiano was born in Africa, and, after buying his freedom in 1766, chose to settle in England. One of the first questions you might raise with students concerns the inclusion of Equiano's *Narrative* in the *NAAL*. What makes it "American" literature? Does Equiano qualify as an "American" writer because he was bought and owned by a Philadelphia merchant, even though he did not choose to emigrate to the New World and left the colonies as soon as he was able? The circumstances of its author's citizenship (or lack of it) give reality to the term "colonial" literature as a category which includes Equiano's *Narrative*. For, as a slave, Equiano was indeed "colonized" in body, and his writing is therefore "colonial."

Like Elizabeth Ashbridge's *Account*, Equiano's *Narrative* gives students a new perspective on life in the American colonies. Servitude and slavery did not begin with the Southern plantation economy, but much earlier, soon after the first colonial settlements. Literature as early as William Byrd's *The Secret Diary*, written between 1709–1712, reflects the presence and ill treatment of slaves, Ashbridge was indentured in 1732, and Equiano was stolen by African traders in 1756. Although the original version of *The Declaration of Independence* includes a reference to the slave trade (see the changes Jefferson notes in the text included in his *Autobiography*), and although, during the writing of the Constitution, the prohibition of the slave trade was discussed, stipulations concerning slavery were omitted from the Constitution and Congress was prohibited from abolishing the slave trade for 20 years. Although Britain outlawed the slave trade in 1807, it was not abolished in the United States until the Emancipation Proclamation of January 1, 1863. Equiano's narrative exists within the context of that history and provides a great deal of information about life in Africa, the internal African slave trade (Equiano's own father owned slaves), and conditions on the slave ships themselves.

One of the most fascinating aspects of Equiano's narrative is the way he creates an African perspective on European life; to cite a term Equiano, in effect, defines for us, even though he would not have used the term, his text embodies the concept of "Afrocentric." His fear of "water larger than a pond or a rivulet" begins when he nears the coast of Africa and encounters a people "who did not circumcise, and ate without washing their hands." The fact that he never learns to swim suggests that the fear of water was early associated, for the 11-year-old boy, with his own enslavement. Much that he sees when he becomes acquainted with Europeans makes him afraid and astonished; he fears being eaten by white men, and he believes that sails, anchors, clocks, and pictures are magic.

The world Equiano depicts enshrines the merchant. King, the Philadelphia merchant, eventually keeps his promise and allows Equiano to buy his freedom. Equiano does so by becoming a merchant himself. Cargo thus becomes central to Equiano's freedom; he begins as "live cargo," becomes a trader in various goods, and literally reverses his fortunes. Unlike the authors of later slave narratives, such as the *Narrative of the Life of Frederick Douglass*, and unlike Elizabeth Ashbridge, Equiano does not achieve freedom by finding his voice. Neither does he feel compelled to keep silent. By including his manumission papers in his *Narrative*, he seems to suggest that, indeed, it is only a reversal of fortune, not his own power, that has produced his freedom, for the "absolute power and dominion one man claims over his fellow" that allowed Robert King to emancipate Equiano equally allowed other white men to enslave the freeman Joseph Clipson, whose story Equiano relates. The reversal of fortune that produced Equiano's *Narrative* remains valuable "cargo" in our attempts to instruct students in the literature of New World colonials.

PHILIP FRENEAU

Freneau's poetry directly addresses the social and historical events of his day and anticipates the influence of the Romantic poets on American writers in poems such as "The House of Night" and "On Observing a Large Red-Streak Apple." "On the Emigration to America and Peopling the Western Country" and "On Mr. Paine's Rights of Man" derive their force from their historical situation. The poems suggest that the American Revolution made the development of American poetry possible, and yet, as Francis Murphy notes in the *NAAL* headnote, Freneau was not "the Father of American poetry." Ask students to think about what limits Freneau. Freneau's brand of eloquence as it survives in his poetry (he also wrote political pamphlets) has not appeared to be as lasting in its significance as our country's founding documents; the political covenant and the autobiography absorb almost all of the literary energy available during the revolutionary and federal period and serve as the major literary genres of the late eighteenth century. Still, Freneau's choice to respond to political and social conditions in "To Sir Toby," written about slavery (although he addresses a sugar planter in Jamaica rather than a Southern slaveholder), demonstrates his faith in the power of language used in the service of political and social change. This faith has its roots in the Puritan belief in the literary authority of the Bible—but it also anticipates the First Amendment to the Constitution, and the idea that freedom of speech is the most important freedom, because it is speech that leads to freedom itself.

PHILLIS WHEATLEY

Wheatley is a fascinating poet for anyone interested in literary history, for she reflects Puritan influence, wrote poetry that imitates Alexander Pope, and was the first black American to publish a book. As the introduction to Wheatley in the *NAAL* points out, "the only hint of injustice found in her poetry is in the line 'Some view our sable race with scornful eye'"; she writes about abstract liberty rather than about freedom from slavery. In "On Being Brought from Africa to America," the kind of enslavement she seems most concerned with is that of her former ignorance of "redemption." She was freed after the death of the Wheatleys, and her circumstances would have been radically different from those of the Southern slaves. Yet the very existence of her poetry may seem evidence to your students that there is a direct correlation between liberty and literary authority. Ask students to compare Wheatley with Bradstreet. What explains the absence of personal voice in Wheatley? Is she writing in imitation of eighteenth-century British poets, or has she chosen a poetic style that calls the least possible attention to the speaking voice? Wheatley does make a connection between achieving exalted language in poetry (or in art, as in "To S.M., a Young African Painter, on Seeing His Works") and rising on "seraphic pinions." Placing Wheatley in her historical context, a reader can see the appeal for Southern slaves of spiritual "rising" and the "liberty" of religious salvation—an appeal that white slaveowners ironically exploited as an effective panacea to silence the slaves' dissatisfactions. In offering the language of "wings enraptured" and "celestial choir," Wheatley resembles the earlier colonial writers (such as Wigglesworth and Taylor) for whom personal concerns and personal voice are largely absent. And yet the imagery of "rising" and racial uplift would reappear in black prose and poetry from Booker T. Washington to Countee Cullen.

ROYALL TYLER

In his exit lines, Dimple summarizes the play's "main chance" when he contrasts himself, "a gentleman, who has read Chesterfield and received the polish of Europe," with Manly, "an unpolished, untravelled American." But long before the closing scenes Tyler establishes contrast as the play's dramatic principle. In opening a discussion of the play, ask students to comment on Tyler's use of contrast. Letitia and Charlotte begin the play by disagreeing on the merits of the pocket-hoop and the bell-hoop; they discuss the contrast Maria finds "betwixt the good sense of her books, and the flimsiness of her love-letters" so that she spoke of Mr. Dimple "with respect abroad, and with contempt in her closet"; and, in Act II, Charlotte describes her brother as "the very counterpart and reverse of me." The servants Jonathan and Jeremy contrast with each other, and mirror the contrast between Manly and Dimple; and the contrast between country and city reinforces the contrast between American style and European influence. Low-life scenes between the servants extend the humor among the protagonists, and the apparent triviality of the play's subject matter—style—contrasts with the seriousness of an American's attempt to write "a piece, which we may fairly call our own."

Some of the play's humor derives, as the headnote points out, from its Americanization of the basic story line of Sheridan's *The School for Scandal.* Tyler also overloads the play with conventions of eighteenth-century comedy, especially at the end, when we discover two eavesdroppers, one of whom hides in a closet, and when the play's *denouement* rests on Van Rough's disclosure that he, too, had eavesdropped from within a closet. The play that begins in disagreement ends in harmony, with the promise of weddings between Jonathan and his Tabitha, and between Maria and Manly.

A literary period which essentially begins with the deaths of all the settlers of Roanoke and half the original settlers of Plymouth, and which predicts a day of doom for sinners in the hands of an angry God, ends, perhaps surprisingly, in comedy. Such is the true contrast in Royall Tyler's play, the reversal of literary fortune from the sermon to the drama. Instead of telling late eighteenth-century Americans how to live, Tyler is more interested in portraying the way they live. Much of the play's value will demonstrate itself if you allow students to experience the comic relief of Tyler and the drama, after what may have seemed to them to be a long struggle with Puritans and historians. If there is time, forgo discussion long enough to assign parts, and allow students to walk through Act V, Scene 2, up to Dimple's exit. The scene includes everyone but Jonathan and Jenny, and walking through it will bring to life the eavesdroppers and the "heroism" of Manly's defense of his sister's honor.

1820–1865

One way of creating a context for discussing early nineteenth-century authors is to analyze closely with students several works related in theme before proceeding to a more chronological examination. I sometimes ask students to read "Rip Van Winkle" (see discussion of Rip's dream below) in conjunction with "Young Goodman Brown" (another story that shows the male protagonist waking from a dream), "Bartleby, the Scrivener" (where Bartleby's "dead wall revery" becomes a variation on the dream motif), and Thoreau's "Resistance to Civil Government" (in which he describes his night in jail as "a change [that] had to my eyes come over the scene. . . ." Students have heard the phrase "American dream" used as a cliché; beginning the nineteenth century with works in which American dreams actually figure in the plot helps them look for new meanings in the theme. In these four works the dreamers share confusion concerning the nature of reality. I ask students to keep in mind the larger historical context—the abolitionist movement, early manifestations of the women's rights struggle in the temperance society, the emerging American economic system, the near-extinction of the American Indians, and the imperialism of the war with Mexico—as they study a literature that explores the power of the imagination at the same time that it often denies or ignores the unresolved conflict at the center of early nineteenth-century American social and political life.

Yet, despite that frequent denial, the literature of the 1820–1865 period gives us evidence of an awakening. As Hershel Parker notes in his period introduction in the *NAAL*, by the 1850s "there was some elusive quality about [the literature of the new country] that was *American*." Even though many of our early nineteenth-century writers may have turned inward, to the world of romance, gothic fantasy, dreams, idealized portraits of the West and the Indians, or the microcosm of individual perception, or the single-sex universe of Melville's sea fiction, even the transcendentalist Thoreau, in separating himself from society at Walden Pond, tries to give imagery of waking literal—and literary—body. Is an American identity the creation of a few early nineteenth-century dreamers, or does it result from the rhythms of dreaming and waking, of separation and engagement, of evasion and confrontation?

As the literature of the 1820–1865 period particularly shows, writing helps Emerson, Hawthorne, Dickinson, and others to discover who they are in what they see and the language they find to express that vision. At this point, I suggest to my students that what we are exploring, in part, as we read American literature is the development of ways of thinking and seeing the world, as well as ways of imagining and creating the self. In rejecting the rationality of the Enlightenment, early nineteenth-century writers yet were evolving their own vision. Thoreau, in Walden, explicitly exchanges Enlightenment thinking for Eastern mystical enlightenment. Can students see the early nineteenth-century writers' rejection of rationality as part of a larger pattern in American literary history? The Puritans were typological; the eighteenth-century writers exalted reason and logic; but the early nineteenth-century writers were analogical in their way of seeing. Perhaps the emergence of an "American" imaginative literature in the early nineteenth century may itself be seen as evidence of evolution in epistemology. Once writers became capable of inventing metaphors for their own imagination or for telling stories about either private or public life, they became equally capable of exploring the meaning of their experience and for defining it as "American."

Transcendentalism took the separatism of early nineteenth-century writers to its extreme limit. Yet, as I try to show in our class discussion of "Nature" and *Walden*, the transcendentalists' theory of language becomes the basis for yet another American spiritual movement, and, in retrospect, every prior moment of separation in colonial and American literary history may be seen as a variation on that pattern. When the Puritan reliance on God's word seems in need of strengthening, Jonathan Edwards rewrites the Bible; when theology fails to solve material problems, Benjamin Franklin invents a language with which to address the common people and to create himself as a blueprint; when Britain no longer speaks for the colonists, Jefferson writes a document that enacts the very independence it declares; and in the early nineteenth century, Emerson calls for a literary separation ("We have listened too long to the courtly muses of Europe," from "The American Scholar") and for an American poet capable of finding the language for the "as yet unsung" American experience ("Yet America is a poem in our eyes . . . ," from "The Poet"). The evolution from typology to logic to analogy is progressive, even though the early nineteenth-century writers were the first to see the pattern. The "forms of being" change, and the theories of language change, but American writers become increasingly aware of their powers to name themselves, and thus to write themselves into being. From Rip Van Winkle's dream to Adrienne Rich's "dream of a common language," the meaning of both American identity and American literary history are intimately tied to the evolution of an American language.

By the end of their study of the first volume of the *NAAL*, students can see that while American writers may continue after the Civil War to struggle with language and literary forms that will make it possible for them to write an American literature, from the Revolution on they learn to look to themselves for their literary authority, and to their own experience for the emotional and aesthetic power of their work. Despite Stowe's comment about taking dictation from God, American writers after the federal period no longer have even the illusion, as Edward Taylor had written, "That Thou wilt guide my pen to write aright." Nineteenth-century authors make creative literature out of the economic and spiritual self-reliance of which Franklin and Emerson wrote. Nevertheless, the prohibitions against writing and speaking that American white women and black men and women suffered throughout the 1620–1865 period in American history would mean that many Americans, then and now, continue to be silenced, and that the act of writing, for white women and for black writers, would reflect acts of heroic rebellion.

WASHINGTON IRVING

"Rip Van Winkle" is the work I choose to open the 1820–1865 segment, and we analyze it closely. Many of my students entirely pass over Irving's references to the American Revolution until we discuss them in class. I call the story the first "American dream" in American literature, and we talk about the implications of that dream. Students make connections between the confused state of mind the earliest colonists must have experienced and Rip's confusion upon "waking" to discover that he is a citizen of a new country, an event that must have seemed to many to have taken place overnight. In one central passage in the story that recurs almost as a template in later American literature, Rip asks, "'does nobody here know Rip Van Winkle?'" Irving writes, "The poor fellow was now completely confounded. He doubted his own identity, and whether he was himself or another man. In the midst of his bewilderment, the man in the cocked hat demanded who he was, and what was his name?" Rip's reply echoes with contemporary resonance to undergraduate students: "'God knows,' exclaimed he, at his wit's end; 'I'm not myself—I'm somebody else—that's me yonder—no—that's somebody else, got into my shoes—I was myself last night, but I fell asleep on the mountain, and they've changed my gun and every thing's changed, and I'm changed, and I can't tell what's my name, or who I am!'" The story suggests as one meaning of the American dream that, like Rip, we are confused and about twenty years behind accepting or understanding our own national history. The new country begins in uncertainty and confusion; the new American's sense of identity falters, then gains in confidence, much as the tale itself shows Rip, by the end, invested with new authority.

But what is the nature of that authority? For Rip, who becomes "reverenced" as a storyteller, a "chronicle of the old times 'before the war,'" is the same person who, twenty years earlier, owned the "worst-conditioned farm in the neighborhood" and was "ready to attend anybody's business but his own." Here Irving shows Rip as a type of the artist before his time; it is only *after* history catches up with him, in a sense, and he manages to wake up after the Revolution that he finds his vocation (the resonance with American literary history seems almost allegorical in this reading of the story). Is the story Irving's comment on the absence of imaginative literature prior to the American Revolution? What happens to Rip's cultural identity that makes it possible for the townspeople to produce their first storyteller? I suggest that the story documents the transition between the moment in which the new country had a potential chronicler (Rip Van Winkle) but no history, to the moment just a "dream" later when its new identity gave it both a storyteller and a story to tell. Like the moment of the decline of Puritanism and the emergence of enlightenment thinking that we see in Franklin's *Autobiography* (where Franklin keeps the form of Puritan introspection and changes its content), there is a similar moment of transition between pre- and postrevolutionary thinking for the new American Rip Van Winkle. In changing only the red coat of King George to the blue coat of George Washington on the sign that used to stand over the village inn (and now advertises the Union Hotel), Irving suggests that the "singularly metamorphosed" country may have undergone radical change, but retains a similar form. What, then, happens to political analysis in the story? Irving writes that "Rip was no politician; the changes of states and empires made but little impression on him."

At the end of the story Irving evades exploring the ironies implicit in the American Dream by turning all of Rip's confusion into a joke at Dame Van Winkle's expense: "But there was one species of despotism under which he had long groaned, and that was—petticoat government." Here Irving establishes a theme that would become characteristic of much nineteenth-century fiction, in which the male character represents simple good nature, artistic sensibility, and free spirit, and the female character all of the forces that inhibit that sensibility and spirit and make Rip miserable. The spirit of American Revolution, in which the colonists threw off the fetters of "mother England," becomes the rationale for nineteenth-century American man, who would rather kill Indians and explore the wilderness than stay home minding his own farm. The American woman becomes the new villain. Dame's "curtain lectures" vie only with Puritan sermons in their severity, and it is her "dinning" voice, her tongue that was "incessantly going," that Irving blames for silencing the budding artist in Rip. ("Rip had but one way of replying to all lectures of the kind . . . he shrugged his shoulders, shook his head, cast up his eyes, but said nothing.") American fiction begins in triumph over the silencing of Dame Van Winkle—for Rip's real victory is not the one he wins over the British, but as a result of Dame's death. One might conclude that for Irving—as for Cooper, Poe, Hawthorne, and Melville—the real American Dream is of a world in which women are either silent, dead, or in some other way entirely excluded from the sphere of action. (See Judith Fetterley, *The Resisting Reader*, for a fuller examination of this story from a feminist perspective.)

Whether you present these readings of "Rip Van Winkle" directly or try to elicit them through questions, I guarantee that the material this single story generates will wake up your own students and keep them awake through many later discussions.

AUGUSTUS BALDWIN LONGSTREET AND "SOUTHWEST HUMOR"

Alone among the four "Southwest humorists" included in the *NAAL* (Longstreet, Thorpe, Hooper, and Harris), Longstreet was the only one who did not publish in *The Spirit of the Times*, a sporting magazine of the 1830s and 1840s that avoided political commentary and references to slavery, and provided gentlemen interested in the leisure pursuits of horse-racing, hunting, and listening to tall tales with a way of gratifying fantasies of upper-class superiority, of ratifying their belief in masculine values and male dominance, and of relegating women to the source, butt, and object of sexual humor. Considering Longstreet's tales along with the works of any of the other three "humorists" of the 1820–1865 period can raise ideological and literary controversy in the classroom, for Longstreet confirms what the *Spirit of the Times* writers assumed—that storytelling is a masculine activity. Further, the "Southwest" writers exclude the moralistic position of their women contemporaries from their fiction (remind students that the 1830s was also the decade of the beginnings of the temperance and abolitionist movements, in which women began to participate as public figures for the first time in American history). Among this group, only Longstreet suggests a lingering fluidity in the relationship between gender and genre in early American fiction, before literature became the self-designated province of men for writers such as Hawthorne and Melville as much as for the "Southwest humorists."

As a way of examining Longstreet's interest in gender, contrast Lyman Hall, Longstreet's narrator of "The Horse Swap" and "The Shooting Match," with Baldwin, the narrator he chooses to relate "A Sage Conversation." Baldwin is an ineffectual moralist, reduced to reporting the cleverness of his friend Ned Brace in fooling the three aged matrons of "A Sage Conversation"; Hall, on the other hand, represents successful masculinity, competence, and the ability to influence others through his storytelling. (In the larger collection in which these tales appeared, *Georgia Scenes*, Longstreet continues to oppose Hall and Baldwin as narrators, and he continues to set up Baldwin as a foil for the masculine Hall's exploits.) In examining "A Sage Conversation," consider how Longstreet links Baldwin to the world of women that he simultaneously mocks. The matrons in the tale do not manage to figure out the mysteries of gender-crossing, much less engage in the actively masculine pursuit of contriving and telling a story; even though they light their pipes and sit around the fire until late in the night, their talking never rises above the level of "old woman's chat." Unlike Longstreet himself, the women miss the narrative potential of their material, and the final message of "A Sage Conversation" offers its own moral: women are "harmless," by which Longstreet means that they are incapable of storytelling and therefore pose no threat, even to the effeminate Baldwin.

WILLIAM CULLEN BRYANT

More than Freneau, Bryant exemplifies the new "Americanness" of nineteenth-century literature; yet Bryant will not serve as Emerson's American poet. Ask your students why; ask them, as well, to compare "Thanatopsis" with Freneau's "The House of Night." Which of Bryant's poems look to eighteenth-century values, both in philosophy and aesthetics? I often closely analyze "The Prairies" in class, for this poem is the most clearly "American" of the selections in the *NAAL*. What aspects of the poem are either neoclassical or derivative of British forms? What marks the poem as American? We discuss the way Bryant draws his imagery from the great plains, takes as his subject the "dilated sight" of the romantic perceiver, and associates the source of perception with change in the "forms of being." The mixture of styles, philosophies, and attitudes toward poetry that students find in "The Prairies" helps them see that evolution in thinking and writing takes place slowly. Some might justifiably argue that the "British" elements in Bryant's poetry contribute greatly to its beauty and power, and that the evidence of continued influence is one valid response to the confusion the new Americans must have felt post-Revolution, as well as a tribute to the enduring cultural and emotional content of the new country's relationship to things British, despite the radical change in our form of government.

RALPH WALDO EMERSON

The Emerson selections in the *NAAL* give us more than any of us can teach in any one course, and therefore you can vary your choices, depending on your model of course organization or what themes or concepts you are emphasizing. I asked my colleague William Shurr, a lover of Emerson and a specialist in the early nineteenth century, how he makes his own choices for the American literature course. He teaches excerpts from *Nature* ("Nature," "Beauty," "Language," and "Prospects" outline one possibility), then chooses essays and poems that will allow students to understand Emerson's basic philosophy. He reported to me that he has found "The Rhodora" to be the single Emerson poem that consistently produces the best student response. In this poem, Emerson addresses the poem as "Dear," and Bill said that he always asks students if they have ever addressed a poem this way, and what it does to the poem. He also suggested a recent article on "Uriel" by Kevin P. Van Anglen, titled "Emerson, Milton, and the Fall of Uriel" (*Emerson Society Quarterly* 30, no. 3) as an essay that "unlocks" this poem and might give instructors help in defining transcendentalism for students.

If you are focusing on the New "Americanness" of American literature in the early nineteenth century, one or more of the following essays will help you develop the theme: *The American Scholar, The Divinity School Address, Self-Reliance,* and *The Poet.* If you are interested in discussing Emerson's philosophy and contrasting it with his commentary on social issues of the day, choose from the list I suggest in Chapter 4. The journal entry of August 1, 1852, in which Emerson rationalizes one of the rare twinges of social conscience in his writing—"I have quite other slaves to free than those negroes, to wit, imprisoned spirits, imprisoned thoughts, far back in the brain of man . . . "—is essential reading for students, however you set up your course. In my own classroom, whatever model of course organization I choose, I ask students to read all of *Nature*, and we then spend several class meetings analyzing it. The key to understanding Emerson for students rests, I have found, in my own success in helping them understand this essay, so I will offer some detailed suggestions from what has worked for me. Following the discussion of *Nature*, I will also comment on two additional essays, *The Poet* and *Fate*, which will help span the chronology of Emerson's career and provide works of particular interest to students.

Nature

Emerson loses many students in the opening paragraphs of *Nature*, and it might be useful to read the "Introduction" with them during the class period before you turn them loose on the entire essay. Certain sentences contain kernel ideas that I work with at length in discussion. One of the earliest—"Every man's condition is a solution in hieroglyphic to those inquiries he would put. He acts it as life, before he apprehends it as truth"—initially gives students difficulty, but as we talk about it, always trying to find something in their own experience that will give them some "felt" affinity for what Emerson is saying, they begin to see that, for Emerson, nature includes our own "condition." He breaks down boundaries between self and body, between our own feeling and the natural world, with the result that he achieves a spiritual vision of unity with nature—"I become a transparent eye-ball. I am nothing. I see all. The currents of the Universal Being circulate through me: I am part or particle of God."

I have found that, pedagogically, the most important single concept in the essay is contained in the following sentence: "Each particle is a microcosm, and faithfully renders the likeness of the world." Students can see this visually by turning to an example Emerson uses earlier in the essay, at the beginning of "Language," in which he writes, "Who looks upon a river in a meditative hour, and is not reminded of the flux of all things? Throw a stone into the stream, and the circles that propagate themselves are the type of all influence." Almost everyone in the class, at some point in childhood, will have done just that—and all will remember the series of concentric circles that radiate out from the point at which the stone enters the water. I ask them to reconstruct what happens as we look further from that central point; they all remember that the circles grow larger but fainter, and some of them will recall from a high-school math class that, theoretically, the circles continue infinitely, even though they might not be visible to the eye. We talk about this example as an analogy for Emerson's entire philosophy, for it contains several essential ideas: (1) that our observation of the finite ripples on the water leads us to "see" the ripples that ease out into infinity; (2) that the concentric circles made by the ripples themselves form a series of analogies; and (3) that in the act of throwing one stone we can manage to contact an infinitely enlarging sphere. This discussion helps with the related ideas that "Man is an analogist, and studies relations in all objects," and "The world is emblematic. Parts of speech are metaphors because the whole of nature is a metaphor of the human mind." Each of these points takes time, but the rewards are great. Students begin to see that, through analogies, we can understand the world and our own relation to it. The chapter, "Language," is important to this discussion, because Emerson sees the very process of creating analogies or metaphors as essential to human understanding. Therefore, he can quote Plato—"poetry comes nearer to vital truth than history'"—and can state, "Empirical science is apt to cloud the sight . . . a dream may let us deeper into the secret of nature than a hundred concerted experiments." Here you can ask students to compare Emerson with Franklin and Jefferson; Emerson's philosophy is deeply antithetical to the "Age of Experiment."

Why do students find *Nature* so difficult? Most of them describe having trouble with Emerson's syntax. Ask them to think about what constitutes the unit of thought for Emerson. Is it the sentence, the paragraph, the section? He uses a linear form, prose, but does not write discursively. I suggest to them that the *analogy* is Emerson's basic unit of thought. His ideas move out from an analogical center like the ripples on the pond, even though he is forced to write about them as if he is thinking linearly and logically.

Another central concept that students need help with is what Emerson means by transcendence. How does an understanding of analogies, or of the microcosm that is nature, help us to transcend the limitations of our material existence and our own finite abilities to "see"? Here, viewing his use of the analogy as the unit of thought is crucial to our understanding, for he seems to be saying that if we focus on the analogy and on the single part, we will be able to understand the whole. To this end, he states, "Whilst we behold unveiled the nature of Justice and Truth, we learn the difference between the absolute and the conditional or relative. We apprehend the absolute. As it were, for the first time, *we exist*." If you have any students in your class who have studied transcendental meditation, or any other Eastern meditative technique, you can ask them to talk about how they have understood and experienced the difference between the "absolute" and the "relative." Sometimes these students can explain what it feels like to begin with a mantra in meditation and then "transcend" into an oceanic feeling of oneness with the universe. (This is also an ideal moment to ask students whether they find any lingering Puritanism in Emerson. Are there similarities in form between Emerson's focus on the analogy as the vehicle for transcendence and the Puritan's search for the black mark or spot?)

I try to describe a series of American themes that Emerson gets at in the essay: reliance on the self; the idea that the possibility of redemption lies within the individual; a belief in the perception of the individual and the intimate connection of human beings with nature (if students have studied the British romantic poets it will help here); the ability, the imperative, of Americans to "build their own world"; and, essential to his philosophy, the conflict between empirical knowledge and intuition, between logic and analogy. We talk about the way that conflict is apparent in students' own lives, even in their own choice of major fields of study at the university: do they become technologists or humanists? do they choose applied or theoretical science? do they elect courses in computer science or poetry? Emerson is certain to challenge their conception of thinking as linear, for he shows that analogy possesses its own logic, and that poetry and imaginative literature can help us to live in the world, perhaps better than science and technology—for, if analogy is the means of transcending, then analogy holds ascendancy over logic and helps us reunite body and spirit, thought and feeling. "What we are, that only can we see" brings the essay back to the beginning, to the idea of "solution in hieroglyphic."

The Poet

With the humanities under increasing attack in our society, students who choose to study literature need some support for their choice. Emerson's essay *The Poet* makes an argument for the value of poetry and the significance of language that remains compelling in the late twentieth century.

As the *NAAL* headnote observes, Emerson considered himself a poet, and I often teach an Emerson essay as if I were teaching the work of a poet; we respond to individual sentences and to Emerson's specific expression of particular ideas, much as if we were trying to close-read a lyric poem. In this essay, we begin with his central idea, that all of us "stand in need of expression . . . we study to utter our painful secret. The man is only half himself, the other half is his expression." Asking students to respond to this idea can lead into a discussion of voice, one of their own specific tasks as undergraduates, as well as the ongoing task of American writers throughout our literary history. Emerson suggests that the poet possesses both a complete vision as well as the tool—language—for expressing what we would all understand if we were just given the analogies for doing so. The poet finds those particular analogies (metaphors, similes, images) which allow us to understand what we might have been just on the verge of seeing, but were never able to fully see without the analogies themselves.

Therefore, Emerson writes, "Words are also actions, and actions are a kind of words." Someone who is able to express the inchoate understandings of other human beings allows us to integrate our being and our experience in the world. (You might digress here to look back to the role expression played in the American Revolution. Would we have been able to articulate *The Declaration of Independence* without Adams, Franklin, and Jefferson?) This idea may generate some controversy for students, unaccustomed to viewing language as action. Ask them to talk about related ideas they find in their reading of the essay, perhaps Emerson's statement that "language is fossil poetry," or that the world is "thus put under the mind for verb and noun." Asking students to explain what it might mean to see the world as "put under the mind for verb and noun" may help them to become more conscious about the relationship between words and actions.

Emerson's poet does more than help us create a bridge between what we see and what we can express; the poet also enables us to recreate ourselves. Thus, Emerson writes, "All that we call sacred history attests that the birth of a poet is the principal event in chronology." In direct challenge to particular theologies, Emerson asserts that, as young Americans (whether we interpret him to refer specifically to the young culture of the new Republic, or more loosely to the process of forming American identity in each of us as one of the tasks of undergraduate intellectual development), we look for a poet who will be able to tell us who and what we are. "Poets are thus liberating gods," he writes, "They are free, and they make free," and they keep us from miserably dying "on the brink of the waters of life and truth."

At the end of *The Poet*, Emerson writes the famous lines, "I look in vain for the poet whom I describe . . . We have yet had no genius in America . . . Yet America is a poem in our eyes." If you are looking ahead to reading Whitman, *The Poet* helps students create a context of continuity between writers of the 1820–1865 period. Emerson would not have to wait long for the particular American poet he longed for; he would be able, after the 1855 publication of Walt Whitman's *Leaves of Grass*, to greet Whitman "at the beginning of a great career" and to see some of his own prophetic hope for the unsung poem of America realized in Whitman's verse.

Whatever your own personal attitudes toward feminism, if you wish to fully include women students in the discussion of Emerson, it will be useful to bring out into the open Emerson's repeated use of masculine imagery to extol the qualities of the poet. How do your students respond to the following statements? "The man is only half himself, the other half is his expression." "The religions of the world are the ejaculations of a few imaginative men." "Hence the necessity of speech and song; . . . that thought may be ejaculated as Logos, or Word." In this context, refer students to Emerson's Journal entry of November–December, 1841, "[Dead Sentences vs. Man-Making Words]," in which he writes, "Give me initiative, spermatic, prophesying, man-making words." Does Emerson's language of action, initiative, and ejaculation include or exclude women from the realm of poetic genius?

Fate

The late essay, *Fate*, is practically guaranteed to elicit controversy among your students, and, at the same time, to give them a rare glimpse of Emerson responding to the current events and spirit of his own times. Throughout the essay, Emerson variously defines fate as the laws of the world, as what limits us, as unpenetrated causes, and he writes that "Once we thought, positive power was all. Now, we learn, that negative power, or circumstance, is half. Nature is the tyrannous circumstance." Contrast what he says here about nature with the essay *Nature* itself. How do your students respond to Emerson's position that the "fate" of our limitations cannot be transcended, except by accepting it and building "altars" to the "Beautiful Necessity"? Is there no hope for reform in the world if "the riddle of the age has for each a private solution"? Is Emerson asking us to accept what he himself terms the "complicity" of "race living at the expense of race" because "Providence has a wild, rough, incalculable road to its end," and therefore it is futile to "whitewash its huge mixed instrumentalities"? Had Emerson been able to imagine a Hitler, would he have included Nazi Germany in his "Beautiful Necessity"? Is there no hope for environment or the "nurture" side of Emerson's portrait of nature? He writes of the ditch-digger that "he has but one future, and that is already predetermined in his lobes, and described in that little fatty face, pig-eye, and squat form. All the privilege and all the legislation of the world cannot meddle or help to make a poet or a prince of him." Is Emerson's own essay itself an ironic example of "organization tyrannizing over character"? If we accept the "Beautiful Necessity" of things, are we enshrining elitism, the New England Brahminism of ideological caste and class? Allowing your students to challenge Emerson is one way of teaching them to take his ideas seriously, to be critical as well as appreciative; it is a way of allowing them to participate in the shaping of ideological debate that characterizes American cultural history.

NATHANIEL HAWTHORNE

Hawthorne presents a special problem for a teacher because students often look for "morals" in his work. They confuse his use of

Puritan subjects and themes with his own values, and conclude that Hawthorne is, himself, a Puritan. They also need help in understanding the concept of allegory and how it works in Hawthorne. "Young Goodman Brown," "The Minister's Black Veil," and "Rappaccini's Daughter" all invite students to find allegorical "equations"—and all deliberately frustrate the attempt. In each of these stories, I challenge students to identify the "good" character, and, in every case, they end by qualifying their initial response. For Hawthorne's moral universe is ultimately ambiguous.

"Rappaccini's Daughter" works particularly well in classroom study of Hawthorne's use of allegory, for students have fun trying to work out the parallels between the Garden of Eden and Rappaccini's garden. The role of the serpent (after the lizard is poisoned by the flower) remains open by the end of the story: who *is* responsible for Beatrice's death? Rappaccini? Baglioni? Giovanni? Hawthorne himself? How does the story, in creating an anti-garden, actually affirm the moral universe of the Garden of Eden, despite its attempt to invert those values? Is the story a variation of "Rip Van Winkle," in which Irving triumphs over Dame Van Winkle's power by silencing her at the end?

Asking students to read Melville's "Hawthorne and His Mosses" can lead into a discussion of the "blackness" Melville saw in Hawthorne's fiction. Is that "blackness" a reference to Hawthorne's moral universe or a reflection of his use of dream imagery (explicitly in "Young Goodman Brown" and implicitly in the atmosphere of his other work)? I suggest to students that the ambivalence they find in Hawthorne actually expresses the mingled self-confrontation and self-evasion that characterize his protagonists. Rather than try to "solve" the ambiguities one finds in Hawthorne, I try to show students, instead, that his choice to be ambivalent is deliberate and conscious. We talk about the way Young Goodman Brown, Reverend Hooper, Rappaccini, and the speaker in "The Custom-House" are all, in part, Hawthorne's self-portraits, or at least portraits of the artist. Unlike Thoreau, who values facing life "deliberately" in *Walden*, Hawthorne goes only so far in trying to see what is *there*—in his characters and ultimately in himself. Hershel Parker, in the period introduction in the *NAAL*, describes the "crucial aesthetic problems" early nineteenth-century writers face, and suggests that Hawthorne's involved his attempt to "strike a balance between the allegorical and the realistic." What might this mean, if we consider the actual moment of confrontation between the writer and the blank page? "The Custom-House" provides a rich opportunity for students to consider the struggles of the writer, and to see that these struggles take place within the depths of the psyche, perhaps at the source of the individual writer's (or the culture's) dream-life.

"Wakefield"

"Wakefield" provides an opportunity to study, in detail, Hawthorne's mingled self-confrontation and self-evasion, and the tale is brief enough for close analysis, either in class discussion or as an essay assignment. In trying to determine what motivates Wakefield, Hawthorne is also exploring what motivates his own story, and if we view Wakefield as a projection of the artist himself, we learn a great deal about Hawthorne. Hawthorne gives us explicit permission to mingle his own projections with his creation of character when he writes, "We are free to shape out our own idea, and call it by [Wakefield's] name."

The point of inception of the tale, as Hawthorne writes in the opening sentence, is a man "—let us call him Wakefield—who absented himself for a long time, from his wife." Although Hawthorne does not explicitly link Wakefield with Rip Van Winkle, the resemblance of Wakefield's twenty-year absence to Rip's twenty-year sleep is unmistakable. In studying Irving, we could view Dame Van Winkle as Irving's allegorical representation of "mother England" and explain away some of the misogyny in Irving's characterization of this character. But "Wakefield" does not have the American Revolution as allegorical underpinning. Wakefield's own twenty-year absence seems unmotivated, and Hawthorne's perception that such an absence is "not very uncommon" leads him to "meditate" on Wakefield.

Hawthorne does not excuse Wakefield's action, using terms like "cold," "quiet selfishness," and "vanity" to describe his character. Nevertheless, neither does he empathize with Wakefield's wife, despite his portrait of the woman as close to death in the aftermath of her husband's mysterious abandonment. Hawthorne approaches self-revelation when he turns away from exploring the effects of Wakefield's behavior on his wife (much as Wakefield himself does) and writes, "But, our business is with the husband." In that single statement, Hawthorne summarizes much of American literature among our classic writers during the 1820–1865 period, and he creates the condition for recognizing his own complicity with Wakefield. He might as well be saying that, in the early years of the American republic, male American writers turned inexplicably away from exploring women's lives and experience, for more than twenty years. Is Wakefield's twenty-year absence from domestic life the true American dream for our earliest classic writers? Hawthorne chooses to analyze Wakefield's "chasm in human affections," but, in omitting any meditation on Mrs. Wakefield's motivations, he veers off from the possibility of self-confrontation. At the tale's end, Hawthorne avoids even considering the possibility that Mrs. Wakefield might not take her husband back. She remains, to the end, a "grotesque shadow," an "admirable caricature," and all Wakefield has to do in order to regain what Hawthorne terms his "place" in the system, is to open the door, stop playing his "little joke" on his wife, and take a "good night's rest."

The moral, "done up neatly, and condensed into the final sentence," allows Hawthorne to side-step the very question he began by exploring: "What sort of a man was Wakefield?" He evades a fuller exploration of the complexity of Wakefield's character by suggesting that it was Wakefield's action, not his failure of empathy, that led him to the brink of becoming the "Outcast of the Universe." In effect, then, Wakefield becomes the self-portrait of Hawthorne the artist. By refusing to explore Mrs. Wakefield as character rather than caricature, Hawthorne repeats Wakefield's act of evasion; and, by averting his gaze from Wakefield's empathic failure, Hawthorne subordinates his portrait of Wakefield to his own projected fears of isolation from the "reciprocal influence" of human sympathies.

The Scarlet Letter

The Scarlet Letter has been interpreted in many different ways, and most of you have probably written about the book at some point, whether as students or as publishing critics. (My own discussion of the novel appears in The Mark and the Knowledge: Social Stigma in Classic American Fiction.) Yet, teaching the book is always, for me, a challenge and a delight. In my classroom, I try to remember what it was like to read the book for the first or second time, and to give students a chance to appropriate its meaning on their own before I turn them loose on a writing assignment that may send them to the library. One of the ways of doing this is to ask questions of the book that link it to discussions of previous authors and to the focal concepts and themes of the course.

I begin with "The Custom-House": the atmosphere of dream or hallucination that accompanies the speaker's discovery of the scarlet letter and his entire memory of the custom-house itself; the differences between this essay and Hawthorne's more conventional use of the preface (in "Preface to The House of the Seven Gables"); the sense of delay the essay gives the reader—and the blame the narrator places on others for his own "torpor" and his inability to write; and the imagery of the essay—the memorable meals Hawthorne describes, the portrait of the Inspector, and his vision of reconciling "the Actual and the Imaginary." I ask them to consider the statement Hawthorne makes early in the essay: "To this extent and within these limits an author, methinks, may be autobiographical, without violating either the reader's rights or his own." Is "The Custom-House" a revelation of its author or a veil like the one Reverend Hooper wears?

The novel itself (or the romance—ask students to talk about what they think Hawthorne means by the difference in "Preface to

The House of the Seven Gables") raises a lot of related questions. Hawthorne bares Hester; does he reveal or conceal Dimmesdale? Examine the imagery of revelation in the book: Hester's first appearance in the prison door, the scarlet letter itself, the scenes on the scaffold, Chapter XXIII, itself titled "The Revelation of the Scarlet Letter." Does Hawthorne's symbol, literally fastened to Hester's breast, allow him to bridge "the Actual and the Imaginary"? Compare Hawthorne's use of tangible symbol with Emerson's use of analogies. Is the scarlet letter also a way of seeing and of knowing, for Hawthorne's characters and for himself? What is the relationship between symbol and stigma? And why does Chillingworth, twice in *The Scarlet Letter*, have the privilege of seeing what is on Dimmesdale's breast, while Hawthorne averts his own eyes—and ours? Who are the "good" or "evil" characters in this book? What limits Hawthorne's sympathy for Chillingworth? What limits his portrait of Hester? In Chapter II he writes, "The women, who were now standing about the prison-door, stood within less than half a century of the period when the man-like Elizabeth had been the not altogether unsuitable representative of the sex." Yet, Hawthorne implies that, by the early nineteenth century, American women have changed. "There was, moreover, a boldness and rotundity of speech among these matrons, as most of them seemed to be, that would startle us at the present day. . . ." Is Hester herself a variation on Dame Van Winkle?—silenced by her author, as much as by her society? And to what extent is *The Scarlet Letter* not "about" Hester Prynne at all? To what extent does she merely catalyze the "real" drama of the dynamic and developing association between the minister and the physician? And how does Hawthorne use Pearl, particularly at the end of the book, to affirm a certain view of femininity and to reject others? He writes that her tears "were the pledge that she would grow up amid human joy and sorrow, nor for ever do battle with the world, but be a woman in it." Is *The Scarlet Letter* itself an indictment of Hester? And a vindication of Dimmesdale? And how do we interpret the "moral" Hawthorne "presses" upon his readers at the end: "Be true! Be true! Be true! Show freely to the world, if not your worst, yet some trait whereby the worst may be inferred!"

EDGAR ALLAN POE

The dream world characterizes Poe's work as well, and students may study his dream imagery in the poems "Introduction," "The Sleeper," "Dream-land," and "The Raven." Is there any connection between Poe's dream worlds and those of "Rip Van Winkle" or Hawthorne's fiction? Many writers in American literary history serve as spokespeople for others; does Poe? What effects does his poetry create in the reader, and how? His poetry lacks specific references to

American places or American life; is it, like Freneau's or Bryant's, derivative of British poetry? I read "The Philosophy of Composition" closely with students, and we compare it with "The Custom-House." How is the act of writing different for Poe and for Hawthorne? Ask them to evaluate Poe's description of the composition of "The Raven" against their experience of reading the poem.

We analyze "Annabel Lee" line by line in the context of Poe's statement, in "The Philosophy of Composition," that beauty moves the soul best when the subject is sad, and that, therefore, the death of a beautiful woman becomes the "soul" of poetry. Why does Poe need to kill Annabel Lee in order to achieve the male speaker's maturity and poetic inspiration? By dying young, she doesn't live to become another Dame Van Winkle for the male speaker; and her death allows him to retain complete control over the way he uses her as material for his poetry, even for the necrophilia the last stanza implies. What reason does the poem give for her death? Poe suggests that the angels—with their associations of being female or possessing "feminine" values—have "coveted" her beauty (as if angels, or women, can never be supportive of each other). And her love has given the narrator status, for she has "highborn kinsmen," and, although they take away her dead body, they cannot take away the class status he has achieved by his conquest. Like those in Irving and Hawthorne, Poe's protagonist/narrators empower themselves by the silencing or death of their heroines.

Among the tales included in the *NAAL*, "The Fall of the House of Usher" and "Ligeia" further demonstrate the effects Poe creates by idealizing women and therefore earns at the expense of his female characters. "Ligeia," in particular, shows Ligeia becoming the male narrator's muse in the process of developing anorexia, in effect conspiring to her own death. How does Poe's use of doubling in "The Fall of the House of Usher" reinforce the effect of the torture and death of Madeline? Ask students to think about the "organic" relationship between human beings and nature, or the supernatural, in Poe, especially "The Fall of the House of Usher," as another form of doubling. In what other tales does Poe use doubling between characters and events? Does he alter the effects of the dream world by portraying events as nightmares (in "The Black Cat," for example)? From the point of view of twentieth-century psychology, do Montresor and Fortunato in "The Cask of Amontillado" represent shadow elements of the same personality?

As Hershel Parker points out in the headnote, Poe created the detective story "with all its major conventions complete." Ask students to analyze "The Purloined Letter," deducing from it some of the conventional elements of the detective story. Compare it with Poe's tales of the supernatural; what are the different effects he achieves in "The Purloined Letter"? How do Dupin's cleverness and rationality go together with his idea that "the material world abounds

with very strict analogies to the immaterial."? Consider the statement in light of Emerson's use of the analogy in *Nature*. Compare
Dupin's language with Poe's in "The Philosophy of Composition": is
the character a double of his author? Compare their relationship
with Hawthorne's relationship to Dimmesdale in *The Scarlet Letter*.
What is Poe trying to reveal and conceal in his own fiction? Does the
genre of the romance, for both Hawthorne and Poe, predetermine
the nature of meaning?

MARGARET FULLER

Unlike Emerson, Hawthorne, and Poe, Margaret Fuller
wrote in direct response to her social and historical context, expressing her concern in particular for women's rights. In "The Great
Lawsuit," Fuller is explicit in her condemnation of constitutional
policy. Ask students to find language of servility in "The Great Lawsuit" and to compare it with the language of slave narrative in *The
Declaration of Independence*. Locate Fuller's commentary on the
fight for the abolition of slavery, and ask students to reflect on her
perception of "a natural following out of principles" by which the
"champions of the enslaved African," "partly because many women
have been prominent in that cause, make, just now, the warmest appeal in behalf of women." Both Fuller and Harriet Beecher Stowe
(in the anthologized excerpt from *Uncle Tom's Cabin*) depict women
as engaged in heroic struggle; ask students to find parallels among
colonial writers. In the early nineteenth century, while white American men were producing the first great imaginative literature, white
women and black slaves were just beginning to find spokespersons,
writers able to articulate the contradiction between constitutional
liberty and their own lack of rights. (Students interested in Fuller
may also want to read Elizabeth Cady Stanton's "Declaration of
Sentiments" [not anthologized but included as an appendix in this
guide] or Sojourner Truth's "Ain't I a Woman?" [not anthologized in
the *NAAL* but included in the *NALW*]).

HARRIET BEECHER STOWE

"The Mother's Struggle" may initially appear melodramatic to
students, but the very fact that Stowe wrote *Uncle Tom's Cabin* in
the first place displays the fierceness with which some Northern
white women fought for the abolition of slavery. And although
Eliza's character is not created by a black writer, she possesses several characteristics that would later appear in the earliest fiction by
black writers—Charles Chesnutt and Zora Neale Hurston (included
in the *NAAL*), and many others of the late nineteenth-century and

Harlem Renaissance period. For Eliza is "so white as not to be known as of colored lineage, without a critical survey, and her child was white also," making it "much easier for her to pass on unsuspected." This detail makes it possible for an instructor to ask some interesting questions: for whom is Stowe writing? Clearly, white Northerners, and, in particular, white women who supported the abolitionist movement. How does Stowe elicit the sympathy of that audience? In large part, by presenting Eliza as a *mother*, as well as nearly white. Some students may want to do background research on the nineteenth-century view of motherhood. Clearly, even in this brief excerpt from Stowe's novel, motherhood parallels Christianity in spiritual significance, and when the white Kentuckian Mr. Symmes helps Eliza and her child up the river bank on the Ohio side, Stowe writes ironically that "this poor, heathenish Kentuckian, . . . had not been enlightened on his constitutional relations, and consequently was betrayed into acting in a sort of Christianized manner, which, if he had been better situated and more enlightened, he would not have been left to do." Stowe directly criticizes the Fugitive Slave Law here, by which Mr. Symmes ought to have returned Eliza to the hands of the slave-catcher Haley instead of pointing her in the direction of a safe house. She is also describing a kind of Christianity that is activist and contextual in its care for the fleeing slave. The nineteenth century gave over the spiritual and moral development of children to women, in their place within "women's sphere"; here Stowe links nineteenth-century Christianity with warrior mothers, for Eliza possesses "strength such as God gives only to the desperate." It is significant for the development of both white and black American literature that Stowe depicts Eliza as a heroic fugitive—a character with the stature of myth. As late as Ralph Ellison's *Invisible Man* (1952), black writers would depict the road north and the fleeing slave as archetypal in American black experience. Like the earliest Puritan settlers, slaves adopted Old Testament typology as a way of understanding their condition—the Ohio River, for Eliza, becomes the biblical Jordan, and the other side, a type of Canaan.

"The Minister's Housekeeper" locates Stowe's stylistic realism and her contributions to the beginnings of literary regionalism. Thematically, you might ask students to compare Huldy with earlier female characters in American fiction, particularly Dame Van Winkle and Hester Prynne. How does the realistic portrait of an American woman differ from her portrait in the romance? You might also raise the question of literary authority and examine one of Stowe's solutions to the dilemma of trying to write professionally as a woman in mid-nineteenth-century America. In one of her letters, she claimed that she didn't write *Uncle Tom's Cabin*, but was merely taking dictation from God. (Recall Edward Taylor's plea for God to guide his pen in "Prologue.") In "The Minister's Housekeeper," she creates a male narrator (Sam Lawson) to tell Huldy's story. Might we consider Sam Lawson a variation on Rip Van Winkle, once he becomes a storyteller after the war? Would the story have had a different effect had Stowe been able to allow Huldy to tell it herself? Compare Irving's creation of Diedrich Knickerbocker with Stowe's need to write in the voice of Sam Lawson.

HENRY DAVID THOREAU

In Thoreau's "Resistance to Civil Government," "Slavery in Massachusetts," and "A Plea for Captain John Brown," we see him as the prominent exception among his white male contemporaries to the pattern of evading confrontation with social and political issues of his day. And *Walden*, despite the premise of separation from society on which it opens, emphasizes the practical aspects of transcendentalism. Ask students to locate Thoreau in a tradition of American writers from Bradstreet through Franklin who speak in a personal voice and address the common reader. How do the effects Thoreau achieves in "Resistance to Civil Government" or *Walden* differ from those Emerson creates in "Self-Reliance" or *Nature*? Ask students to compare and contrast *Nature* and *Walden* as literary works: how are they conceptually similar but technically different? Many who found it difficult to find logical discourse in *Nature* will perceive a narrative design in *Walden*. How does Thoreau manage a happy balance between logical and analogical thinking?

Walden

I organize my own class periods on *Walden* around the following series of points:
(1) Focusing on "Economy," ask students to address Thoreau's practical concerns. What, for Thoreau, is wrong with the daily life of his contemporaries? What were his motives for going to Walden? What led him to write the book? How does his version of writing in the first person compare with Hawthorne's in "The Custom-House"? Find evidence that he is making a pun on "I" and "eye"; recall Emerson's "transparent eye-ball" in *Nature*. Are Thoreau's criticisms of his own society applicable to ours? How seriously are we to take his suggestion that students ought, quite literally, to build their own colleges? Compare Thoreau's list of materials for his house at Walden with Franklin's list of virtues in *The Autobiography*. Is there evidence in "Economy" that Thoreau is constructing an analogy, or is he writing a "how-to" book in the tradition of "The Way to Wealth"?
(2) In "Where I Lived and What I Lived For," I ask students to consider again the creation of analogies in *Walden*, suggesting

here that analogy becomes a method of introspection and religious meditation for Thoreau. Stanley Cavell in *The Senses of "Walden"* suggests that *Walden* is a scripture. We review the ways various American writers before Thoreau achieved literary authority, and what different relationships writers have to scripture, especially the Bible. Does Thoreau achieve literary authority by going back to what he sees as the very source of creation, in nature at Walden? Ask students to comment on the following quotation from Hershel Parker's headnote: "The prose of *Walden*, in short, is designed as a practical course in the liberation of the reader." Thoreau's experience at Walden becomes a record of his way of seeing the world; as it is for Emerson, the process of learning, for Thoreau, involves making the analogies he discovers as a result of going to the woods. In Thoreau's very ability to create the analogy he has the experience; transcendentalism can thus be seen as the first American spiritual movement based on a theory of language. That theory is Emerson's as well as Thoreau's, but Thoreau is able to find the analogies he wants in the life he is living on an hourly, daily, and seasonal basis at the pond.

Crucial to considering *Walden* as scripture are the frequent references Thoreau makes to Eastern religious experience. He writes that every morning "I got up early and bathed in the pond; that was a religious exercise, and one of the best things I did." How can bathing in the pond be a religious exercise? (He seems to mean that it is a spiritual experience, not just part of his routine that he follows religiously.) Following his own inclination toward analogy, bathing in the pond metaphorically suggests his daily immersion in the meaning of the experience of the pond. To jump into it suggests, by means of analogy, his daily attempt to understand it—at the same time as he is *literally* (like Emerson's stone) entering the pond. It cleanses, renews, wakes him up—provides a rippling effect by which he can reach Eastern enlightenment, to "reawaken and keep [himself] awake, not by mechanical aids, but by an infinite expectation of the dawn." Bathing in Walden becomes an interim "mechanical aid"; when he becomes able to keep himself awake without the pond, he won't need it any more. You can ask students, at this point, how Thoreau's meditation differs from Puritan meditation. Thoreau (like Franklin) is also focusing on a single mark or spot—but instead of looking for his theological or economic salvation, he is attempting to transcend the world of literal limits, what Emerson calls the relative world. Yet, there is so much of the literal world in *Walden*. There is a sense in which the very rhythm of working in the physical world, finding an analogy in that work to spiritual life and feeling, temporarily, at least, at one with the universe, becomes cumulative for Thoreau. The process enables him to make successive leaps between relative and absolute worlds, to transcend the limits of material existence, to truly become eccentric (a word that he cites as particularly important at the end of *Walden*). Walden Pond becomes his eye (see the chapter "The Ponds").

(3) Beginning with "Brute Neighbors," I trace Thoreau's deep submergence into the character of Walden Pond as nature's "face." Then the last three chapters, "The Pond in Winter," "Spring," and "Conclusion," all build to Thoreau's description of the transcendent moment in which he has the experience of confronting absolute truths. In "The Pond in Winter," Thoreau makes the analogy between sounding the depths of a pond and "sounding" the depths of the human mind, as one might theoretically do by pursuing Eastern meditation techniques. Thoreau has no mantra but his pond; his "depth" of knowledge of the pond prepares him for an even deeper dive into his own imagination, his own consciousness.

"Spring" heralds new life at the pond and new light in the writer. Here he discovers that "the day is an epitome of the year"; the small scale of Walden Pond (and ultimately of *Walden* as book or scripture) is what makes it useful as an analogy. He concludes, at the end of "Spring," that "We need to witness our own limits transgressed, and some life pasturing freely where we never wander." Becoming eccentric, getting outside our own limits, trying to transcend the narrowness of our own experience, can give us the vision of larger life, of some life "pasturing freely where we never wander." The exploration of life by means of analogy possesses a spiritual dimension that logic does not.

But he leaves the pond because he has learned its lessons. When the person becomes enlightened, the vehicle of enlightenment is no longer necessary. The religious technique, or the poetic analogy, is viewed not as an end in itself, but as means to an end. The basic idea, then, in *Walden*, is that of self-expression, Thoreau's attempt to find a way to make visible and concrete his sense of who he is. His greatest fear, as he expresses it in "Conclusion," is that his expression "may not be *extra-vagant* enough. . . . " It's hard to get students to be "extra-vagant" themselves, because it means encouraging them to "wander outside" the limits of everything they have learned as received knowledge, prescribed feelings, and "right" and "wrong" ways to think.

FREDERICK DOUGLASS

Douglass wrote his 1845 autobiographical *Narrative* the year before Thoreau began to write *Walden*. Ask students to consider the following quotation from *Walden* in connection with *Narrative*: "I sometimes wonder that we can be so frivolous, I may almost say, as to attend to the gross but somewhat foreign form of servitude called Negro Slavery, there are so many keen and subtle masters that enslave both north and south. It is hard to have a southern overseer; it is worse to have a northern one; but worst of all when you are the slave-driver of yourself." Would Douglass agree? Are there conceptual and thematic similarities between *Walden* and *Narrative of the Life of Frederick Douglass, an American Slave*? Do Douglass's escape to freedom and Thoreau's transcendence at Walden Pond suggest connections between abolitionism and transcendentalism? Both narratives imply that the experiences that are their subjects also confer literary authority on their narrators. Evaluate the *Narrative* as autobiography; what are its formal and thematic similarities to Franklin's *Autobiography*? Is the slave narrative a variation on autobiography or a distinct genre? The central feature to focus on in Douglass's *Narrative* is the way he, like many white writers before him, articulates himself into being, creates an ontological model for black male identity: "You have seen how a man was made a slave; you shall see how a slave was made a man," he writes. And he makes himself a man by refusing to submit to Mr. Covey. Therefore, Douglass achieves ontological freedom before he escapes to actual freedom, and in portraying his own courage in fighting Mr. Covey, he sets himself up as a model for other slaves much as Franklin did in his *Autobiography*. Douglass portrays himself as a "heroic fugitive" for others to imitate. Contrast Douglass and Stowe. Might we consider "The Mother's Struggle" a form of the slave narrative? Can the warrior mother be a heroic fugitive? Douglass and other escaped slaves wrote their stories with the encouragement and support of the Northern abolitionist press, and there is clear didactic intent in Douglass's *Narrative* (as there is in *Uncle Tom's Cabin*). Does didacticism weaken the narrative as a work of literature? Students may find it interesting to discuss the contrasting effect didacticism has in works produced under the umbrella of a reigning theology (such as Puritan literature) and works that are clearly trying to change people's ideas. From the literary perspective, the year 1845 is as important as 1776 because it shows a former slave writing in his own voice, and naming and claiming his own liberty. Douglass's *Narrative* and Fuller's "The Great Lawsuit" suggest that, while going to Walden may be an effective technique for some Americans to achieve transcendence, black Americans and white women must first adopt defiance.

WALT WHITMAN

In teaching both Whitman and Dickinson, I try to show students how these two poets are pivotal figures, summarizing in their work many of the themes and concerns of earlier writers, yet looking ahead to the twentieth century in their poetic technique and the high level of self-consciousness that each brings to the act of writing. How, in particular, does Whitman express a culmination of American impulses in poetry? Ask students to reread Emerson's "The

Poet" and to evaluate Whitman; is Emerson prophesying the kind of poetry Whitman would write, especially in "Song of Myself"? Or are both writers responding to the same cultural need? I ask students to discuss the detailed catalogues of American people, places, and human feelings that Whitman creates in "Song of Myself." How does Whitman's portrait of human life differ from those of earlier writers? I introduce the concept of realism and suggest elements of realism in Whitman's language, looking ahead to the "local color" impulse of some of the post–Civil War writers that students will read in the second course or second half of the course in American literature. We consider aspects of dream in Whitman, particularly in "The Sleepers," which illustrates the process by which Whitman works through the "night" of his analogy to "awaken" into a diffused and enlarged sense of self; students can then trace the same pattern through the much longer "Song of Myself," at the end of which the poet transcends even his physical body, becoming effused flesh that drifts "in lacy jags." How does Whitman's use of analogy compare with Emerson's or Thoreau's? And how does reading Whitman compare with reading earlier writers? What is the conceptual unit of a Whitman poem?—possibly the catalogue? What is the effect of the repetitions? What evidence can students find of discursive reasoning in Whitman? I suggest that Whitman requires immersion ("religiously," the way Thoreau bathes in the pond). My colleague, George Hutchinson, has explained to me that he sees Whitman as a shaman-figure. Is "Song of Myself," like *Walden*, a kind of scripture?

Students understand Whitman better when they locate the same image in several different poems; the imagery I ask them to focus on shows Whitman's vision of physical life. Harold Aspiz's *Walt Whitman and the Body Beautiful* is extremely useful reading as you prepare to teach Whitman. Aspiz suggests that "Whitman's physical self *is* the authentic vital center of *Leaves of Grass*. By idealizing his body, Whitman created a model that his fellow Americans could emulate" (Aspiz, 1980, p. 239). Such a reading of the poems makes it possible to suggest pedagogical connections between Walt Whitman and Benjamin Franklin, for Whitman clearly "invents" himself as *the* American poet in the same way that Franklin invents himself as American man. And it may lead students to see that *Leaves of Grass* is as much a poetry of evasion (Aspiz makes the point that for all of Whitman's pretense to health in his poems, from childhood on he had physical problems, was fascinated by physical illness, and spent many years as a sick man) as it is of self-disclosure (as in "I celebrate myself and sing myself"), in its own way another "Minister's Black Veil." I ask students to examine "Trickle Drops" and other *Calamus* poems included in the *NAAL* for evidence that Whitman's analogue for vision is male sexuality. In "Trickle Drops," they can see most clearly and succinctly the way Whitman views poetry as spermatic fluid; the image is pervasive in his work, including his discussion in

"Preface to *Leaves of Grass*." Male physical health and robustness, in general, becomes a metaphor for vision. Does that make male sexuality, for Whitman, as much a product of the creative imagination as Walden is for Thoreau? Is the version of sexuality Whitman proposes (and suggests, throughout his work, that women share) another variation on the early nineteenth-century American Dream?

HERMAN MELVILLE

The Melville selections in the *NAAL* give students a sense of Melville's range, and the set of letters to Hawthorne will help create obvious connections between the two writers. Students respond particularly well to "Bartleby, the Scrivener" and can see Melville, in contrast to Hawthorne, being more courageous in confronting and exploring "dead-wall" reflections of the self. In the narrator's discovery of a "fraternal melancholy" with Bartleby, and in his depiction of the scrivener as "absolutely alone in the universe. A bit of wreck in the mid-Atlantic," a teacher can suggest connections with *Moby-Dick*. "The Town-Ho's Story" is an interesting choice for an excerpt from that novel, partly because it takes place *after* the events in the novel have passed but *before* Ishmael begins to write *Moby-Dick*. So the chapter uniquely shows Ishmael "rehearsing" the larger story he wants to write before the audience of sailors in Lima. The chapter is anomalous in *Moby-Dick*—but usefully suggests the way a major author's works are often rehearsals, prefaces (like "The Piazza"), or sketches ("The Encantadas, or Enchanted Isles"). Students may speculate on nineteenth-century gender roles in "The Paradise of Bachelors and The Tartarus of Maids." Is Melville writing social commentary here? Point out to students that most of his fiction depicts a single-sex universe. What happens to values associated with "women's sphere" in *Moby-Dick*, or in *Benito Cereno*, or *Billy Budd, Sailor*? Is Melville, too, engaging in the silencing of women? Or does his single-sex universe actually allow him to break down gender boundaries in the ways that different (male) characters reflect attributes often culturally assigned to male *and* female behavior? Is *Benito Cereno* social commentary? What cultural assumptions does Captain Delano bring into the fiction? How does Babo compare with the autobiographical narrator in *Narrative of the Life of Frederick Douglass*? Are Melville's portraits of black characters realistic?

Billy Budd, Sailor

Billy Budd, Sailor may be the most difficult for students of the long works by Melville included in the *NAAL*. In addition to discussing central characters, trying, with my students, to figure out whether the novel is an allegory, and, if so, of what, and tracing Melville's elegiac tone in his last work, I also focus on some specific points somewhat off the main track that, yet, lead into interesting discussion. The digression on Nelson—Chapters 3 and 4—is one of the most interesting. Is Melville associating Nelson with Captain Vere? or with himself? At his report of Vere's death, he alludes again to Nelson, stating about Vere that "Unhappily he was cut off too early for the Nile and Trafalgar." Is Melville undercutting the value of Vere as heroic commander here, and, if so, what fascinates him so much about Nelson's type of heroism? He suggests at the end of Chapter 4 that "the poet but embodies in verse those exaltations of sentiment that a nature like Nelson, the opportunity being given, vitalizes into acts," and perhaps Melville sees Vere as triumphant in part because he makes an absolute judgment and proceeds to enact it. But there are dramatic contrasts in style between Nelson and Vere that might inspire a bit of student research. Melville, digressing on Nelson and confessing to having committed a "literary sin" in doing so, suggests a compulsion to model himself on Nelson rather than Vere. Vere lacks above all Nelson's passion; but Melville shares it.

Yet Vere's judgment concerning Billy, despite its apparent rationality, seems spontaneous, if not altogether passionate. What might Melville have been trying to understand, in weaving a fiction based on the arbitrary, even vengeful, judgment of an otherwise intelligent and human man? Students recalling Jonathan Edwards might find the atmosphere of the drumhead court familiar; when Vere states that "'We must do; and one of two things must we do—condemn or let go,'" he expresses the absolute Calvinist separation between damned and elect, guilty and innocent. The sailors listen to the results of the deliberations of the drumhead court "like that of a seated congregation of believers in hell listening to the clergyman's announcement of his Calvinistic text." In giving us his portrait of Captain Vere's rigidity, Melville explores the effect of a continuing and pervasive Calvinism—fictionally transposing its visible effect on the nineteenth-century American mind to the deck of a British warship in 1797, a year belonging to a period of transition from one conceptual view—neoclassicism—to another, romanticism.

The question of Billy Budd's guilt can lead into lively classroom discussion, particularly if students are guided to see the terms of the debate as absolute vs. conditional or contextual justice. Carol Gilligan's *In a Different Voice* assigns gender categories to moral development that can lead to these mutually exclusive perceptions of justice; interestingly, Melville characterizes Billy as a type of the Handsome Sailor, a beardless, "feminine" martyr—possibly Christlike, possibly "female." Students might find it interesting to apply Poe's statements on beauty and sadness to *Billy Budd, Sailor.* For, in some ways, Melville, too, achieves his tragedy by the silencing and death of a beautiful sailor (students can list the many ways in which Melville gives Billy female characteristics, and can consider the effects on their tragic feeling had Billy and Claggart retained their own characters, but exchanged physical types). And what of the evasion in the final interview between Vere and Billy?—we are told only that they are "briefly closeted." Does this resemble the way Hawthorne averts his eyes at crucial moments in his fiction? *Billy Budd, Sailor* remained unfinished at Melville's death; does this affect our ability to interpret its meaning? Does the work itself—like Billy—retain a stammer and a hesitancy in its "speech"? It's difficult to teach Melville without including *Moby-Dick*, and if you have somehow found class time to include this novel, then students will more easily be able to understand the problem of Billy's death within Melville's larger work. For, in the earlier novel, Melville suggests that tragedy for Ishmael is not death but a return to the necessity for vision. Unlike Thoreau, who leaves Walden after he no longer needs the pond as a vehicle of transcendence, Ishmael, after his brief moments of oceanic vision in the vortex in the "Epilogue" to *Moby-Dick*, gets picked up by the *Rachel* and returned to the landed world of what he calls, in the opening chapter, his "hypos," his nebulous depression of spirit. Melville himself, as his biographers have made clear, fell into deep depression after finishing *Moby-Dick*, as if the tragedy of his own life resembled Ishmael's: the vehicle he chose to achieve his vision, writing, served only temporarily to ward off his creditors in the physical world and his own metaphysical despair. No wonder he wrote, in the letter of June 1851 to Hawthorne included in the *NAAL*, "all my books are botches." A teacher doesn't need to be an expert in Melville biography to engage students in biographical speculation: why does Melville portray, as his final tragic vision in Billy Budd, Sailor, a world in which only absolute justice prevails? Might he be making an attempt to justify or explain the fate he received as a writer—that of obscurity during most of his life?

EMILY DICKINSON

Dickinson's poems are transcendental in method; ask students to select a favorite and discuss affinities with Emerson and Thoreau. At the same time, Dickinson is often considered an early modernist, because of the way her poetic technique calls attention to itself and reflects a high level of self-consciousness. I often begin discussion of Dickinson by asking students to contrast her with Whitman. Both poets reverse students' expectations concerning traditional poetic form, and comparing and contrasting the ways they do this leads to an extensive discussion of what each poet might have been trying to do in poetry. Sheer size is one of the most striking features. As Dickinson writes, in 185, "'Faith' is a fine invention / When Gentle-

men can *see*— / But *Microscopes* are prudent / In an Emergency."
Compared to Whitman's "Walt Whitman, a kosmos" and the "mag-
nifying and applying" of "Song of Myself," Dickinson's small poems
seem microscopic. Exploring the freedom with which Whitman
creates the vast catalogues in "Song of Myself" and allows himself
endless repetition, then contrasting that freedom with 185, or with a
poem like Dickinson's 1099, "My Cocoon tightens—Colors teaze—,"
can move the discussion from formal differences to thematic ones,
here to the question of literary authority. Where does Whitman find
his? How does it appear as an assumption in his poetry, although
Dickinson, as in 505, "I would not paint—a picture—," must struggle
to achieve it? How does the smallness of her poetry suggest her own
assumptions about the nature of literary authority?

Unlike Whitman, Dickinson appears uninterested in the
physical body, grounding many poems in a specific natural image
that she then proceeds either to transcend, as in poems 328, "A Bird
came down the Walk—" or 348, "I dreaded that first Robin, so," or to
despair in finding her own inability to transcend human limitations
and the limits of poetry, as in 465, "I heard a Fly buzz—when I
died—" or 1400, "What mystery pervades a well!" Like Whitman,
Dickinson also writes analogically, following Emerson's technique
for transcendental vision. Many poems illustrate her use of analogies
to express and contain her vision, particularly the poems that appear
to be about death, but actually show the poet trying to see beyond
the limits on human vision that death, as life's limit, symbolizes for
her. 510, "It was not Death, for I stood up," 754, "My Life had
stood—a Loaded Gun—," and 465, "I heard a Fly buzz," are just
three of the many poems that illustrate this pattern, and many others
write thematically about the process, as 67, "Success is counted
sweetest" or 528, "Mine—by the Right of the White Election!"

Many of the Dickinson poems that initially appear so elusive
to students can become deeply revealing of the consciousness of the
woman who wrote them—and of the fact that they were written by a
woman. 1129, "Tell all the Truth but tell it slant—" becomes another
Dickinson variation on Emerson's use of the poetic analogy to
achieve transcendental vision. But her reasons for choosing analogies that move in "slant" fashion rather than in concentric circles
(like the ripples that result when Emerson throws a stone) suggest
that Dickinson, unlike Whitman, may have seen herself as self-con-
ceived, self-born—not because she has invented a new kind of poetry
but because she has dared, as a woman, to write at all. For who are
her female precursors? If she does view herself this way, how does
she differ from those other self-inventors, Franklin and Douglass?
Does she imagine setting her life up as model for others? And does
the biographical fact that she published only seven poems in her
lifetime imply self-censorship? Ask students to reread Bradstreet's
"Prologue" and "The Author to Her Book." To what extent does

Dickinson's use of smallness in her imagery reflect her sense of inadequacy at the same time that it gives her the analogical vehicle for transcending that sense? Despite the fact that the editors of the *NAAL* have already provided a rich selection of Dickinson's poetry, I recommend placing on reserve and adding to your syllabus some of the poems on smallness, diminutiveness, hunger, deprivation, and repression, such as 61, 77, 146, 178, 182, 248, 439, 540, 579, 612, and 613 (available in *The Complete Poems of Emily Dickinson*, ed. Thomas Johnson), all of which portray the ways in which Dickinson wrote out of her experience as a woman in nineteenth-century American society. And for some intriguing contradictory readings of Dickinson that are certain to provoke discussion in the classroom, see, in particular, William Shurr, *The Marriage of Emily Dickinson*, and essays by Adelaide Morris and Joanne Dobson in Suzanne Juhasz, ed., *Feminist Critics Read Emily Dickinson*.

REBECCA HARDING DAVIS

Davis's rediscovered story "Life in the Iron-Mills" allows you to end your course by making a lot of thematic connections with earlier writers and introducing your students to an early work of literary realism. Ask students to compare the atmosphere in Davis's mill with Melville's "The Tartarus of Maids"; to evaluate the nightmarish realism of Davis's description against Poe's tales of the supernatural; to contrast Hugh Wolfe's creation of the korl woman with women characters created by Irving, Poe, and Hawthorne; to think about the korl woman's special hunger in light of Dickinson's own poems about hunger and deprivation; to see "Life in the Iron-Mills" as a story about what happens when a man like Wolfe or a woman like Deborah are denied liberty and equality by others; to analyze similarities between the bondage of Davis's mill workers and Douglass's portrait of actual slavery; to recall Thoreau's view from inside his prison cell in "Resistance to Civil Government" with Hugh Wolfe's view—which is more powerful?; Wolfe's last moments in his cell with Billy Budd's "God rest Captain Vere!"; and the last lines of *Walden* ("Only that day dawns to which we are awake. There is more day to dawn. The sun is but a morning star"), and of "Life in the Iron-Mills" (" . . . its groping arm points through the broken cloud to the far East, where, in the flickering, nebulous crimson, God has set the promise of the Dawn"). Discuss in particular Davis's appeal to her readers to accept the realism of her description of Hugh Wolfe ("Be just: when I tell you about this night, see him as he is") and of his korl woman ("A working-woman,—the very type of her class"). What might have led Davis to write realism in a literary era still influenced by the British romantic poets and the work of the American authors Hawthorne and Poe in the romance form? What gave Davis another view of American life than that of the New England transcendentalist writers? What differentiates Davis's realism from Stowe's indictment of slavery in the earlier *Uncle Tom's Cabin*? And where did Davis find her own literary authority? How did she manage to write realistically about what it means to be working class, female, and hungry in a country still dominated, in its literature, by the attempt to define white American male identity?

VOLUME 2

1865–1914

The question of realism and the genre of narrative fiction dominate the concerns of post–Civil War writers. The meaning of the term "realism" is complicated by the fact that, as the general introduction to the period in the *NAAL* suggests, there were "other realists," and there were critical categories that seem somehow both related and different: regionalism, "local color" writing, and naturalism (which at the turn of the century was often termed "new realism"). The traditional approach to teaching the period is to begin with the triumvirate of Clemens, Howells, and James and then touch on the "others." One of the difficulties with this approach is that American authors (as a reading of "Life in the Iron-Mills" at the end of Volume I suggests) began writing in a realistic mode decades before Clemens, Howells, and James published their major works. If we begin teaching the period not with Clemens, but with the realistic literary works that were published in the 1860s and 1870s, we can give students a better sense of the evolution of American literary realism, which began as a mode of perception and a way of thinking about indigenous American life. It only achieved the stature of "theory" when Howells (and James) wrote so many editorial columns (and prefaces) in an attempt to define the American "art of fiction." In the notes on specific authors that follow this general discussion, I have kept to my practice of following the chronology in the *NAAL*. But, in my own classroom, I teach the authors who represent the various genres in the order in which the genre developed, even though this often means teaching writers out of strict chronological order. I begin with regionalism and "local color" writers; then teach Clemens as part of a group of realists; and end with naturalism and turn-of-the-century nonfiction.

The earliest writing in a realistic mode begins with Harriet Beecher Stowe (illlustrated by "The Minister's Housekeeper" in Volume I) and some of her contemporaries, Alice Cary and Rose Terry Cooke (not anthologized), as well as Rebecca Harding Davis. Literary historians also trace strains of early realism in the "Southwest humor" writers (anthologized in Volume 1), Augustus Baldwin

Longstreet, George Washington Harris, T. B. Thorpe, and Johnson Jones Hooper. In order to understand the evolution of American realism, students need to see what happens to these early strains; and what happens is that a group of writers, mostly women, beginning with Cary, Stowe, and Cooke, develop the genre of regionalism, represented in Volume 2 by Sarah Orne Jewett, Mary Wilkins Freeman, Charles Chesnutt, and Kate Chopin (although the anthologized novel, *The Awakening*, shows Chopin's strengths as a realist rather than a regionalist). In my attempt to convey the nature of the earlier literary tradition, I teach Jewett and Chesnutt before Clemens, even though all of the anthologized works by regionalist writers were published after *Adventures of Huckleberry Finn*. The chronological point I try to make is that regionalism preceded realism as a literary genre and serves as a bridge between early and late nineteenth-century American writers. Then, regional elements of Clemens's work (and its strain of anecdotal humor) can be placed in their context, and students can also understand the differences between the realism of Henry James and that of writers like Jewett and Freeman. But even within writing that contains regional elements, students will find the "local color" fiction of Bret Harte and Hamlin Garland to contrast with the regionalism of Jewett and Freeman. In my own discussions of these writers I make one major distinction between regionalism and "local color" writing based on where the author locates the center of perception in the story. Regionalist writers tell the story empathically, from within the protagonist's perspective; "local color" writers often stand back from their characters and look at, not with, them. This distinction prepares students well to think about point-of-view in Henry James.

What all of the writers in realistic modes share is a commitment to referential narrative. Despite the evidence of invention, the reader expects to meet characters in the fiction who resemble ordinary people in ordinary circumstances, and who often meet unhappy ends. (The pattern of the unhappy ending is much less prevalent in regionalism, however.) The realists develop these characters by the use of ordinary speech in dialogue, and plot and character development become intertwined. Some writers make use of orthographical changes in order to convey particular speech rhythms and other elements of dialect peculiar to regional life. They all set their fictions in places that actually exist, or might easily have actual prototypes, and they are interested in recent or contemporary life, not in history or legend. Setting can become conspicuous as an element of theme in "local color" and regionalist fiction. And the realists rely on first- or third-person-limited point of view in order to convey the sensibility of a central character or, in the case of the "local color" writers, the altered perception of the outside observer as he witnesses the scene.

SAMUEL CLEMENS

Adventures of Huckleberry Finn

Clemens defies classification as humorist, "local color" writer, or realist; *Adventures of Huckleberry Finn* is all of these. I usually spend several class periods on the novel and focus more on close analysis than on trying to definitively identify the book's genre. I urge students to slow down in their reading and to pay attention to the development of the text. In this novel, where one of the significant questions concerns the extent to which Huck Finn develops or doesn't develop in his moral character and depth of self by the novel's end, the process of focusing on the way Clemens unfolds his fiction can highlight, at any given moment, whether Huck himself has developed or whether he has just moved on to another adventure. As part of a "warm-up" discussion, I ask my students to consider why so many critics have called the book particularly American, and make a running list (if they have studied the 1820–1865 period with me, they are used to thinking about this question): the contrast, from the beginning, between Huck's love of wildness and the Widow Douglas's attempt to 'sivilize' him; the central problem of the book once Huck and Jim start down the river on the raft—namely, that Jim is trying to escape to the free states; Samuel Clemens's use of various dialects and of vernacular language, both in Huck's own narrative and in the book's dialogue; the "back woods" humorous presentation of characters and events; the importance of the longest North American river to the plot. In close analysis we discuss the novel according to the following general outline:

Chapters 1–7

● Read closely the opening passages and evaluate the language: Huck is an ordinary boy, uneducated, a plain speaker; he feels the need to introduce himself and doesn't claim either reputation or literary authority; his idea of story simply concerns the actual events; moves from one report to the next, using very few subordinate clauses.

● Discuss the way Huck's language resembles the novel's plot—events, like clauses, are strung together in linear fashion rather than woven together; discuss Tom's allusion to Cervantes's *Don Quixote* (the first novel) as his own model and Clemens's choice of the picaresque form (from the Spanish *picaro*, wanderer).

● Contrast the adventures Huck has as a member of Tom's "boys' gang" and the real escape he makes from Pap's cabin; compare Huck's search for adventure and his quest for his own identity (one of his "American" characteristics); ask why Tom's gang doesn't work very well for Huck: even if the boys did manage to have some real adventures, Tom would offer no real alternative to the life the Widow Douglas wants for Huck; Tom still tries to regiment Huck—whether the rules are based on boys' books or on the Bible (cite Huck's conclusion after the adventure with the "A-rabs" and elephants—"as for me I think different. It had all the marks of a Sunday-school").

● Evaluate the attraction Tom holds for Huck: what does Huck want from Tom that he can't find in Miss Watson's world? Consider Tom's values as companion, his cleverness (he manages to live in both the world of the boys and the world of the grown-ups); discuss Tom's limitations: while Huck may tell a few "stretchers," Tom Sawyer actually lies and won't admit even to himself that he is pretending; Tom doesn't face the raw necessity that governs Huck Finn's life (Tom has a family; Huck, despite the existence of "Pap," is for all practical purposes an orphan).

● Talk about Clemens's class analysis here. In Miss Watson's world, where Tom manages to feel comfortable, Huck will always be an outsider. The son of a bum, Huck will always be lower class in the widow's world; it's only when he manages to slip away to sleep in the woods, or to imagine himself escaping for good, that he can free himself both from the constraints of "sivilization" and from its class system, which places him at the bottom. Note Huck's commonality with Jim here; when Huck finds himself in real trouble with Pap, he goes not to Tom but to Jim for some of his "magic." (A related discussion of the Uncle Remus tales and Chesnutt's use of folklore can lead into a consideration of the extent to which Jim "teaches" Huck.)

● Discuss the sequence of events with Pap: how does the previously humorous tone change? Huck here becomes homeless and friendless. Analyze the social commentary in these chapters, in which Huck is beaten and abused, enslaved and imprisoned by the drunken Pap. Focus on Huck's increasing need for separateness. Escaping the widow seemed necessary if Huck were to be free to live without having his spirit stifled; escaping his father is necessary if he is to avoid imitating him.

● Analyze Huck's symbolic death: how does he forge a new identity for himself? how does it separate him from Tom Sawyer as well as from Pap?

● Discuss the final metaphor of Chapter 7, in which Huck floats down the river lying in the canoe, then writes: "I run the canoe into a deep dent in the bank that I knowed about; I had to part the willow branches to get in; and when I made fast nobody could 'a' seen the canoe from the outside." Connect the image to the tale the Widow Douglas tells Huck in the novel's opening pages, the story of Moses in the bulrushes that Huck cared so little about because "he had been dead a considerable long time." Suggest Huck Finn as an American Moses: newly born, an orphan, and, if not a prophet, at least prophetic in his attempt to express the nature of experience.

Chapters 8-15

• allusions to *Robinson Crusoe*; shipwreck as a motif to characterize human loneliness and isolation, and discussion of Jim as Huck's Friday.

• the relationship between Huck and Jim; ways in which Jim's flight from slavery comments on Huck's own need for freedom.

• the quality of experience Huck and Jim have, at first on the island, and then on the raft; connections with New World settlements and (ironically) with the middle passage for American slaves; Leslie Fiedler's argument from "Come Back to the Raft Agin', Huck Honey"; discussion of single-sex relationships in other American works (Dimmesdale and Chillingworth in *The Scarlet Letter*, Ishmael and Queequeg in *Moby-Dick*) and the extent to which the single-sex world in the nineteenth century frees the protagonist to develop gender characteristics of both sexes; thematic connections to "Rip Van Winkle" or the stories of Harte and Garland that show a male writer portraying women characters as limiting human freedom.

• close analysis of Chapter 15, in which Clemens gives us what becomes yet another American dream. The "dream"—more precisely, Huck's successful attempt to convince Jim that he was asleep and only "dreamed" his separation from Huck in the fog—opens a complex discussion of the possibility of friendship between Huck and Jim. Some students will not have noticed the age difference between the two until you point it out to them. But they will see Huck wavering on the subject of slavery. Here, and later, whenever Huck views Jim as a slave, or as a "nigger," Jim loses his individuality. So what is at stake as the two make their way down the river is not only Huck's identity, but Jim's as well; and since Jim's individuality is dependent on Huck's willingness to recognize his humanity, Huck comes closest to being human and in full possession of his own identity in the moments when he recognizes Jim as a person. In the dream scene at the end of Chapter 15, students can see the complex irony Clemens is portraying here. For, as they will find out in Chapter 16, Huck and Jim miss Cairo in the fog, and therefore Jim's "American dream" of becoming a free man has evaporated. Jim's loss of his hopes and his loss of individuality (as Huck turns him into the butt of his own joke) is nothing more than a game for Huck. The contrast here between Jim, the slave, and Jim, the person, is never again too clear: when Jim realizes he has been duped, he tells Huck, "'trash is what people is dat puts dirt on de head er day fren's en makes 'em ashamed.'"

Chapters 16-33

In this section, Clemens concentrates on social commentary. The Shepherdson-Grangerford feud (itself a comment on the Civil

War) divides the novel roughly in half, and also marks a shift in the novel's focus that neatly parallels historical contrasts between antebellum romanticism (which can be linked to the idyllic scenes of freedom on the raft) and the Reconstruction period (marked by the carpetbagger morality of the king and the duke). The analysis of the king and the duke that is possible in the classroom is far too comprehensive to do more than sketch in some of the central points here:

• the historical commentary, in which, although the American Revolution appeared to throw off monarchy, the new government doesn't really protect the common man.

• the social commentary, in which the king and the duke seem just as "American" as Huck and Jim, and so the new country seems to have replaced a hierarchical system (in which everyone might know who is privileged and who is colonized) with a more insidious system of human oppression, made even more so because the "innocents," Huck and Jim, can't tell the difference between what is real and what is not. The Royal Nonesuch is just one incident that illustrates the chameleonlike qualities of some new Americans, in which their apparent sincerity proves to be a sham and a worse form of humanity than Huck tried to escape. Here the book sets up a hierarchy of its own, in which Huck encounters worse forms of degradation than he had ever suspected (previously viewing his own father as the lowest form).

• the epistemological commentary in which Huck learns the use of disguises as a means of self-preservation, and in which the raft itself (invaded by the king and the duke) becomes only an illusion of freedom. Here the book (like the river) has also shifted shape, possibly like the shape shifting of Negro folktales (see Joel Chandler Harris), and Huck's identity becomes mercurial, indeterminate.

• the literary commentary, in which the Shakespearian parodies (the king and the duke are themselves parodies of the traveling Shakespearean actors of the late nineteenth century) suggest the inability of American art to "render" experience in the same forms that the greatest British writers chose. Just as there is no certainty for Huck Finn once he moves outside a world that has rules, there is none for Mark Twain, except the shape-shifting form of creating for the first time a fictional character with an American voice. The literary commentary can lead into a discussion of the way Clemens refers to fate's wheel and the dramatic sense in which tragedy and comedy are inversions of each other. America seems to be a place, the novel suggests, where one day a crook can become a king, a slave can become a freeman, a man within sight of freedom can become a slave again. The security and freedom of life aboard a raft can be transformed into their very opposites and the raft a kind of prison—a literal prison for Jim, who is tied up as if he were a runaway slave. The irony, of course, is that he actually is a runaway slave, and in any world but the novel (where the boards of the raft become the "boards" of the stage) Jim's ropes would be appropriate and would signify that the author was adhering to the conventions of realism.

● the central theme of "pretending," in which the absence of any reality that doesn't shift shape begins to unify the entire novel. Students here can go back to the "pretending" of the boys' gang; can discuss the king's and the duke's scams; can see "pretending" as one of the ways Huck eases his conscience when he tries to "pray a lie"; and can think about the way "pretending" can lead to self-invention (making connections back to Benjamin Franklin's "real," as opposed to Huck Finn's "fictional" autobiography).

The king and the duke sequence finds its end in the scene at the Wilkses, where Huck's conscience finally starts working and he sympathizes with the plight of the Wilks "orphans." It's as if he is able to put himself inside another's clothes for the first time—literally, when he hides among Mary Jane's dresses. But wearing women's clothes, for Huck, makes it possible for him to perform a kind of literary transvestism, a costume change that alters his moral sense—and all of Miss Watson's teachings come back to guide him when he decides to turn in the frauds.

Chapter 33–Chapter The Last

The final section of the novel always generates discussion in the classroom, and I ask students to take sides on the problem of the novel's ending. Many readers of *Huck Finn* consider the ending flawed—Hemingway, for example, said that Mark Twain "cheated"—while other readers have praised it, and I ask students to defend or to criticize the ending.

At issue for the defense: The ending completes the novel, provides unity, since it returns the reader to Tom Sawyer's world, and actually shows Tom in a successful adventure; the ending completes the novel's form as well, starting roughly in the same place where it began, with another woman, Aunt Sally, wanting to adopt Huck Finn, and ending with Huck's reaffirmation of his own need for freedom in the novel's famous closing lines, "I reckon I got to light out for the territory . . . "; and for readers who view the novel as picaresque, the ending appropriately sets the hero out on another adventure.

At issue for the critique: The novel moves back from Huck's initial quest for separation, shows him once again under the influence of Tom Sawyer, and, therefore, prevents him from developing further. In fact, the entire sequence of events at the Phelps farm seems to portray him as having regressed. He doesn't think twice about imprisoning Jim, treating him like property again; and either his character is presented inconsistently—since as late as Chapter 31, he was ready to go to hell for Jim's sake—or Clemens has backed off

from confronting the moral dilemma of slavery within his novel's social commentary. The novel finally treats Jim's freedom unrealisti-
cally, since Clemens achieves his "happy ending" by revealing that
Tom has known since his arrival at the farm that Miss Watson set
Jim free in her will. Students may see the ending as Clemens's own
evasion, and may make connections in particular with Hawthorne
(the boys and Jim persist in describing the escape as an "evasion").
When Aunt Sally asks Tom why he wanted to set Jim free when he
was already free, he replies that it is "*just* like women" to ask such a
question. Earlier, when Huck, Jim, and Tom are running from the
armed men and Jim volunteers to stay with the injured Tom even
though he knows he is risking his own freedom again, Huck writes, "I
knowed he was white inside."

At the end, the novel can seem to confront none of the serious issues of inequity in American society. But, as one student re-
cently pointed out to me, perhaps that makes *Adventures of Huckleberry Finn* most realistic. Although the novel has a happy ending,
Clemens doesn't manage to achieve what he seemed to be setting
out to do: to create Huck as a developing individual, capable of
managing reality, able to shift for himself in a new country. The
novel's realism here becomes Mark Twain's problem, not Huck
Finn's; the novel's form becomes as elusive as the "real" identity of
the king and the duke, and what the novel demonstrates historically
is that realism itself proves too confining a form within which to
contain the changing shape of American reality.

"The Man That Corrupted Hadleyburg"

Clemens wrote "Hadleyburg" at the end of his career, and it
reflects the despair he fought in his own personal life. Ask students
to contrast the tone of "Hadleyburg" with the tone of *Huckleberry
Finn*. The *NAAL* headnote calls "Hadleyburg," "preachy." Ask students to evaluate the negative view of human nature that Clemens
portrays in the story. Recall Jonathan Edwards's sermon, "Sinners in
the Hands of an Angry God," and consider the effects, for Clemens,
of the difficulty in believing in human goodness. Trace the process of
Hadleyburg's corruption, step by step throughout the story, and explore what Clemens has to say about the complications of being
honest: the town is "narrow, self-righteous, and stingy." Does
"Hadleyburg" approach the stature of social satire, or does it rather
express the author's misanthropy? What has happened to Clemens's
roots in the "Southwest humorist" tradition? Read "How to Tell a
Story" (published just 5 years before "Hadleyburg") and set the essay
up as a standard for Clemens's own later work. Clemens himself
refers to Stowe's storyteller of "The Minister's Housekeeper," Sam
Lawson, which invites comparison between the moralism of "Hadleyburg" and the moralism which Clemens spent so much of his life

trying to turn into humor, namely the moralism of the abolitionist and reform movements that Stowe's work represents. Clemens omits empathy and compassion as well as humor from his tale of Hadleyburg's decline. Consider the possibility that humor, for Clemens, is too frail a defense against despair; examine, in particular, the scene in section III, in which Burgess begins the reading of the notes from the nineteen "principal citizens" of the town. In this scene Clemens appears to try out some of the stylistic techniques he describes in "How to Tell a Story." Burgess uses repetition and strategic pauses, and his audience of townspeople laughs with great "jollity." What about Clemens's readers? Do we laugh? In "How to Tell a Story," Clemens suggests that it is not content, but the failure of technique which ruins a story. He criticizes the teller of the comic story who must shout "the nub" at the reader, and he concludes, "All of which is very depressing, and makes one want to renounce joking and lead a better life." Does the revised motto at the end of "Hadleyburg" constitute a joke, or does it serve as final evidence that Clemens renounces joking?

BRET HARTE

In "The Outcasts of Poker Flat," Harte creates central characters who become the object of perception by someone outside the setting or region. Oakhurst is the outsider, and the reader's views of Madam Shipton, Piney Woods, and the others are all filtered through Oakhurst. When Oakhurst kills himself at the end of the story, Harte presents this scene, as well, as a tableau for other outsiders—his readers—to see. Ask students to consider the humor of the story: does Harte achieve it at the expense of any particular characters more than others? Had he tried to depict the experience of western life from Mother Shipton's point of view, would "Outcasts" have been a different story? How much does Harte assume that his readers will find women, in general, and western prostitutes, in particular, laughable? Is he laughing at or with his characters?

W. D. HOWELLS

"Novel-Writing and Novel-Reading" gives students a chance to read some of Howells's literary theory, and then to test the application of that theory in "Editha." Howells's definition of realism requires that fiction be "like life," and the central statement in his essay is the following: "The truth which I mean, the truth which is the only beauty, is truth to human experience. . . . It is a well ascertained fact concerning the imagination that it can work only with the stuff of experience. It can absolutely create nothing; it can only compose."

For students who come to Howells after studying *Adventures of Huckleberry Finn*, notions of "like life" and "truth to experience" will seem justifiably naive. For all of the complexities of the world in which he lived, Howells's own view of reality remains a simplistic one—that somehow reality may be verified and agreed upon. However, Howells's theory makes more sense if we focus on the word "compose." He seems to be saying here that the novelist must "place together" elements from real life that he is unable to create, that the novelist's art reveals itself in the relative placement of real things. Later in the essay he draws the analogy of a cyclorama to explain what he attempts in his fiction. He describes beginning "with life itself" and then going on to "imitate what we have known of life." The good writer will "hide the joint. But the joint is always there, and on one side of it are real ground and real grass, and on the other are the painted images of ground and grass." The realism of Howells describes the way existing elements are placed together. But composing implies assertion. To pose a question is to assert it, to propound it, to put it forth for examination. Therefore, in the very process of "composition," Howells and his hypothetical realistic writers are trying to set forth reality itself for examination, as if it were the proposition of an argument.

"Editha," for all of the realism of its portrayal of sexist stereotypes in late nineteenth-century American society, is superficial in its attempt to find and define motivation in Editha's character. Is Editha a real person or a "painted image"? And if she is a "painted image," does she project social reality or her author's distorted view of women? Compare her with Dame Van Winkle, Ligeia, Freeman's Louisa Ellis in "A New England Nun," and James's May Bartram in "The Beast in the Jungle."

HENRY JAMES

"The Art of Fiction" shows that James shares Howells's theory of fiction, in part. He writes, "The only reason for the existence of a novel is that it does attempt to represent life." However, what James means by "life" and what Howells means by it are two different things. Unlike Howells, who asserts a reality that is referential and shared, James suggests that creation resides in the author's perception. Without the perceiving eye there is no art. James implicitly links realism with point of view and with the "quality of the mind of the producer." He writes, "A novel is in its broadest definition a personal, a direct impression of life: that, to begin with, constitutes its value, which is greater or less according to the intensity of the impression." Thus, reality is subjective for Henry James, and he suggests that, far from being referential, realism reveals aspects of life that cannot be seen. He insists on "the power to guess the unseen

-124-

from the seen, to trace the implication of things, to judge the whole piece by the pattern," and he writes, "Experience is never limited, and it is never complete; it is an immense sensibility, a kind of huge spiderweb of the finest silken threads suspended in the chamber of consciousness, and catching every airborne particle in its tissue."

If, as Howells writes, the reader is the arbiter of a fiction's realism, and if "the only test of a novel's truth is his own knowledge of life," then many of our students will have difficulty seeing realism in Henry James. The challenge in teaching James is to try to get students to follow the psychological complexity of the relationships James creates—between Daisy and Winterbourne in "Daisy Miller," and between John Marcher and May Bartram in "The Beast in the Jungle"—as well as to see his interest in relationships, per se, as an aspect of realism that makes James stand out among many of his contemporaries. Compare James's analysis of the complexity of emotional and psychological development with Clemens's in *Adventures of Huckleberry Finn* and with Howells's in "Editha." The regionalists link emotional development to the development of community—here portrayed by Mrs. Todd's empathy with the French woman in Jewett's "The Foreigner." And Freeman and Kate Chopin show that the individual develops emotionally within the context of human relationships, but their focus remains the quality and development of individual or shared vision. Only James, among his contemporaries, focuses on human relationships themselves as the source of experience. The single context within the meaning of human experience may be explored. In the shorter works anthologized here, we see relationships that are primarily dyadic. In the novels, James interweaves pairs of intense personal relationships with each other to form the "huge spiderweb" of his psychological fiction. Although instructors will probably want students to read "Daisy Miller"—it establishes James's themes of the innocence of Americans in Europe and the way individuals are bound by convention, and it focuses on a female protagonist in a way that is representative of many of the novels—the works anthologized in the *NAAL* that I find more successful as a way of demonstrating James's power as a storyteller are *The Turn of the Screw* and "The Beast in the Jungle."

The Turn of the Screw

As students conclude from studying Clemens and Howells, the 1865–1914 period may be viewed, in part, as a series of experiments in how to tell a story. In *The Turn of the Screw*, Henry James offers his own theory of fiction, demonstrated in the telling. As much as any work by James, *The Turn of the Screw* illustrates the idea, from "The Art of Fiction," that the perceiving eye creates the artistic impression.

Many critics have attempted to unravel the meaning of this short novel, and students may find their own ingenious ways of interpreting the governess, Mrs. Grose, the children, or the apparitions, but in my own teaching I present the work as a *tour de force* of narration rather than a work with explicit thematic content. We begin by reading closely the opening prefatory chapter, in which the first-person narrator describes the way Douglas prepares his audience to be receptive to his tale. We talk about the way James's own narrator is also preparing his reader, and I suggest that eliciting reader response is James's primary objective in the tale. We trace the stages of offering up and withholding that Douglas engages in, and I comment that the prefatory chapter "trains" James's own reader in the act and art of reading the work that will follow.

Critics have made much of the concept of the "unreliable narrator" in Henry James, but rather than dismiss any of James's narrators in this tale as unreliable—the first-person narrator, Douglas, or the governess herself—I read the novel as a series of stages in the development of an engaged reader: the governess establishes her own literary authority; engages the trust of Mrs. Grose, who becomes a type of the innocent and unsuspecting hearer or reader; begins to "read" or to interpret the events of the narrative for herself, for Mrs. Grose, and for James's own readers; formulates a "theory" based on that reading; comes up against ambiguity, or difficulty in fitting both her own perceptions and the perceptions of others (Mrs. Grose, Flora) into the theory that evolves from her progressive acts of interpretation; becomes unable to tolerate ambiguity and acts in such a way as to "kill" both little Miles and the illusion of being "at the helm" in her own fictional creation.

James's prose style masters the art of building a believable fiction based on empirical inference—both the governess's inferences or "reading" from the events she experiences, and our own reader response to the inferences we draw from her own incomplete disclosures to Mrs. Grose. In the process, James suggests a depth and quality to human interaction that is representative of his "major phase" fiction, for he documents how much human relationship is based on the art of "reading" and interpreting from the inferences we make about other people. The governess makes this explicit when, at the end of Chapter XII, she tries to interpret Mrs. Grose's response to her latest revelation about the children's danger, and, thus, concludes from the expression on Mrs. Grose's face "as a woman reads another" that "she could see what I myself saw." James draws a fine line, at the end of the novel, between a well-articulated interpretation and a delusion. Ultimately he throws his own reader back on the difficulty of interpretation and leaves us with two choices: either we accuse James himself of betraying us with an "unreliable" narrator (and if we do this, we become as "mad" as the governess herself seems to be at the end of the novel), or we are forced to accept the potential unreliability of a theory based on empirical interpretation, no matter how persuasive or internally consistent the theory itself may be, and no matter how worthwhile are our motives for formulating the theory—the governess herself believes that she wants to "save" the children.

Among the numerous approaches that critics have taken to *The Turn of the Screw*, several may intrigue your students, or they may offer them as their own interpretations of the novel. Various approaches focus on the governess herself: (a) The novel explicates the governess's sexual repression (the Freudian approach); (b) The governess's social isolation has made her insane (a social systems approach); (c) The governess is searching for her own identity: who *is* the "governess," that is, the "person who cares for children"?; (d) The governess has frightened the children to death in a display of the undercurrent of distrust, and even hatred, that characterized the Victorian attitude toward children. Other approaches focus on the text itself. I have explicated one approach to reader-response criticism of the novel. In addition, you may identify the novel as working out problems in realism for Henry James: the use of narrative point-of-view characterizes the development of realism as a genre. A psychological approach suggests that James blurs the boundaries between inner and outer, anticipates the concept of projective identification defined by twentieth-century psychoanalytic theorists, and questions our ability to distinguish between perception and reality. Finally, James also anticipates the birth of modernism in the twentieth century by asking us to consider what happens when we can't believe a story that has been so convincing. In essence, James rejects both Clemens's despair and Howells's optimism; *The Turn of the Screw* confronts his readers with the idea that realism itself is a comforting fiction—no more than a fiction—in a world in which we may ultimately be unable not only to control or save others from the powers of evil, but even to recognize or to substantiate the existence of good and evil except as we project out of ourselves images of our own inner psychic structures.

"The Beast in the Jungle"

In this story, James fully develops his theory of the novel as "a personal, direct impression of life," for it is actually such an "impression" that Marcher expects to have, and by which he figures his "beast." James's use of third-person limited point of view to define the unfolding of Marcher's perception serves as a laboratory of the use of technique. Marcher's point of view gives the reader a sense of reality as being bounded by the limits of perception and consciousness; yet James so skillfully creates May Bartram that, without ever entering her consciousness, we know what she is think-ing and feeling—even more than John Marcher, despite the fact that he sees and hears everything the reader does.

I like to ask students "what happens" in this story. The wide range of responses creates a spectrum of the kinds of experience that constitute "reality" for James. Some will reply that nothing hap-pens—which, in a sense, is true enough. Others will wonder whether Marcher dies at the end of the story—a valid speculation. Some will reply that he discovers he has been in love with May Bartram all along—an assertion that seems both true and false in light of the story. A few will focus on the developing portrayal of character as "what happens" for James. You can help them see what interests James in the relationship between his two characters by asking them which character they, as readers, most resemble. They will certainly align themselves with May—for, in a sense, Marcher and May are acting out the ideal relationship between author and reader. He is his own author, like many American male protagonists before him; she is his ideal reader—she grants him his *donnée*—as, James states in "The Art of Fiction," the reader must do for the novelist. So that when the two meet again after ten years' time and May Bartram re-members Marcher's old impression, he asks, "'You mean you feel how my obsession—poor old thing!—may correspond to some pos-sible reality?'" "Corresponding to some possible reality" is the precise problem of the story, of James's other work, and of realism itself. If reality is only "possible," and if two different characters within the same story, in which nothing else happens but their relationship, have such different perceptions of what is real, then what happens to realism itself?

James's interest in convention and social forms in "Daisy Miller" is apparent in "The Beast in the Jungle" as well. Marcher's very "unsettled" feeling about the nature of reality makes it difficult for him to go along with social forms. And so he lives with his "figure" of the beast as the hypothesis by which he understands his life. When the beast springs, in a sense, he will be able to live; until then he can't consider marriage. The beast becomes his disfiguring quality—he calls it "a hump on one's back"—and it is necessary for May to "dispose the concealing veil in the right folds." James, here, continues Hawthorne's fascination with the contradictions between apparent self-confrontation (Marcher tries to think of himself as courageous) and actual self-evasion (even when the beast finally springs, he turns "instinctively . . . to avoid it" as he flings himself, face down, on May Bartram's tomb). Ironically, his relationship with May contributes to that process of self-evasion. For she helps him "to pass for a man like another"; with her, Marcher appears to be conventional and to be living an ordinary life. He says to her: "What saves us, you know, is that we answer so completely to so usual an appearance: that of the man and woman whose friendship has become such a daily habit—or almost—as to be at last indispensable." Although they aren't married, Marcher believes that he has the "appearance" of it. He uses May to "cover" his apparent deficiencies. But certain kinds of experience and certain kinds of psychological development cannot be acquired by what "passes for" living, and neither can they be taught; they must be lived. Therefore, although the reader perceives that May Bartram understands much more of Marcher than he does of himself, she restrains herself, as James restrains himself, from telling him what it all means. He has to figure it out for himself—or not know it at all.

The story ends "happily" in a sense, because, although Marcher discovers the limitations of his fate, James manages to achieve his own goal—namely, that of portraying a character having a "personal, direct impression"—a literal *impress* of "letters of quick flame." The question becomes, How does Marcher finally achieve that impression? What is responsible, what is the catalyzing moment? Students will remember the scene in the cemetery, when Marcher sees the ravaged mourner, who is apparently a widower, and whose manifestation of grief makes Marcher ask, "What had the man *had*, to make him by the loss of it so bleed and yet live?" The apparent answer, and perhaps the only "right" answer, is that the other man has been touched by passion, has loved, whereas Marcher "had seen *outside* of his life, not learned it within." And he concludes, "The escape would have been to love her; then, *then* he would have lived."

But it seems curious that the other man at the cemetery seems—possibly, to Marcher—aware of an "overt discord" between his feelings and Marcher's. The significant thing, to Marcher, is that the other man showed his feelings, "*showed* them—that was the point. . . . " And he is aware of his own presence as "something that profaned the air." In my own reading of this scene, I see James as more interested in Marcher's inability to find the appropriate *form* for his feeling than in his inability to feel at all. He describes Marcher at May's funeral as being "treated as scarce more nearly concerned with it than if there had been a thousand others." As the author of his own fate, Marcher has failed in its execution. He has failed to find any manifest form for his own "personal, direct impression" that would have allowed him to "learn from within." And James links that failure with Marcher's refusal to make "real" what is only "appearance"—his "daily habit" of relationship with May Bartram. For James, consciousness requires a social context. Therefore, "It was as if in the view of society he had not *been* markedly bereaved, as if there still failed some sign or proof of it. . . . " James's characters may defy convention, as Daisy Miller does, but they don't escape having to confront it. The intrusion of convention in James's fiction establishes its social realism, the limitations within which his characters may establish themselves as conscious.

JOEL CHANDLER HARRIS

The "Uncle Remus" tales depend for their narrative success on the contrast between black storyteller and white audience. Harris includes in his work "instructions" to his readers; writes for a white audience; and yet, manages to avoid caricaturing his black characters or turning them into mere entertainment. In his extensive use of southern black dialect and Negro folktales as the source of his subject matter, Harris might easily have been perceived in his time, and in ours, as a "local color" writer. I explain my own distinction between regionalism and "local color"—that the regionalist narrator looks *with* the regional protagonist, while the "local color" writer looks *at* regional experience—and ask students to consider the location of Harris's own perspective on his characters.

SARAH ORNE JEWETT

In the traditional presentation of late nineteenth-century American fiction, Sarah Orne Jewett and Mary Wilkins Freeman are often grouped with the "local color" writers and "regionalism" becomes a descriptive term for the entire group. A closer look at American literary history reveals that regionalism and "local color" writing developed as distinct but parallel genres, and that if we look at chronology, regionalism was the first of the late-nineteenth-century fictional genres to emerge. Harriet Beecher Stowe published *The Pearl of Orr's Island*, the work which influenced Jewett's own development, five years before Clemens's "The Notorious Jumping Frog of Calaveras County," and during the same decade that Hawthorne and Melville were publishing their most significant work (the 1850s), Alice Cary, Rose Terry Cooke (not anthologized here), and Stowe herself were establishing regionalism as a genre. By the time Jewett published *Deephaven*, in 1877, she already had a regionalist tradition to write within, and, although, by the chronology of birth order, she and her work appear to follow Clemens, Howells, and James, *Deephaven* precedes publication of *Adventures of Huckleberry Finn*, *The Rise of Silas Lapham*, and *The Portrait of a Lady*. A brief discussion of the early appearance of regionalism and Jewett's significant contributions to the genre opens my own discussion of Jewett's work in the classroom. The two Jewett stories included in the *NAAL*, "A White Heron" and "The Foreigner," represent her work at its best.

"A White Heron"

In "A White Heron," Jewett chooses as her center of perception a character who lives within the region she is writing about. In

"A White Heron," Sylvy (whose name means "woods") is indigenous to the setting (even though she has moved there from the city) because she speaks the language of nature; it is the ornithologist who is the outsider, implicitly resembling the "local color" writer in his quest to come into the rural scene, shoot and stuff a bird, and bring it back for urban people to see. In refusing to reveal the secrets of the white heron's nest, Sylvy protects the regional perception from exploitation. The contrast between Sylvy's desire to allow the bird its freedom and the ornithologist's desire to kill and stuff the bird provides a focal point for a discussion of the contrasts between regionalism, realism, and "local color" writing. Consider Bret Harte's story, "The Outcasts of Poker Flat," and James's "The Beast in the Jungle" in conjunction with "A White Heron," and ask students to describe differences in point-of-view, the extent to which the story includes the perspective of other characters, and the text's depiction of female characters. Ask them to imagine that "The Outcasts of Poker Flat" included the perspective of the Duchess, Mother Shipton, or Piney Woods, instead of turning them into caricatures, or to imagine that "The Beast in the Jungle" included May Bartram's perspective and gave her a voice, and you will begin to convey some of the particular features of regionalism as a genre. In "A White Heron," Jewett shifts the center of perception not only to a poor, rural, female character, but also to a nine-year-old child, and makes it possible for her reader to understand the disenfranchised perspective.

"The Foreigner"

"The Foreigner" depicts the relationship between the female narrator of *The Country of the Pointed Firs* and her guide in that novel, Mrs. Todd, but Jewett wrote "The Foreigner" after publishing the novel and the story stands alone. In this text, students can experience the power of the earlier, longer work. Like Clemens, Howells, and James, Jewett as regionalist also experimented with storytelling, but "The Foreigner" adds empathy to the requirements of relationship between storyteller and reader/listener/audience. In characterizing the tale Mrs. Todd relates in "The Foreigner" as a "ghost story," Jewett's narrator invites us to contrast her approach with James's narrators in "The Turn of the Screw." For James, the "impression" the teller makes on the listener becomes the standard of the tale's success. For Jewett, the tale becomes a medium for relationship between teller and listener, and although the narrator of "The Foreigner" says very little while Mrs. Todd tells her story, her choice to remain silent at crucial points in the narrative establishes her as a partner in the telling. The listener/reader has a role to play, in Jewett, that goes beyond the reader response James's narrator tries to teach in "The Turn of the Screw." Without relationship between teller and listener, there is no text. The power of Jewett's narrator is that she does not attempt to "read" the meaning of Mrs. Todd's narrative but allows the other woman to tell the story as its meaning deepens and dawns on her. Ask students to contrast the tone of "The Foreigner" with "The Turn of the Screw." In James, the suspense builds; in "The Foreigner," students may find at several points that they think the story is over. The appearance of the "ghost" at the end is not Mrs. Todd's attempt to frighten her listener, or to create a narrative effect, but to move beyond her storm fear for her aged mother, who, with Mrs. Todd's brother William, lives on one of the "outlying islands." The story begins with Mrs. Todd, separated from her mother by the raging gale, and dramatizes her use of storytelling to ease her anxiety and to regain inner peace. By the end of "The Foreigner," Jewett has taught her readers how to feel a different kind of suspense than they might have expected in a "ghost story." The story's climax occurs not with the appearance of the ghost, but in Mrs. Todd's recognition that Mrs. Tolland has been reunited with her mother. In the larger story, the narrator also feels the strengthening of her ties to Mrs. Todd, and fiction, for the regionalist Jewett, becomes reparative and inclusive. Neither Mrs. Tolland nor Mrs. Todd are caricatures set up for readers to laugh at; the comedy of "The Foreigner" makes possible the continued "harmony of fellowship" that eases separation anxiety and social isolation.

KATE CHOPIN

In seeing Edna Pontellier as yet another American on a quest to become self-reliant and to establish her identity within a hostile society, students might consider whether the novel could be titled "Adventures of Edna Pontellier." This can lead into a brief discussion of Huck Finn, and students can see essential differences in design between the two novels. Briefly, Edna Pontellier is not a "picaro" —and Chopin does not present her awakening as a linear series of adventures but rather as an interwoven account of the relationships Edna has with other characters and the way in which her awakening becomes her own "education." Conversely, you may ask students whether Clemens might have subtitled his book "The Awakening of Huckleberry Finn"—and the incongruity of the two portraits of nineteenth-century life becomes even clearer. (If you have taught Volume 1 to the same group of students, you can also make connections between Chopin's novel and earlier "American dream" fictions, especially "Rip Van Winkle," "Young Goodman Brown," Thoreau's "Resistance to Civil Government," and certainly to Jim's dream in Chapter 15 of *Huckleberry Finn*.) In Chopin's successful attempt to present Edna's life from her own point of view—so that students can see that even physical sex is not an end in itself for Edna, but rather only one aspect of her artistic and spiritual awakening and her struggle to achieve autonomy—she uses the technique of shifting the center that characterizes the best of regionalist writing. (One essay that will help students place Edna's attempts to reach toward limits that seem radical for women in her time is Elizabeth Cady Stanton's 1896 "The Solitude of Self," which is brief enough to photocopy and circulate as background reading.)

But Edna's attempt to achieve her own limits is thwarted—by her husband, by the attitudes of men, like Robert, whom she respects, and by the society in which she lives. In describing the limitations Edna constantly comes up against, Chopin writes literary realism; for, in *The Awakening*, Edna's identity is finally so contingent on her social context that it becomes impossible for her to reconcile her sense of her own individual identity with society's expectations. But does she commit suicide? Some students may want to argue that her death is not actually suicide, but rather the consequences of Edna's choice to immerse herself quite literally in a context (the sea) that is the only place she can transcend her own limits (with connections here to Thoreau's "immersion" in Walden Pond). To put it another way, if Edna's death is suicide, then Huck Finn's choice to evade the conflicts of civilization is suicide by other means.

I find it profitable to close-read one scene in the novel (the closing scene of Chapter 23, in which Edna and Leonce have dinner with Edna's father and Dr. Mandelet) as a way of demonstrating Edna's inability to transform the world she lives in into one that will seem real to her. In this scene, each of the four characters tells a story that reveals a great deal about the teller's character. Leonce tells an antebellum tale of "some amusing plantation experiences" and casts himself as a paternalistic Huck Finn; Edna's father depicts himself as a "central figure" in the Civil War; Dr. Mandelet tells a tale of a woman who moves away from her husband, but whose love returns "to its legitimate source"; and Edna tells a romantic story of two lovers who paddle away one night and never come back. What is interesting about the scene is that only Edna's story engages the imaginations of her audience. Despite its romanticism, the story possesses some compelling truth. Ironically, the anecdotes the other three relate are equally romantic projections of themselves or, in the doctor's case, of his ability to "cure" Edna; but in each case, the society has provided mirrors that appear to confirm the self-portraits. Leonce can depict himself as Huck Finn without seeming ridiculous; the colonel can aspire to having a war-hero's reputation without attracting scorn; the doctor can presume to understand the nature of women without losing patients. But Edna cannot find in her culture—except in the invention of her own imagination—any ratification of her self-concept.

Edna's confusion can be viewed as a variation on DuBoisean

"double consciousness," for throughout the book she constantly lives in a state of tension between her emerging sense of self and the limitations her society imposes on her. You might ask your students if Chopin is portraying Edna as the victim of social forces over which she has no control, and if the novel can therefore be viewed as naturalistic. But I always feel the need to point out, here, that sexism (a view of human beings that divides consciousness into "masculine" and "feminine" and prescribes that certain individuals manifest only certain sets of attributes) does not evolve from scientific thinking of the day (in the way that both Stephen Crane and Theodore Dreiser are influenced by Darwin) but rather from conceptions of men's and women's "spheres" that become crystallized in nineteenth-century society. To call it a social force in the same way that Darwinism might be seen as a social force obscures the fact that theories of separate spheres were viewed as the underpinnings of American culture, rather than as new "discoveries." The force over which Edna has no control leads her to look for some other form within which to make manifest her "double consciousness." In the "real" world of Edna's family and society, the only person capable of understanding her death on its own terms might be Mlle. Reisz—another woman who has engaged in a similar struggle and taken the life of the artist as her own form within which to express the tensions of the solitude (also the title of the piece of music she plays) of self. From a realist's view, Edna's last act appears to be meaningless suicide. From a regionalist's view, however, it becomes the only form of expression available to her.

Yet, perhaps the novel's limitations partly reside in Chopin's limited vision of what an American woman might achieve. Edna isn't strong enough or talented enough to live like Mlle. Reisz, and Chopin doesn't even present this as a serious possibility for her. Neither does she perceive the possibility of extending her own desire for awakening to the countless, and generally nameless, women of color in the novel. (I have often suggested to students looking for a paper topic on *The Awakening* that they count and study the great variety of servant women who pervade the novel's background, but no one has ever done this.) Neither Edna nor Chopin herself seems to perceive Edna's concerns as applicable to women of color or different social class. Perhaps Edna's limitations are Chopin's own: for Chopin, implicitly viewing sexism with the naturalist's eye, cannot achieve the full shift of the center of perception that would be necessary to produce works of regionalism in the nineteenth century or modernism in the twentieth, a shift that in Chopin would have to focus on Edna's perception as normal and the perceptions of other characters as skewed. The only nineteenth-century work by a woman writer that really accomplishes this is Sarah Orne Jewett's 1896 *The Country of the Pointed Firs*—not anthologized but available in paperback in a Norton edition (with my introduction).

Like Jewett, Mary Wilkins Freeman wrote in the genre of regionalism, and, also like Jewett, Freeman places women's lives as well as regional vision at the center of her stories. Freeman's "A New England Nun" makes a useful companion story to Jewett's "A White Heron." Ask your students to evaluate the motivations and final choices of Louisa Ellis and Jewett's Sylvy. Compare and contrast "A New England Nun" with Bret Harte's "The Outcasts of Poker Flat." Although Freeman focuses on Louisa Ellis's experience, she portrays her male character, Joe Dagget, more sympathetically than Harte or Hamlin Garland do their female characters. "A New England Nun" presents Louisa Ellis's vision and decision not to marry as valid and normal, but Freeman doesn't earn the reader's sympathy for her female character at Joe Dagget's expense. She portrays Joe as well-meaning and honorable, if typical of his time and place (many young men left New England in order to make their fortunes elsewhere in the years following the Civil War). Some critics have called Louisa sexually repressed. A lively discussion will follow if you ask your students whether they agree.

"The Revolt of 'Mother'" earns Freeman a place in the humorist tradition, with a difference. Once again, she includes "Father's" perspective in her story of "Mother's" revolt, and suggests "Father's" ability to enlarge his own capacity for empathy. Unlike writers of the "Southwest humorist" school, for whom "local color" implied acceptance of "off-color" jokes about women, Freeman does not elevate Sarah Penn by caricaturing Adoniram and making him the object of ridicule. Like Jewett's "A White Heron," "The Revolt of 'Mother'" may be read as Freeman's response to "local color" writing. From the opening line of the story, what Sarah Penn seems to want most of all is to engage her husband as her audience and to find acceptance for her own voice. "Revolt" may be too strong a word to describe Sarah Penn's attempt to make herself heard; she remains within the family structure, even if she has managed to redefine its terms, and Nanny's impending marriage, not Sarah's own frustration, moves her to act.

Freeman contributes to the development of regionalism by collapsing narrator and female protagonist. Ask students to consider the absence of narrators in Freeman's stories and to contrast this with the reliance on narrators by her contemporaries, most notably Jewett and James. Where Jewett makes it possible for a reader to empathize with a regional character, and to imagine that character speaking in his or her own voice, Freeman actually stands back from her own regional canvas, allowing her characters' voices, not a narrator's perspective, to create their own stories. Unlike Jewett, Freeman does not dramatize a shift in the center of perception, from, say, the ornithologist of "A White Heron" to the nine-year-old rural child; instead, Freeman writes from a position where such a shift has already occurred. She frames her stories carefully—Louisa Ellis's window and the Penns' barn door carefully limit the world she depicts—but within that frame, she creates a fictional territory in which characters can articulate the perspective of marginal women as central. The tight form of her fiction both fences out and fences in; she writes as if regionalism both opens up and protects that small space within which late nineteenth-century women were free to express their vision.

BOOKER T. WASHINGTON

Washington, like his contemporary W. E. B. DuBois, is searching in *Up from Slavery* for a theory of human identity that would both explain the forces on which black identities are contingent and offer programs for future action. He tries to explain the forces ranged against black people and to evolve a plan to counteract these forces. In the Washington-DuBois controversy, Washington's position of "Atlanta Compromise" presents the powerlessness of black people as *donnée* and proposes to accept "severe and constant struggle" rather than "artificial forcing" in the question of social equality. Contrast his position with that of DuBois. Consider whether the black polemical writers of the late nineteenth century, in their attempts to explain social forces, share the perception of naturalists Stephen Crane or Theodore Dreiser, who also turned to theories in order to try to explain our human position in the universe.

CHARLES W. CHESNUTT

The problem of aesthetic distance is more complex for Chesnutt, a black man, than for Joel Chandler Harris, a white. Like Harris's tales, Chesnutt's "The Goophered Grapevine" and other stories from *The Conjure Woman* might have been perceived as "local color" writing. However, Chesnutt, in particular, deliberately works in opposition to the expectations of "local color" writing as his way of realistically portraying the experiences of black people in slavery and Reconstruction. Students can see Chesnutt inventing his own form. For Chesnutt must write as if his white readers might be as obtusely condescending as the Yankee who buys the plantation in "The Goophered Grapevine." How does Chesnutt avoid the anxiety of writing in the first person as a black man? (Students may need to consider his historical situation in order to perceive that anxiety before responding to the question.) He embeds Uncle Julius's narrative within the larger story, in which the white man officially narrates "The Goophered Grapevine," thereby allowing the white narrator to reveal his own limitations. Still, the story manages to portray Uncle

Julius's reality—one dominated by the need to use folklore and the cunning of the powerless as a way to get what he wants, which, in this story, is a job that will continue to give him free access to the grapevine, despite the fact that, as Theodore R. Hovet points out in an interesting essay ("Chesnutt's 'The Goophered Grapevine' as Social Criticism," *Negro American Literature Forum*, Fall 1973), Julius is also aware of the "cycle of exploitation" that will "begin again with the appearance of the Yankee." Hovet sees the story as the continuation of slavery by the means of wage-slavery—an interpretation that he also admits may be buried "a little too deeply within the folk tale," but perhaps not too deeply for students taking a historical perspective on Chesnutt.

HAMLIN GARLAND

Garland's "Under the Lion's Paw" usefully contrasts with both Jewett's "The Foreigner" and Freeman's "The Revolt of 'Mother.'" Although Stephen Council initially helps Haskins get a good start, Garland focuses on the futility of Haskins's labor, and the concluding scene creates a tableau similar in effect to the end of "The Outcasts of Poker Flat." Haskins is "under the lion's paw," and Butler (and Garland) leave him "seated dumbly on the sunny pile of sheaves, his head sunk into his hands." The reader views Haskins—like Mother Shipton, Piney Woods, and ultimately Oakhurst, as well—from the outside. Contrast this with the perspective Jewett offers in "The Foreigner," in which she depicts the growth of sympathy between characters, and in which Mrs. Todd explores and tries to repair the social exclusion of Mrs. Tolland; Haskins ends as an object of exclusion, viewed from outside the story, whereas Jewett's characters expand their circle of community. Or contrast the poverty of the homeless characters in "Under the Lion's Paw" with the inadequately housed Sarah and Nanny Penn in Freeman's "The Revolt of 'Mother.'" Garland bases the power of his story on its portrait of the bleakness of poverty; Freeman bases hers on her protagonists' awareness of their own strengths.

CHARLOTTE PERKINS GILMAN

Like *The Awakening*, "The Yellow Wallpaper" also shows a woman trying to find some alternative context for self-expression. The speaker in the story looks in vain for any referential reflector of her own reality—until she is incarcerated by her husband in a room with yellow wallpaper, and over the course of the story comes to identify with or project herself onto the figure of a woman who stoops down and creeps about behind the pattern on the wallpaper.

Gilman presents her narrator's "double consciousness" as the tension the woman artist must live with in a context that refuses (with absolute denial of her husband) to mirror her self-concept. Like Edna's suicide at the end of *The Awakening*, Gilman's narrator's madness becomes understandable as her only means of self-expression. Ask students to contrast the story with Poe's "The Fall of the House of Usher" and James's "The Beast in the Jungle," or "The Turn of the Screw." Consider the narrator as a type of the artist, and apply to her Howells's dictum that the imagination "can work only with the stuff of experience." Does the narrator "compose" elements from real life, and, if so, are both her madness and her work of art—the story itself—realistic? What happens to a writer when she wants to write referentially about experience that the world refuses to recognize? What does the story tell us about the prevailing medical attitudes toward women in the late nineteenth century?

JANE ADDAMS

In reading the excerpts from *Twenty Years at Hull-House*, students have the opportunity to examine the dialectic between writing and social action. Although Addams challenges the usefulness of literature, she herself also wrote—about her decision to open Hull-House, and she explores the divergent paths open to educated, middle-class women at the end of the nineteenth century. Ask students to take on Addams's challenge. Read her description of her impressions of the poverty of East London in "The Snare of Preparation," and her "disgust" that in order to respond to the scene before her, she recalls an image from DeQuincey that intervenes or mediates between what she sees and how she perceives it. She wishes to act other than "through a literary suggestion," and she states that literature "only served to cloud the really vital situation spread before our eyes." Ask students to comment on this scene and Addams's reactions; if there is truth to Addams's challenge, what, then, is the purpose and use of literature? Some may argue that Addams herself uses writing to pose her challenge, and may see in other turn-of-the-century writers (Chopin, Washington, DuBois, Norris, Crane, and Dreiser) a kindred attempt to use writing to change social conditions. Is Addams rejecting all writing, or only that which does not engage social problems? Would she also challenge the importance of literary naturalism? The excerpts from *Twenty Years at Hull-House* become an implicit commentary on Addams's contemporary literary figures. Ask students in particular to examine her statements about women's education, and her sense that "the first generation of college women . . . had developed too exclusively the power of acquiring knowledge and of merely receiving impressions," and to comment on James's *Daisy Miller*, in light of Addams's critique. Addams's solu-

tion to the disengagement of women's education is to found the settlement house movement in this country, "in which young women
who had been given over too exclusively to study, might restore a
balance of activity along traditional lines and learn of life from life
itself." In doing so, she appears to define social welfare as emerging
from a crisis between culture and conduct, especially for middle-
class women. Does her version of social work become applied literary studies, despite her apparent rejection of literature and culture
as more than "preparation" or foundation education? Critics often
move outside the discipline of literary study and find in other
fields—psychology, sociology, philosophy, anthropology, history—a
perspective by which they read and interpret a particular text. Might
we view Jane Addams's choice to open a settlement house and, in
effect, to found the field of social welfare as itself a "reading" or
"interpretation" of American literature? If so, then *Twenty Years at
Hull-House* is, in part, a new form of literary criticism, and in the dialectic between literature and social action, literature provides the
basis for knowledge in social welfare, while social work itself becomes a form of literary criticism.

EDITH WHARTON

In the "Introduction" to *Ethan Frome*, Wharton describes her
characters in the novel as her "*granite outcroppings*; but half-emerged
from the soil, and scarcely more articulate." It is the "outcropping
granite" that she states has been overlooked in the New England of
fiction, and implicitly, then, *Ethan Frome* is Wharton's challenge to
the regionalists Jewett and Freeman who were her contemporaries.
Edith Wharton joins the group of late nineteenth-century writers
who concern themselves with point-of-view, she shares with James a
sense of the world's increasing complexity, and she contributes her
own version of how to "read" or see the world in light of the decline
of omniscience that characterizes the transition to modernism.

You may begin your discussion of the novel by asking students to characterize Wharton's narrator and the stance that narrator takes toward his material. In the "Introduction" she characterizes
her narrator as a sophisticated "looker-on" and contrasts him with
the "simple" people of her story, and she writes that while each
chronicler contributes "just so much as he or she is capable of understanding," only the narrator "has scope enough to see it all." How
does Wharton's attitude toward her characters contrast with that of
Jewett and Freeman? In the opening chapters of the novel, the narrator hopes to get Frome to "at least unseal his lips," establishing the
theme of silence as one of Wharton's concerns. And, in writing the
novel, the narrator claims to present "this vision of [Frome's] story."
Instead of drawing Frome out to hear his own story in his own

words, the narrator tells it for him; ask students how this contrasts with the regionalists' attempt to listen to rural characters speak in their own voices. In further contrast, discuss Wharton's use of the Starkfield landscape in the novel. What relationship to landscape do her characters have? Part of what distinguishes the regionalist writers from the "local color" writers is their attitude toward women, acceptance of women's vision, and attempt to give women their own voice. Ask students to comment on Wharton's treatment of Zeena and Mattie. The two seem like split images of woman throughout most of the novel. Zeena is the bad mother figure, "already an old woman," and she turns "queer" on Ethan, an example of what the narrator calls "pathological instances" in Starkfield; Mattie elicits Ethan's "passion of rebellion," and in her request that they die together in the sleigh ride, expresses both sexuality and submission. Zeena is the cold, repressive mother; Mattie, the warm, sexual daughter. Or are both only projections of Ethan's (and the narrator's) imagination? *Ethan Frome* focuses not on the female characters, but on Ethan himself, and just as "all the intercourse" between Ethan and Mattie is made up of "inarticulate flashes," so is the narrator's acquaintance with Ethan. Together, character and narrator paint a portrait of humbled manhood, male suffering (the narrator tells us that, in this story, Ethan himself has suffered the most), and a reprise of themes from early nineteenth-century fiction: flight from domesticity, the idea that the best American woman is a dead one (Ethan tells Mattie, "I'd a'most rather have you dead than [married]!'"), and the American hero as male. By the end of the novel, at the point in the story's chronology when the narrator meets the principals, Mattie Silver has become interchangeable with Zeena, proven herself unable to take care of herself, and, like Zeena, has lapsed into silence. However, as Ruth Varnum Hale implies to the narrator in the novel's final sentence, the last indignity for Ethan Frome is that the women at his farm aren't able to "hold their tongues" with each other. Ethan's final "punishment" at the hands of his womenfolk is that for all his suffering, he is doomed to hear their voices; he has not managed to "silence" them, even though the novel itself succeeds in doing so.

W. E. B. DUBOIS

In the anthologized selection from *The Souls of Black Folk*, DuBois summarizes the history of black leadership in the nineteenth century and proposes nothing less than full suffrage, civic equality, and education as the means to achieve progress. How does this conflict with the position Booker T. Washington articulates in his "Atlanta Compromise"? DuBois writes about the curious "double movement" within the leadership of social groups in which "real progress may be negative and actual advance be relative retrogression," and he describes Washington "as essentially the leader not of one race but of two,—a compromiser between the South, the North and the Negro." Instructors can point to these statements as an extension of DuBois's most provocative idea, one he expresses in "Our Spiritual Strivings" (Chapter I of *The Souls of Black Folk*—not anthologized, but it can be placed on reserve), in which he describes the "double consciousness" of the American Negro. As my colleague R. Baxter Miller explains this concept, DuBois sees black consciousness as existing in some midpoint between two conflicting perspectives. Black consciousness is independent both of a self-contained culture and of mainstream culture and therefore exists in a state of constant tension between "black" and "white" worlds. DuBois moves well beyond Frederick Douglass's ideal of "ultimate assimilation *through* self-assertion, and on no other terms"; DuBois asks, On whose terms do we define assimilation? Miller explains that, unlike Douglass, for whom slavery was a physical reality, DuBois can envision slavery in other than physical terms, and therefore he is really asking for pluralism in *The Souls of Black Folk*, not assimilation—and not compromise. Like the regionalists, DuBois has also shifted the center of his perception to a pan-ethnic or pan-African view of culture rather than seeing consciousness as centered in western thought.

The necessary two-ness of Washington and the "double-consciousness" that DuBois expresses are just one of several points in the anthologized selections where students can begin to see the emergence of real stress-points in the concept of a referential, universal, or reliable reality. While it would not be accurate to say that the "double consciousness" of American blacks and of American women, beginning with Elizabeth Cady Stanton's address to the Seneca Falls Women's Rights Convention and the "Declaration of Sentiments" in 1848, led directly to ways of thinking that would produce modernism, it was certainly one of the real aspects of the social environment that made and continue to make central concepts of modernism seem directly relevant to American experience. So DuBois, then, while neither a naturalist nor a modernist, still can be interpreted as a transition thinker—someone who observed social forces at work, who wrote and spoke in the tradition of Benjamin Franklin in order to move common people, and who located his vision within the increasing sense that reality might not be inherited, but rather, like myth, invented.

FRANK NORRIS

Like realists Howells and James, Norris tried to describe his "art of fiction," in essays such as the anthologized "Weekly Letter."

Discuss with students what Norris means by making his distinction between "accuracy" and "the impression of Truth." Comment on his implication that the purpose or place of fiction is to express those "feelings under stress" that he states people are generally unable to express in "real life." Then, in discussing the excerpt from *Vandover and the Brute*, test out Norris's definition of naturalism as lying "midway between the Realists and Romanticists, taking the best from each." Ask students to identify elements of realism and romanticism from the excerpted chapter. How do the terms "accuracy" and "truth" characterize the distinction between realism and romanticism in Norris? Perhaps what Vandover sees, feels, and experiences, narrated from his third-person-limited point-of-view, expresses the realism of *Vandover*, and the way Norris generalizes Vandover's perception as a depiction of human experience expresses its romanticism. Vandover becomes both an individual and a type. The prevalence of animal imagery in *Vandover* underscores Norris's naturalism, as he suggests that in moments of crisis, "it was the animal in them all that had come to the surface in an instant." Norris also portrays human beings caught in a hostile environment over which they have no control. In Vandover's struggle, the ship, which becomes the "brute," is also an emblem for the larger environment. Ask students to think about the various forces Vandover must combat and how he changes his behavior in response to these forces. Does his behavioral change signify the capacity for deeper changes in character? In surveying the four major narrative fictional genres—regionalism, realism, "local color" writing, and naturalism—ask students to consider the extent to which each genre frees or constricts the development of character. In Norris, the narrative acts upon Vandover in the same way that the environment does; Norris brings into the act of fictional creation basic assumptions about the limitations of human character, and therefore he has no interest in the growth of Vandover's perception or his attempts to speak in his own voice. For better or for worse, Norris's characters reflect his own view of human nature; how "realistic" do students find that view?

STEPHEN CRANE

For Crane, even our most intimate self-concepts are contingent on our social context, and on the forces of natural environment. The selections in the *NAAL* allow students to see the variety of forces against which the protagonist in the Crane universe must fight. "An Experiment in Misery" demonstrates the forces of poverty for its characters who have been derailed from the pursuit of economic prosperity. Crane uses many of the same devices in this story that he uses in *Red Badge of Courage*: his protagonist wanders the city as if in a dream; the characters are referred to by their prominent characteristics—"a youth," "the seedy man," "the assassin"; and the misery is personified as a malicious force—"a nation forcing its regal head into the clouds, throwing no downward glances; in the sublimity of its aspirations ignoring the wretches who may flounder at its feet." Students can see some of the differences between realism and naturalism if you ask them to compare Huck Finn with the youth in "An Experiment in Misery." Who is more "real"?

"The Open Boat" presents the forces of nature as the elements against which the characters are pitted, and "The Blue Hotel" reveals the rage and ultimate lack of control that govern human behavior; "An Episode of War," read with "An Experiment in Misery," can give students an even fuller experience of Crane's interests in *Red Badge*. "The Bride Comes to Yellow Sky" is anomalous in the collection. Where does the story get its humor? What are the "local color" elements in the story? Crane suggests that marriage itself is a force; how does the story suggest that each character is controlled by that force?

THEODORE DREISER

The selections in the *NAAL* introduce students to Dreiser; and "The Strike" chapter from *Sister Carrie* conveys Dreiser's own sense of forces ranged against the individual. Without suggesting that students can get anything like a real introduction to Dreiser without *Sister Carrie* or *An American Tragedy*, you can still ask them to compare Crane's "An Experiment in Misery" with "The Strike" chapter to deepen their awareness of what the naturalists were trying to do in their fiction. "Old Rogaum and His Theresa" is a useful story to analyze closely in the classroom. It reveals Dreiser at his most subtle, for the forces Theresa and her father must battle are revealed to them indirectly. Unlike Carrie Meeber of *Sister Carrie*, Theresa is not "ruined" during her night out but is given a glimpse of how she might be. Unlike Hurstwood, Old Rogaum does not lose "his Theresa"—but the blonde girl who shows up groaning on his doorstep gives him a similar glimpse of how the night might have turned out. And Dreiser reveals the forces within the family as well. Old Rogaum himself is both a force, for his daughter, and is taken over by forces of rage and powerlessness beyond his control. His wife is no force at all; compare her with the bride in Crane's "The Bride Comes to Yellow Sky."

GERTRUDE SIMMONS BONNIN (ZITKALA-SÄ)

Bonnin's three autobiographical essays invite comparison with other autobiographies by women writers. Students may find it interesting to read Mary Rowlandson's "Narrative" (*NAAL*, Vol. 1), in which Rowlandson describes her capture by the Indians, or Elizabeth Ashbridge's "Some Account," in which she describes her own indenturing and "enslavement" in marriage (*NAAL*, Vol. 1), against Bonnin's narrative of "capture" by the "palefaces." Suggest that Bonnin's account of her removal from the reservation and attempted assimilation into white culture provides an ironic twist on the Indian captivity narrative of the Colonial period. It's also interesting to think about Bonnin as a Native-American Daisy Miller, particularly in light of what Jane Addams says college education does to women in the first generation (see the excerpt from *Twenty Years at Hull-House*). Like Addams, Bonnin invested most of her energy in social action in order to improve the lot of Native Americans. Ask students to locate hints, in Bonnin's essays, of the same disenchantment with education that Addams writes about. Although Bonnin's work does not, strictly speaking, belong to the genre of regionalism—it is autobiography, not fiction—nevertheless, there are elements of fictional form, especially in "Impressions of an Indian Childhood." She uses images—learning the "art of beadwork" or the cropped and "shingled hair"—that characterize both her own life and the larger plight of other Native Americans as well. "Impressions of an Indian Childhood" also possesses an aesthetic distance which students might associate with fiction. At the end of the third essay, "An Indian Teacher among Indians," Bonnin herself acknowledges that "as I look back upon the recent past, I see it from a distance, as a whole." Perhaps the reason for this distance is that, at least in "Impressions of an Indian Childhood," she writes about a developing child whose path of development as an Indian becomes so pinched off that the older child and adult narrator cannot even repair the discontinuity. She also writes in English about events that took place when "I knew but one language, and that was my mother's native tongue." The act of rendering her Indian childhood into English creates its own fiction, for she writes about herself at a time in her life before speaking and writing in English was even imaginable. Like the regionalists, Bonnin depicts a female-centered universe and her own refusal to be silenced, and she triumphs on behalf of the disenfranchised "squaw" when she writes of winning the oratory contest; but unlike Jewett's world of "The Foreigner," in which Mrs. Todd can ease her separation anxiety from her mother by telling a comforting story, Bonnin's estrangement from her own mother only deepens as she proceeds with her autobiography. She loses her connection with the world of nature, becoming a "cold bare pole . . . planted in a strange earth."

HENRY ADAMS

Whether or not Henry Adams ever read or heard W. E. B. DuBois, for pedagogical purposes we can see the excerpts from *The*

Education as thematic variations on the DuBoisean theme of "double consciousness." Like DuBois, who summarizes nineteenth-century black thinking in 1903, Henry Adams writes as one born in 1838, yet wanting "to play the game of the twentieth" century. *The Education* is another book in the tradition of Franklin's *Autobiography*, but interesting because of the new directions Adams takes. "As it happened, he never got to the point of playing the game at all; he lost himself in the study of it, watching the errors of the players; but this is the only interest in the story, which otherwise has no moral and little incident. A story of education—seventy years of it—the practical value remains to the end in doubt. . . . " The development of self-reliance in the American writer and thinker leads Adams to write that "every one must bear his own universe." Unlike Franklin, Adams does not become a politician, but rather finds literary symbols that, as the introduction to Adams in the *NAAL* asserts, make *The Education*, to many readers, "the one indispensable text for students seeking to understand the period between the Civil War and the First World War." Students can see this clearly in Chapter I, where Adams writes, anticipating modernism, that the twentieth century is a world without design: "Often in old age he puzzled over the question whether, on the doctrine of chances, he was at liberty to accept himself or his world as an accident. No such accident had ever happened before in human experience. For him, alone, the old universe was thrown into the ash-heap and a new one created. . . . " And Adams traces his perception to early events (railroad and telegraph) that presented his six-year-old eyes with a "new world." Even as a boy, he developed "a double nature. Life was a double thing . . . . From earliest childhood the boy was accustomed to feel that, for him, life was double."

Chapter XXV, "The Dynamo and the Virgin," crystallizes the doubleness he feels, presaging modern life, in the symbols that express the split between technology and spirituality. Adams writes clearly, and I ask students to prepare a summary of the argument of this chapter. In class, we continue to focus on Adams's early modernist ideas—what happens to human energies, symbolized by the force and power of the Virgin and of ancient fertility goddesses, in an age and in a country that replaces human with technological power; and whether it is possible to state, "with the least possible comment, such facts as seemed sure," and to "fix for a familiar moment a necessary sequence of human movement."

1914-1945

The realists' inability to determine whether or not there exists a certain reality that can be "fixed" limited the applicability of Howellsian realism to turn-of-the-century life. But the regionalists' interest in shifting the center of perception (producing an early form of DuBoisean "double consciousness" that the "local color" fiction of the period did not possess), James's use of point of view to create the unfolding of the central consciousness in his fictional characters, and the perceptions of the naturalists and turn-of-the-century polemical writers would all influence the twentieth-century debate over the existence of reality. However I make my choices for any given course from the selections available in the 1914–1945 period, I try to convey three different aspects of modern literature over the course of studying individual writers: (1) how and why modern writers see the world differently than writers from earlier periods and centuries—what we might call a thematic approach to understanding modernism; (2) how and why they choose their images and their narrative and poetic forms—an approach that focuses on modernism as technique; (3) how their gender, ethnic, or class backgrounds influence their writing—how pluralism, both within American culture and as it derives from international influence (particularly by Joyce, Woolf, and Yeats), emerges as a determining factor and a consequence of modern literature.

BLACK ELK

In opening discussion on the anthologized excerpts from this work, begin by asking students questions that will help them explore the very interesting narrative form. To the question, Who is speaking?, they will answer, Black Elk. But who is narrating? Black Elk or John Neihardt? I underscore for them points of information from the *NAAL* headnote, namely that Black Elk could neither read nor write nor speak English when he told John Neihardt the story of his great vision. We talk about the context within which *Black Elk Speaks* was created: Black Elk telling his story to his son, Ben Black Elk, who then translated it into English for Black Elk's "adopted" son, John Neihardt, while Neihardt's daughter Enid wrote it all down and other tribal elders contributed their memories of events. Then, later, Neihardt worked from his daughter's transcriptions to produce *Black Elk Speaks.* How do the circumstances of composition affect students' perception of authorship of the work? We discuss differences between Neihardt's work and the work of early twentieth-century social scientists who often paid Indian informants to tell their stories. Neihardt was himself a poet; in agreeing to tell his story to Neihardt, holy man Black Elk was recognizing a kindred spirit.

"Heyoka Ceremony" provides the text within which to explore the concept of tribal identity for Black Elk and the extent to which his personal life story is also deeply connected to the history of his people, even though, as the *NAAL* headnote points out, by the time of Black Elk's birth, forced removals of eastern Indian tribes to the American West had already dissipated tribal identity. Although performing the dog vision (enacting the entrance of truth "with two faces" into the world, so that the ceremony becomes a kind of Indian drama) records an essential rite in the development of Black Elk's own power, Black Elk focuses his account of the ceremony on making it possible for the power to come to the people. His participation in the ceremony reflects his commitment to his own religious vision, and he performs and describes each step in the ceremony with great care and seriousness, but his own role is integrally connected with the participation of the people and the power of the ceremony "to make them happier and stronger." "Heyoka Ceremony" thus records the interrelation between Black Elk's vision, his enactment of the ceremony, and the needs of his tribal group.

"The First Cure" expresses the meaning of the Sioux Indian's relation to the universe and Black Elk's own ability to tap into the powers of the universe to become both a holy man and a healer. It also begins to record the decline of Sioux powers in face of the progressive loss of Sioux land to the "Wasichus" (the white men) in the 1870s and 1880s. For Black Elk's people are forced to live in square houses instead of teepees, which begins to cut them off from the Power of the World that works in circles. In his description of his first cure, Black Elk reveals his role as a medium—"I could feel the power coming through me"—and as an empathic reflector of the sick boy's pain—"I could feel something queer all through my body, something that made me want to cry for all unhappy things." His position as healer allows him to mediate between the clouded vision of his people, expressed in their pain, and the inner knowledge of the spirit world which is located in the "living center" of the sacred hoop, or of all other round things, including the shape of the teepee, the circle around which Black Elk passes the sacred pipe, and the human life cycle which "is a circle from childhood to childhood." The pipe itself acts as a symbolic conduit to the inner center of the powers of the universe. And in discussing the power of Sioux religious beliefs, it becomes possible to make a literary leap to the power of Black Elk's and Neihardt's collaborative text. Neihardt's attempt in *Black Elk Speaks* is to create a character who is as "round" as his vision; in so doing, Neihardt will be capable of contacting and revealing the Power of the World which works in circles.

Black Elk Speaks records only the first 27 years of Black Elk's life, ending with the battle of Wounded Knee. "The Butchering at Wounded Knee" portrays even more strikingly than the two earlier chapters how much Black Elk's identity is intimately connected with his tribe's history. Students will be extremely moved by his description of the "butchering" of Sioux women, children, and warriors, and by Black Elk's ability to feel in his own body the danger, the terror, and the pain of his own people, as well as his own powerlessness to "cure" the ultimate disease—the "dirty work" of the white soldiers. Neihardt ends *Black Elk Speaks* with an image of drifted snow in "one long grave" at Wounded Knee. Although Black Elk himself lives long (another 41 years) into the early years of reservation life for the Sioux, Neihardt ends his text with what some readers have described as Black Elk's spiritual death, as well as the end of tribal independence, for as Black Elk himself states in "The First Cure," after the end of Sioux freedom, he and his people become simply "prisoners of war while we are waiting here."

Black Elk Speaks therefore shapes the form of Black Elk's story as Neihardt works to create the full effect of Sioux tragedy "in" his white readers, just as Black Elk himself was capable of feeling "in" himself the pain of the people. The act of the bicultural collaborator creates empathy in the modern reader. Furthermore, the act of teaching *Black Elk Speaks* places the instructor, as well, in the position of bicultural translator, using the classroom and discussion of the text as a way to complete the circle between the American undergraduate student and the text that "writes" Black Elk's name in our canon of collective attempts to define the American identity.

ELLEN GLASGOW

"The Difference" uses the technique of literary realism to express how Margaret's world view changes in a moment. Living with a change in world view is a theme that many modern writers share; ask students to recall earlier moments in American literary history when world views and self-concepts changed rapidly. Explore Glasgow's use of point of view to convey "the difference"; ask students to compare the story with Gilman's use of point of view in "The Yellow Wallpaper" or James's in "The Beast in the Jungle." Glasgow frames her story with the same image in its first and last sentences. Narrative framing is a technique that modern prose writers, as well as poets, frequently use. What is its effect in the story? How does the repetition of the image underscore "the difference" in Margaret's perception? Comment on the following quotation in light of Crane's and Dreiser's insistence on forces that overpower human life: "Somewhere beneath the civilization of the ages there was the skeleton of the savage." Does "The Difference" show Glasgow to be sensitive to social injustice? Consider the following quotation: "Suffering outside of herself made no difference to her. Her throbbing wound was the only reality." Is it possible to be aware of one kind of injustice and oblivious to others? Compare "The Difference" with Chopin's *The Awakening* as examples of the way women's oppression has ironically isolated them from being able to take a larger view of social forces and therefore from being able to understand their oppression.

WILLA CATHER

Unlike most of Cather's narrators, who are male, the narrator of the novella *My Mortal Enemy* is Nellie Birdseye. The story, like "The Difference," portrays a series of changes in perception. Ask students to locate some of these: the narrator's "first glimpse of the real Myra Henshawe," and her first glimpse of the Henshawe's marriage, in which "everything was in ruins." How surprising it may seem to some readers, as it does to the narrator, that when she meets Myra again, in her "temporary eclipse" ".she looked much less changed than Oswald." What are some of the objects, images, or motifs that provide continuity for Myra, and for the narrator's view of her? How in particular does the amethyst necklace serve to frame the story? The central love relationship appears to be that between Myra and Oswald; the narrator has her own passion for Myra Henshawe. How does the story reveal it? How does Cather suggest that passion, perception, and self-revelation are interconnected emotions or faculties? The priest says of Myra, "'She's not at all modern in her make-up, is she?'" What does he mean by this? What does Cather mean?

Rosicky of "Neighbour Rosicky" represents pastoral values in a losing battle with an increasingly urbanized, mechanized world. As a young man living in New York, Rosicky "found out what was the matter with him," and decided to join the Czech community in Nebraska. In the face of his own declining health and the "cruelty" of the cities, Rosicky tries to keep his son Rudolph on the land. How does Cather condemn the materialism, rapaciousness, and cruelty that Rosicky associates with urban life? How does his gift of loving people (his "gypsy hand") offer a corrective? The story ends on a note of tragedy. How long will Rudolph be able to hold out against the forces of nature? How long before he will join the exodus from the farms to the cities?

In both of these stories Cather portrays women's lives as complex and various, rich in love, but contingent on other things—worldly position, friendship, self-esteem, family, the ability to adapt to circumstances. Compare her portraits of women (Myra, and Mary and Polly from "Neighbour Rosicky") with the women in Jewett and Freeman. What are the regionalist elements of Cather's stories—even of *My Mortal Enemy*, in which the setting moves from urban to rural, East Coast to West Coast? Like the narrator of *My Mortal Enemy*, Doctor Ed of "Neighbour Rosicky" seems to love Rosicky, but the second story creates more aesthetic distance than the first (and is actually more representative of Cather's other work). Does the change affect the dramatic power of the story?

GERTRUDE STEIN

The Good Anna

The Good Anna provides students with an excellent introduction both to Gertrude Stein and to modernism itself. While Stein experiments with prose style in this early novel, her experimentation does not make the work inaccessible to students. Ask them to describe their impressions of The Good Anna. Such an open-ended request may elicit from them the significant words for a study of Stein: repetition, stream of consciousness, slow emergence of identification with Anna, empathy, transformations, erotic encoding, self-reflexivity. These become themes to develop in an ensuing discussion of the novel, and prepare students to read the more experimental excerpt from The Making of Americans. For example, consider the numerous "repetitions" of "large and careless" women in Anna's life and of the even more numerous animals and people Anna comes to take care of. Ask students how we come to know Anna in the narrative; focus on the present-time aspect of Stein's characterization. What does character development mean with respect to Anna? How do we know how she thinks and feels? Examine the differences between persons and actions that seem to be repeated experiences for Anna. To what extent do the others, especially women, in Anna's life reflect back to her some of her own personality traits, including some she finds hard to accept in herself? Suggest that Anna herself exists as a continuum on which we may locate the other women in her life, and consider the interplay of Anna's projections and introjections of aspects of these women.

Miss Mathilda and Mrs. Lehntman may particularly intrigue students. Examine Stein's portrait of Miss Mathilda as her own self-portrait (she, too, was "large and careless," collected art, and had a "careless way of wearing always her old clothes") and raise questions about the self-reflexivity of the text. In writing about Anna, Stein is also writing about aspects of herself; she is also writing about the way to write a story. Locating images of Stein in the various characters in The Good Anna alerts students to looking at the relationship between the modernist writer and her text. Of particular interest here is the passage at the end of Part I, in which Stein writes about the "troubles" Miss Mathilda has with Anna. Miss Mathilda wants both to have her mind read and have everything done for her, and to rebel against the rules she accepts when she allows herself to be dependent on Anna. The conflict between spontaneity and reliability characterizes the relationship between the two characters in the fiction, between Stein and her own text, and between the reader and what modernist art will, and will not, satisfy. There is no perfect attunement in any of these dyadic conflicts; character, writer, and reader all suffer jarring discontinuities, just as Anna herself does when she tells Miss Mathilda, "I don't see how people can go on and do things so" when she has lived her life with the "old world sense of what was the right way for a girl to do."

Mrs. Lehntman's presence in the novel, and Stein's reiteration that this woman has served as Anna's "romance," may lead some students to pursue Baym's headnote comment that the eroticism in Stein's lesbian love poems (not anthologized) remains "obscure" and "needs to be decoded." Despite the novel's title and the narrator's presentation of Anna as "good," Part I opens with Anna's equation of "bad" with sexuality. What other evidence exists to suggest that Anna has an erotic life, or at least is capable of an erotic awareness? In studying the pre-Freudian writers of the previous century, twentieth-century readers may speculate on erotic and homoerotic undertones in American literature, but Gertrude Stein is the first American writer both to live outwardly as a lesbian and to write fiction with lesbian erotic content. Do students find homoerotic passion in Anna's feelings for Mrs. Lehntman, or do they prefer to characterize the relationship as friendship? Whether or not Stein is asking her readers to "decode" this relationship, she at least has the courage to write about strong feelings between women, unlike Cather, who appears to have encoded her own erotic life with women into relationships between male and female characters in her fiction, or onto her own passion for the Nebraska or Southwest landscape. To what extent did Stein's choice to live as a permanent expatriate in Paris and as an experimentalist in art, as well as in life, make it possible for her to write about love—of whatever kind—between women?

The Making of Americans

The excerpt from *The Making of Americans* becomes readily accessible to students after reading and discussing *The Good Anna*. The anthologized "[Introduction]" serves as a description of Stein's technique in the novel, a way of using Stein's own language to talk about what she attempts in *The Good Anna*. At the same time, reading the novel gives students a feeling for Stein's "love of repetition," so that they may carry with them into the more experimental work the sense of already having experienced the truth of Stein's statements in the excerpt that "Always from the beginning there was to me all living as repeating," and "Sometime every one becomes a whole one to me." The footnotes in *NAAL* help students gloss Stein's self-reflexivity. Ask them to do some work with her use of language. In the *NAAL* headnote on Marianne Moore, Baym notes that Stein worked with the word as the unit of composition. Ask students to trace the linguistic transformations of similar sentences in *The Making of Americans*, to note single word changes, and to comment on alterations in meaning. Look also for the development of ideas.

Does Stein's insistence on continuing to begin prevent her from developing a concept? Watch in particular for the ways Stein very slowly begins to expand the vocabulary she uses. One word which startles me when I read it is "earth," which makes a sudden appearance as an adjective for "feeling," then quickly modulates into "earthy," and then becomes available for use in the essay's lexicon. What words startle your students? Can they describe their reader response to Stein's use of repetition?

ROBERT FROST

Like Glasgow and Cather, Frost retains elements of realism, and, like them, he portrays moments in which his speaker's perception changes as central to his poetry. In my classroom, I spend several class periods on individual poems and read representative poems by other twentieth-century poets through the fulcrum of our analysis of Frost. I prepare for a discussion of "The Oven Bird" by reading "Nothing Gold Can Stay," with its allusion to Eden and human mortality. I give "The Oven Bird" an important place in our discussion because Frost's other poems, his essay "The Figure a Poem Makes," many other works of literature by modern writers, and even the concept of modernism itself seem contained and articulated in the poem's last two lines: "The question that he asks in all but words / Is what to make of a diminished thing." The bird and the poet ask questions that express the central modernist theme: how do we confront a world in which reality is subject to agreement, or lacks referentiality altogether? how do we express the experience of fragmentation in personal and political life? how do we live with the increasing awareness of our own mortality—whether we face the prospect of human death, as the speaker does in "Home Burial," "After Apple-Picking," or "'Out, Out—'"; the death or absence of God, as Frost considers that possibility in "Desert Places" and "Design"; or mere disappointment at our own powerlessness, as in "An Old Man's Winter Night" or "Stopping by Woods on a Snowy Evening"? In "The Oven Bird" I ask students to hear contrasting ways of intoning the last two lines. I read the lines, first, with emphasis on the phrase "diminished thing"—and the pessimism in Frost and in his conception of modern life receives most of our attention. I read it again, emphasizing the infinitive "to make," and the poem seems to reverse its own despair, to create the possibility that creative activity can ease the face of the lessening, the "diminishing," of modern perception.

Other works offer this positive response to the bird's question. In "The Figure a Poem Makes," Frost defines the act of writing poetry as "not necessarily a great clarification," but at least "a momentary stay against confusion." Students who have studied the Volume 1 material may see Frost's solution to his own metaphysical problem as one more variable in Edward Taylor's attempt to sustain a metaphor through the length of one of his *Preparatory Meditations* in order to arrive at the language of salvation. Frost emphasizes, though, that he wants to be just as surprised by the poem as the reader. And his description of the thought process that a poem records applies to our own endeavors in the classroom as well—whenever we try to engage students first, and then teach them how to order their engaged perception. When Frost contrasts scholars, who get their knowledge "with conscientious thoroughness along projected lines of logic," with poets, who get theirs "cavalierly and as it happens in and out of books," most students prefer to identify with the poets. And Frost might, indeed, be describing an American epistemology, as it works best with students: "They stick to nothing deliberately, but let what will stick to them like burrs where they walk in the fields."

No study of Frost, at any class level, is complete without close analysis of the great poems "Birches" and "Directive." Depending on our time and the students I have in the course, I choose one or the other for a full class period. "Birches" works better with sophomores; even so, students at any level profit from line-by-line discussion of "Directive," particularly in contrast with the earlier poem, "After Apple-Picking." In this poem, the speaker's troubled sleep results from his realization of the imperfection of human power to "save" fallen apples (or fallen worlds) or to fully complete any task as someone with godlike power (or any "heroic" human being before the modernist era) might have been able to do. "Directive" transcends those limitations, offers a specific path to take ("if you'll let a guide direct you / Who only has at heart your getting lost"), and arrives at a vision of spiritual regeneration unparalleled in any of Frost's other poems: "Here are your waters and your watering place. / Drink and be whole again beyond confusion." How does Frost contain *both* American dream and American nightmare? How does his poetry, as he writes in "Two Tramps in Mud Time," allow him to "unite / My avocation and my vocation / As my two eyes make one in sight"? How do Frost's images suggest that, long after the apparent decline of transcendentalism, the analogical thinking of Emerson and Thoreau would become a permanent part of the American imagination?

SHERWOOD ANDERSON

Looking at the egg on the table—as Anderson's narrator does at the end of "The Egg"—characterizes Anderson's own contribution to developing American fiction in the early twentieth century. He wants to know where it all begins, to focus on a particular house in a particular street, and to try to figure out, by examining origins, who he is and who we are. Anderson's life before he declared himself a writer illustrates a classic theme in nineteenth-century fiction by white male writers; ask your students to recall Irving's "Rip Van Winkle," Hawthorne's "Wakefield," or Clemens's *Huckleberry Finn*. Like the characters in that earlier fiction, Anderson also seems to have suffered a form of amnesia, sudden disappearance, or inexplicable departure, one day, from his life with his wife and his job at the paint firm. In leaving his life in Ohio so abruptly, Anderson expressed the incompatibility of living conventionally and also writing an American book. How does this define the role of the writer, for Anderson? *Winesburg, Ohio*, though fiction, emerges from an autobiographical impulse, and the reporter in that work, George Willard, experiences the young writer's conflict. Later in life, Anderson would write a memoir titled *A Storyteller's Story*; *Winesburg, Ohio*, itself, tells the story of Anderson himself still within the eggshell, before his "hatching" as a storyteller.

Several related themes characterize the anthologized stories from *Winesburg*. Anderson portrays conflict between inner emotions and outward behavior; Alice Hindman and Elmer Cowley share this conflict although they express it differently. Sexual repression and displaced aggression enter American fiction in *Winesburg*, and each of the anthologized stories shares this theme. In Elizabeth Willard, sexual repression and repressed identity become interconnected; and in "Adventure," Anderson hints at "the growing modern idea of a woman's owning herself and giving and taking for her own ends in life," although his own fiction explores the stunting of women's lives, not their "modern" alternatives. Writing itself becomes the American passion for George Willard; the "queerness" that interests Anderson in some of his characters (Elmer Cowley and Mook in "Queer") suggests an American illness caused by inarticulate inner lives that the fiction writer might be able to "cure." At the end of "Rip Van Winkle," Rip takes his place as the "chronicler" or storyteller of the village, and, thus, moves from margin to center in his position in the town. Anderson's portrait of the American storyteller—in his character George Willard and in the events of his own life—addresses the marginality of the white male writer. Anderson's marginality is central to his vision; despite his portrait of the way American life has twisted and thwarted individual development, he chooses to portray it from without, not envision recreating it from within. Like Huckleberry Finn, George Willard escapes Winesburg, and, in the process, becomes capable of telling a story.

WALLACE STEVENS

Poems such as Frost's "The Oven Bird" and "Desert Places"

allow students to experience modernist feeling; Stevens translates the central thematic concern of modern writers into an intellectual framework. We begin by reading "Of Modern Poetry" line by line and make connections between the idea of "finding what will suffice" and making something "of a diminished thing." This poem links modernist thought to World War I, breaks with the realists' "script," and ends with actions that appear referential ("a man skating, a woman dancing, a woman / Combing") but can be understood only as manifestations of what is spoken "In the delicatest ear of the mind," not as semantic symbols. Students' greatest difficulty in reading Stevens is to move beyond the apparently referential quality of his language and to learn to read it as dynamic forms of abstract ideas. "Anecdote of the Jar" works well to analyze closely. This poem forces them to push beyond the referential features of the language, for its meaning resides not in the jar, but in its placement, and in the larger design the poem creates and imposes. But that larger design is an arbitrary creation of the poet, not the manifestation of divine presence in the universe, and we work through other Stevens poems that illustrate the poet's power to make his world's design. "Thirteen Ways of Looking at a Blackbird" can help students see the problem of perception in a modern world in which there is no shared reality; in "The Idea of Order at Key West," the woman makes order out of the diminished thing by singing, thereby becoming "the self / That was her song, for she was the maker"; and "The Emperor of Ice-Cream" proposes as the modernist's reality a world that lets "the lamp affix its beam" to show, as "The Snow Man" states, "Nothing that is not there and the nothing that is." Ask students how the idea that nothing is there—except what the imagination invents—becomes a manifestation of American self-reliance. For Stevens, all forms of order are created by human perception; nature itself reflects human values only as we project our image onto the natural world.

Stevens responds to the oven bird's question directly in the first line of "A High-toned Old Christian Woman": "Poetry is the supreme fiction." In discussing this concept, I put together some of the ideas from the Stevens headnote in *NAAL*. The editor, Nina Baym, directs the reader's attention to two repeated activities in Stevens's poems: (1) looking at things, and (2) playing musical instruments or singing. I ask students to identify poems in which these activities appear (for the first, see in particular "The Snow Man," "The Emperor of Ice-Cream," "Thirteen Ways of Looking at a Blackbird," "Study of Two Pears," excerpts from "An Ordinary Evening in New Haven," and "The Plain Sense of Things"; for the second, see in particular "A High-toned Old Christian Woman," "Peter Quince at the Clavier," "The Idea of Order at Key West," "Of Modern Poetry," and "Asides on the Oboe"), and we identify as parallel concepts making music or singing and writing poetry, and perceiving or observing and giving existence to reality. These parallel activities replace the Christian god, create new gods or mythological forms (see "An Ordinary Evening in New Haven"), and allow us to devise our own "supreme fiction." The new mythology or fiction, for whom the poet is both creator and secular priest, explains the presence of so much continually unexpected imagery in Stevens. Further, Stevens's own poetry provides an answer to the woman's musings in "Sunday Morning."

In "Sunday Morning," Stevens creates a dialogue between a woman and a narrator, or a dialogue of one that shows the woman thinking within her own mind, and he alters the meaning of Christianity. The poem transforms the religious connotations of Sunday into those of a human-centered "day of the sun," in which, since we live in an "island solitude, unsponsored, free," we invent, as our "supreme fiction," our god or our explanation for the way the universe works, the very mortality that is the only "imperishable bliss" we know. Stevens proposes making ritual of the diminished thing, creating fellowship "of men that perish and of summer morn," and seeing "casual flocks of pigeons" not as "homeward bound" but rather as nature's "ambiguous undulations." Nature has no message for us; but in the act of writing (and reading) poetry, we can create our own order, one that becomes more beautiful because it is the projection of "man's rage for order," and therefore as fragile as human life. "Death is the mother of beauty" for Stevens because it intensifies the act of "arranging, deepening, enchanting night" (in "The Idea of Order at Key West"), or of taking momentary "dominion" (in "Anecdote of the Jar"), or in the "old chaos of the sun." Poetry serves Stevens (from his book of collected lectures *The Necessary Angel*) as a "means of redemption." What should we make of a world in which there is not external order? Project onto it human mortality and make art out of the moment of sinking "Downward to darkness, on extended wings"; create a "jovial hullabaloo among the spheres."

The images of the sun that form the focus for the woman's meditations in "Sunday Morning" also provide Stevens's central image in other poems. Build class discussion around a group of these poems ("Gubbinal," "A Postcard from the Volcano," "The Sense of the Sleight-of-hand Man," "An Ordinary Evening in New Haven"), and examine the way Stevens builds his real image of what the "supreme fiction" might look like on the sun itself. In "Sleight-of-hand Man," he writes, "The fire eye in the clouds survives the gods," and in "New Haven," calls "imagining of reality / Much like a new resemblance of the sun." The "supreme fiction" takes the form of human flesh in "Peter Quince at the Clavier." Give students time to work through the experience of Stevens's concept of the "supreme fiction." For many, reading Stevens will seem like heresy, a fundamental challenge to their own religious practice. Allow them to compare notes on their various perceptions of Stevens's work. Use class discussion as an exemplum of modernist thought; a class of any size may approach "Thirteen Ways of Looking at Stevens," or "a visibility of thought, / In which hundreds of eyes, in one mind, see at once."

WILLIAM CARLOS WILLIAMS

How does Williams answer the question, what to make of a diminished thing? We begin with "A Sort of a Song," which directs its reader to write a poem about the thing. Make nothing of it but the thing itself. Since there may not be meaning, don't insist on it. And we talk about characteristics of Williams's poems, trying to elicit, in discussion, some of the central features of imagism: exactness, precision, compression, common speech, free verse. "The Red Wheelbarrow," "The Widow's Lament in Springtime," "The Term," and "Portrait of a Lady" work well for this discussion. We analyze "Spring and All" closely, suggesting that the process Williams describes becomes, in part, analogous to the creation of a poetic image. Some students have difficulty understanding the concept of the image, and, in teaching Williams, I often take time out to talk about the eidetic faculty—what happens in the mind when we read a visual description. "Portrait of a Lady," read aloud with appropriate emphasis ("Agh!"), can help them "hear" another kind of image. We talk about some themes in Williams—love and death—and how the poems strip those themes of sentimentality. What happens to Williams's view of human life in poems such as "Death," "The Dead Baby," and "Landscape with the Fall of Icarus"? Compare Williams and Frost; students may suggest that, despite his objectivity, Williams lacks the pessimism of some of Frost's poems. How does Williams's use of poetic technique develop his themes? Critics often compare Williams with Whitman. Ask students to discuss this connection. Several modern poets try to write longer poems, perhaps with the epic form in mind. The excerpt from *Paterson* shows Williams at his most experimental. What aspects of the poem mark it as self-consciously "American"? Does the poem have form? Is the poem an example of "free verse"?

EZRA POUND

We read a few Pound poems to see how he uses the image: "In a Station of the Metro" and "The River-Merchant's Wife: A Letter" work well, although students sometimes have difficulty actually seeing Pound's image in the first poem. Does the poem's second line only work if one sees a contrast between the faces and the black bough? Does Pound assume light-skinned faces? "To Whistler, American," "A Pact," and "The Rest" are easily accessible to students; but what response do they have to "Hugh Selwyn Mauberley: Life and Contacts" or *The Cantos*? How do students without a classical education understand Pound's dictum, "make it new"?

H. D.

Given the possibility of such a modernist myth, trace H. D.'s attempts to construct it in "The Walls Do Not Fall." She defines poets as "discoverers of the not-known, / the unrecorded"; how does she use images from the historical world as her means of discovery? Nina Baym's headnote suggests that "the personal and the historical had always been one" to H. D. How does the speaker in "The Walls Do Not Fall" record her own personal voice?

ROBINSON JEFFERS

Jeffers's poetry contrasts sharply with that of both Frost and Stevens; ask students to discuss his ways of transforming poems about nature into philosophical meditations. Jeffers appears to have disdained modernism; is his poetry traditional? Comment on the end of "Boats in a Fog," where Jeffers writes that "all the arts lose virtue / Against the essential reality / Of creatures going about their business among the equally / Earnest elements of nature." How does Jeffers's view of "reality" differ from that of many of his contemporaries? Compare Jeffers's use of free verse with Williams's poetic line. How is Jeffers's poetry unique? Discuss his use of the physical landscape of the central California coast. Is Jeffers a regional poet? Identify the source of his cynicism and compare it with Frost's pessimistic poems. Jeffers seems to suggest that "what to make of a diminished thing" is to diminish it still further: "We must unhumanize our views a little." Consider what he means by this. In my own classroom I discuss "Shine, Perishing Republic" line by line—or alternatively assign it to students to explicate in an essay. The poem stands out in contrast to many of the modernist works we read, both in what it lacks (any sense that classical mythology holds the key to understanding our present) and for what it offers (as a view of twentieth-century American life and values). This poem and others ("November Surf," "Carmel Point") seem to some students to comment on our own contemporary life. How does "Shine, Perishing Republic" suggest what it means to be an American in the twentieth century?

MARIANNE MOORE

Baym comments in her headnote that, in Moore, "the reader almost never finds the conventional poetic allusions which invoke a great tradition and assert the present poet's place in it." If there are no allusions, in what other ways does Moore's poetry address poetic tradition? Like many of her contemporaries, she tried to reinvent poetry for herself, or to find a new form for what she thought poetry should be. Locate and discuss some of Moore's statements on the act and art of poetry. Analyze, in such a discussion, "The Past Is the Present" and "To a Snail." What happens to poetic language when "expediency determines the form," and where there is an "absence of feet"? Analyze closely, as well, the frequently anthologized "Poetry." Often students have difficulty understanding why a poet such as Moore would write with such passion about the nature of poetry itself. Build on previous discussions of the image to help them find the contrast, in the poem's middle stanzas, between the discursive statements Moore makes ("we / do not admire what / we cannot understand" and "all these phenomena are important") and her use of images drawn from precise observation of the animal world. What does she mean in trying to create "imaginary gardens with real toads in them"? Analyze "The Fish" and "Bird-Witted" to see what Moore does with form in poetry. Comment on the kind of stanza she creates in "The Fish" and ask students to locate rhyme in "Bird-Witted." Most will not have discovered rhyme (as students, in reading Frost, do not immediately perceive rhyme in "After Apple-Picking"). What is the effect of the use of rhyme? Compare "Bird-Witted" with Frost's poem. Is "Bird-Witted" a poem about birds or about poetry? What is Moore's "uneasy new problem"? Does one possibility cancel out the other for her? Which poems illustrate Moore's response to the modern way of seeing the world? Compare "In Distrust of Merits" with Jeffers's earlier "Shine, Perishing Republic." Which poem seems to be more referential? Discuss Moore's views of war as an "inward" struggle in "In Distrust of Merits." How does her image of the world as an "orphans' home" comment on the modernist themes of her contemporaries?

T. S. ELIOT

"The Love Song of J. Alfred Prufrock" works well to read closely with students. Find images in the poem that serve as Eliot's "objective correlative" for Prufrock's particular emotions, and for the state of feeling in the modern world (as Eliot saw it). In my own classroom, we read "The Waste Land," but I recommend that students take an upper-division course in modern poetry if they want to study it in detail. The poem raises a problem students have with modernism generally—that so many twentieth-century poets make extensive use of classical allusions or interweave references to Renaissance painters, or quote writers in languages other than English. Berating students for not having a classical education doesn't help them much. Discuss the poem in context with "Tradition and the Individual Talent," where Eliot defends his own method and describes the good poet as the one who is able to "develop or procure the consciousness of the past." Although Eliot presents a "waste land" as his variation on the "diminished thing" that symbolizes human personality and culture in the modern world, his answer to the oven bird's question is not to make something (entirely) new or to show Stevens's snow man confronting "the nothing that is not there" and inventing a "supreme fiction," but rather to surrender the individual personality of the poet. The poem becomes a medium that expresses the essential history of the culture. Eliot writes in his essay, "Impressions and experiences which are important for the man may take no place in the poetry, and those which become important in the poetry may play quite a negligible part in the man, the personality." How does Eliot depersonalize the poet in "The Waste Land"? He combines traditions from mythology and legend, anthropology (with references to vegetation myths and fertility rites), classical literature and culture (including Shakespeare and Wagner), the Tarot, and comparative religious cultures, and he juxtaposes these traditions with images of isolation, fragmentation, uncertainty, and waste, hoping to use "these fragments" to "shore against" the ruins that are Eliot's variation on Frost's "diminished thing."

EUGENE O'NEILL

Long Day's Journey into Night demonstrates that one of the strong features of twentieth-century American literature is the continuation of what O'Neill's Edmund calls late in the play "faithful realism." But O'Neill's realism differs from that of the late nineteenth-century writers, even as it seems to extend some of their concerns. In fact, O'Neill's play sometimes seems a compendium or a spectrum of American ideas that long precede the late nineteenth century, for he presents the Tyrones both as deeply conditioned by their past and as characters who face in their daily life (in this classically one-day's play) the fragmentation that is one symptom or consequence of modernist sensibility. In discussing the play, I focus on Mary and Edmund as central figures, and we talk about the different historical influences on each of their characters.

Mary's descent into the madness of morphine addiction becomes the play's emblem, and although O'Neill is writing, in part, about his own mother here, he is also sensitive to Mary's position as woman in the American family and in American history. As the play unfolds the history of Mary's medical treatment and of her husband's attitudes toward her condition, students will make connections between Mary Tyrone and both Edna Pontellier and the narrator of "The Yellow Wallpaper." O'Neill suggests that modern life is more difficult for women than for men: Mary might have played the piano, but married instead, thereby depriving herself of the coherence of vocation; in marriage, and especially in marriage to the peripatetic James Tyrone (rootlessness itself becomes a modern condition), she cuts herself off from having woman friends with whom she might ease her loneliness (O'Neill adds early scandal to the fact of marriage as a way of doubly cutting Mary off from other women); and in choosing to ease her loneliness by following Tyrone on his tours, she is forced to reject even the traditional solace of making a home for her children, so that the series of choices becomes irreversible, and her need for something to ease her emotional pain and to dull her perception of her own meaninglessness increases.

Within the family structure, Mary also suffers the anachronism (in the twentieth century) of not being able to move beyond the scrutiny of external forces that seem to control her. When she tells her husband, "You really must not watch me all the time, James. I mean, it makes me self-conscious," she is experiencing the radical emotion that led the deist founding fathers to revolution in the 1770s. But, unlike the deists, who experienced a fundamental shift in world view when they accepted the idea that God might not be watching them all the time and fought for self-determination from the system of divinely ordained British monarchy, Mary Tyrone is only made "self-conscious" by Tyrone's scrutiny. She suffers self-consciousness and is not inspired by it. She is not self-conscious in a way that leads other modernists to insight; she is only increasingly made aware of her own worthlessness. O'Neill underscores that worthlessness by presenting the role of wife as one based on constant humiliation and defined by Tyrone's need to feel he has made "good bargains" in life—he makes others pay the price he won't pay.

Throughout the play, O'Neill presents Mary as someone living in a dream (especially as she becomes more and more detached by the effects of taking morphine) that might have made sense for Rip Van Winkle, but, protracted into the twentieth century, simply increases her sense of disorientation and alienation. She says at one point, early in the play, "None of us can help the things life has done to us. They're done before you realize it, and once they're done they make you do other things until at last everything comes between you and what you'd like to be, and you've lost your true self forever." For students who have studied Irving, the language Mary uses here will seem reminiscent of Rip's "identity crisis" when he returns to the village after his twenty-year sleep. Later in the play, thinking aloud to the hired woman Cathleen, Mary ties that disorientation to the death of what students might see as her own American dream. She says, about the fog, "It hides you from the world and the world from you. You feel that everything has changed, and nothing is what it seemed to be. No one can find or touch you anymore." Her language clearly echoes Irving's here, but it also conveys the isolation of American self-reliance carried to its historical extreme and ironically epitomized in the role of twentieth-century American wife and mother—Mary must be self-reliant in order to survive and must do so in a world devoid of human context other than her own family. She asks the play's central question: "What is it I'm looking for? I know it's something I lost."

Her son Edmund, the autobiographical voice for O'Neill himself, is the only character who understands his mother's drug addiction as the play progresses, and who suffers the consequences of trying to articulate the kind of pain she feels. In Edmund's statements, students who have read twentieth-century European literature will hear connections to Camus and Beckett. Edmund also feels the absence of home, and referring to his nebulous, nameless lack of power to control his life, he says, "They never come back! Everything is in the bag! It's all a frame-up! We're all fall guys and suckers and we can't beat the game!" Later he calls himself "a stranger who never lives at home." Like Mary, he would like to "be alone with myself in another world where truth is untrue and life can hide from itself," but he chooses poetry rather than morphine to ease his own pain, and then must confront his own failure as a poet. In a scene with his father, Edmund says, "I just stammered. That's the best I'll ever do. I mean, if I live. Well, it will be faithful realism, at least. Stammering is the native eloquence of us fog people!" In depicting Edmund's "stammering," O'Neill underscores both the need to express modern consciousness and the difficulty in finding the words for it. Other twentieth-century writers will take some comfort in making the attempt; Edmund's "faithful realism" prevents him from idealizing his "stammering." In brother Jamie's cynicism ("The truth is there is no cure . . . ") and father James's despair ("A waste!, a drunken hulk, done with and finished!"), O'Neill completes his portrait of the disintegration of the American psyche and American family life and, yet, presents that portrait within the conventions of literary realism.

KATHERINE ANNE PORTER

Miranda, like Mary Tyrone in *Long Day's Journey into Night*, learns in *Old Mortality* to characterize her problem as homelessness. The story is about life not fulfilling its dreamy promise for women like Miranda's Aunt Amy, and about Miranda's own series of disappointments. The ending of the story echoes the language of "Rip Van Winkle" and Mary Tyrone, when Miranda asks, "It is I who have no place. . . . Where are my own people and my own time?," and in posing her final question, she expresses her own version of the oven bird's: "Oh, what is life . . . and what shall I do with it? It is something of my own. . . . What shall I make of it?"

ZORA NEALE HURSTON

Hurston worked as an anthropologist as well as a writer, and wrote "The Eatonville Anthology" after graduating from Barnard College and returning to her birthplace in Eatonville, Florida, in order to collect and transcribe the folktales and folkways she remembered from childhood. Like her later *Mules and Men* (1935), both the "Anthology" and the essay "How It Feels to Be Colored Me" explore origins of consciousness—both collective and individual—that Hurston transforms into mythology, her attempt to explain the creation of the universe, to understand why the world is the way it is. By writing down the folktales she remembered from the black community in which she grew up, she created a bridge between the "primitive" authority of folk life and the literary power of written texts. (See my "Introduction" to Marjorie Pryse and Hortense Spillers, ed., *Conjuring: Black Women, Fiction, and Literary Tradition*, 1985, for a fuller discussion of Hurston and literary authority.) Mythology does not overpower Hurston's fiction; rather, it empowers her use of folk history. Ask students to locate suggestions of mythology in "The Eatonville Anthology"; see, in particular, the opening of section XIV, "Once 'way back yonder before the stars fell all the animals used to talk just like people." Compare and contrast Hurston's depiction of life against a backdrop of talking animals with the earlier Joel Chandler Harris tales (*NAAL*, Vol. 2). Hurston writes out from folklore as a source of literary power.

Their Eyes Were Watching God, Chapters 2-3

This excerpt illustrates Hurston's reliance on folklore as a source of literary authority and creates a black woman, Janie, as a powerful speaking voice. Ask students to describe the narrative context in Chapter 2. Who is telling the story, and to whom? Although Pheoby does not emerge as a clear character in this excerpt, she does become the "hungry" listener who helps Janie tell her story. By implication, the presence of a sympathetic ear makes it possible for Janie to discover her own literary authority; and Hurston also suggests, in using the word "hungry," that Janie's story serves an essential need of Pheoby's. The relationship between narrator and listener—which replicates the relationship between Hurston and her own reader—is one of intimate friendship, self-disclosure, and mutual need. Women turn to each other's stories for understanding and consolation.

Chapter 2 also depicts the generational roots of women's fiction. Before Janie can begin her own story, she must first tell her mother's and grandmother's stories. Discuss the statement, "She thought awhile and decided that her conscious life had commenced at Nanny's gate." Hurston is one of the first American writers to write fiction out of the need to portray the origins of black women's consciousness. Here I note again connections between mythology and fiction for Hurston. We discuss the many elements that create Janie's "conscious life," her attempt to locate herself in a universe that has "a personal answer for all other creations." Hurston weaves together in Chapter 2 the source of Janie's burgeoning sexuality; her connection with the natural world as a way of knowing; her recognition of Nanny as a "foundation of ancient power"; the history of black women's oppression during slavery by white men and women; the burden of sexual as well as racial oppression for Janie's mother; the impulse (in Nanny) to accommodate to a world in which " 'de nigger woman is de mule'" by finding "protection" in a responsible man; the imperative (in Janie) to strike out on one's own in a world in which "the familiar people and things" have failed.

We discuss the novel as Hurston's "sermon"—Nanny had envisioned herself as a preacher—and the act of writing fiction as akin to making a sacred text. After Leafy runs away, Nanny thinks to herself about Janie, "'Ah said Ah'd save de text for you.'" Janie finds herself in telling Pheoby the story of her life; "saving the text" is precisely what Janie learns to do for her friend, and what Hurston does for the black and white women writers who would come after her. Hurston focuses on a black woman's need to write stories that mirror her own image—unlike the first photograph Janie sees in which she cannot find herself—and in this way she expresses a black woman's modernist concern. What happens to a black woman—or to a woman of any color—when the "familiar people and things" fail? Hurston offers one answer to the question in the rest of her novel; and she suggests Janie as a prototype for the modern female child. As long as Janie has not discovered for herself that what her grandmother wants her to believe is a lie—that in marrying Logan Killicks she will come to love him—she is willing to go along with another's script or formula for her life. But when she walks out to the gate a second time, in Chapter 3, she has a more realistic view of the road. Hurston suggests that it is only by rejecting the conventional scripts that Janie "became a woman." And for Hurston, "woman" is synonymous with "independent person." In *Their Eyes Were Watching God*, Hurston creates a modernist myth of origins; the process of becoming a woman, for Janie, involves making her own dream, her own story.

DOROTHY PARKER

Discuss Parker's place in the tradition of American humorist writing. Analyze how Parker achieves her linguistic effects, both in her short poems and in "The Waltz." Does her humor rely on mockery, exclusion, or the "put down"? Is she writing to entertain? Comment on Baym's suggestion that her poems' "wit and elegance costume moods of emptiness and despair." Compare Parker's "The Waltz" with Charlotte Perkins Gilman's "The Yellow Wallpaper." What strategies does each narrator choose to deal with her situation?

E. E. CUMMINGS

Consider what it would mean to ask whether Cummings is a "serious" poet. Describe the ways in which he experiments with language in poems such as "anyone lived in a pretty how town" or "my father moved through dooms of love," and consider their effects. Ask students to read "Buffalo Bill's" or "'next to of course god america i'" out loud, and discuss what happens to poetry that is meant to be read, not spoken. Locate modern themes in Cummings; place him in context with Frost (compare "nobody loses all the time" with Frost's "Departmental"), Jeffers ("i sing of Olaf glad and big" or "pity this busy monster, manunkind" with "Shine, Perishing Republic"), or Moore ("Poem, or Beauty Hurts Mr. Vinal" with "Poetry").

JEAN TOOMER

Discuss "Georgia Dusk" as a variation on Emerson's call for an American poet a century earlier. What, for Toomer, will be the characteristics of that "genius of the South"? And what will be the literary tradition for that "singer"? Locate Toomer in the context of other black writers or writers about black experience in the *NAAL*—Joel Chandler Harris and Charles W. Chesnutt. What does it mean, in Toomer, to make "folk-songs from soul sounds"? Analyze "Fern," first from the narrator's point of view, and then focusing on Fern herself. What is happening within the speaker as he imaginatively recreates Fern? What is the literary analogue in Toomer for DuBois's "double consciousness"? How does Toomer evoke "the souls of black folk" in this excerpt from Cane? Place Fern herself in the context of other works by American male writers, such as Poe's "Ligeia" or Anderson's "Mother." Toomer gives Fern a moment of speech when she asks, "Doesn't it make you mad?," and then his narrator interprets what she means. Does he give her voice? Consider the last sentence in "Fern": "Her name, against the chance that you might happen down that way, is Fernie May Rosen." What, in this sentence, gives the reader more clues to Fern's identity than Toomer's earlier idealization of her? Is there any "real" Fern beneath Toomer's portrait of her as his narrator's muse? Note Toomer's reference to the black woman who "once saw the mother of Christ and drew her in charcoal on the courthouse wall." The allusion is one piece of evidence to suggest that black women, as well as men, have tried to record their visions; they have been artists as well as inspirations for art.

F. SCOTT FITZGERALD

Disappointment abounds in modernist fiction, and Fitzgerald's narrator characterizes Dexter Green's story in "Winter Dreams" as a story of life's "mysterious denials and prohibitions." What does life "deny" Dexter? Some students may say that it denies him Judy Jones and the "satiety" Dexter believed she aroused in him. Others may pity this protagonist; despite the welcomed "liberation from webs of tangled emotion" that he feels when he goes off to the war, he ends by regretting his inability to cry or care. Has he therefore lost his ability to feel? Explore student interpretations of Fitzgerald's title, "Winter Dreams." Does he lose Judy Jones herself or the ability to project onto her his own dreams? Consider the various portraits or interpretations of Judy Jones in the story. How do we know her? Which Judy is real, the woman who is Dexter's ideal or the woman who seems to have "faded" in Devlin's anecdote at the end of the story? Does Dexter's achievement of the American dream (he makes a lot of money) ironically cause him to lose his ability to engage in dreaming?

WILLIAM FAULKNER

As I Lay Dying

As students begin to read *As I Lay Dying* they experience fragmentation and dislocation. After assigning only the first five or ten monologues, I spend much of the first class period allowing them to discuss the expectations they bring to a novel as readers, and how *As I Lay Dying* disrupts those expectations. The initial confusion they feel as a result of Faulkner's disparate narrative sections and points of view can help them understand modernism as a challenge to their ways of seeing the world. If allowed to express their own disorientation, they begin to use Faulkner's novel as an exploration of ways of knowing (epistemology), as well as of ways of being (ontology) in a disordered universe.

We begin with a preliminary discussion of the book's title in light of earlier thematic discussions of modernism. What does the reader expect, given this title? And how does the novel, from its opening sections, thwart those expectations? Who *is* the "I" of the title? Just Addie Bundren? What or who else does that first person point-of-view include? And how does the past tense of the title create a preliminary absurdity before the reader begins the novel? In eliciting students' initial confusion about opening sections, I try to give them the experience of posing Faulkner's own questions as he lets his characters speak. What do they know as they read, and how do they know it? We "close-read" Darl's opening section. Where does Faulkner "locate" the reader? Part of what "lies dying" for readers new to Faulkner is any reliance on the author as someone who will facilitate knowing. Faulkner shows readers only what his characters know, not what readers may feel the need to know.

As students proceed through the novel (over the span of an additional two or three class periods), we spend class time describing what Faulkner is doing. We consider novelistic conventions—character development, plot, use of a narrator, chronology, narrative form—and assess the extent to which Faulkner adheres to or deviates from traditional elements of the novel. In the collective act of description, students make numerous statements about *As I Lay Dying*: they note the number of narrators (15 by the novel's end) and sections (59 separate monologues); they distinguish among the narrative voices by making descriptive observations: Darl has, by far, the most sections; some central characters—Jewel and Addie—have only one monologue; monologues by Darl, Jewel, Dewey Dell, Anse, Vardaman, Cash, and Addie create a nexus of family dynamics; other characters—Cora, Tull, Peabody, Samson, Whitfield, Armstid, MacGowan, Moseley—express a wide range of possible social responses to the Bundrens. These descriptive statements may make some students feel that they have "figured out" the novel, and I may observe that their attempts to "solve" the novel may be premature and may actually be covering over their uneasiness as readers, lest they become lost in a work without omniscient authority.

They also establish collective understandings about the characters in the novel that become shared "facts" and which serve as a prelude to interpretation. The attempt to bury Addie becomes the family members' ostensible reason for the journey to Jefferson, which provides Faulkner with his novel's narrative structure, but most of the Bundrens also have other reasons for the trip. Cash wants the free ride back to Tull's, where he is supposed to work on his barn, and he dreams of a "talking machine." Vardaman remembers something in a store window (the toy train) that Santa wouldn't have sold to town boys. Anse wants to get some new teeth. Dewey Dell hopes to buy a drug-induced abortion. Darl twice narrates events at which he could not have been present, and in other sections appears to "know" things that others have not told him (he knows Dewey Dell is pregnant and that Anse is not Jewel's father). Among all of Addie's survivors, Jewel seems best able to feel the depths of his connection to his mother, to mourn her death, and to achieve emotional resolution. (At the end of Cora's section just preceding Addie's monologue, Addie tells Cora that Jewel "is my cross and he will be my salvation. He will save me from the water and from the fire"; and, indeed, Jewel first saves Addie's coffin in the ford, and later from the fire Darl has set to Gillespie's barn.) The group effort to "figure out" what can be known in reading the novel becomes a pedagogical analogue to the Bundrens' own journey. The parallel tensions of burying Addie (for the Bundrens) and figuring out what is happening in the novel (for the members of the class) comment on the act of modernist reading: without the storyteller/guide of traditional narrative, the task of arriving at an understanding of Faulkner's text (analogous to bringing the coffin to Jefferson) places much of the burden of creation on the act of reading itself.

As a result of description, students move toward interpretation. The elements of form they observe lead to their perceptions of character. For example, they note the repetition in the form of the images Jewel and Vardaman create as a way of grieving for Addie: "Jewel's mother is a horse" and "My mother is a fish." Then they can ask, which image works best to help the character resolve grief? In responding to the question, they explore the relationship between image and feeling, between word and meaning, between the novel as a form and the attempt to order the fragments of human consciousness.

Central to exploring Faulkner's search for theme, meaning, and order is Addie's single monologue, placed off-center in the novel in the second half, long after Addie has died and the Bundrens have begun their journey to Jefferson. To what extent does Addie exist in the novel? Although she gives the other characters their ostensible reason for action, she herself does not act. Neither does she speak, except to acknowledge Cash as he builds her coffin. Her monologue in the novel may appear to give her a voice, but her death has already silenced her and prevents her from making her genuine presence known. She exists for others as their own projected need. Interestingly, what occupies her thinking in her monologue is the uselessness of words. Discuss Addie's various statements about words: "words don't ever fit even what they are trying to say at"; a word is "just a shape to fill a lack"; a name is a "word as a shape, a vessel . . . a significant shape profoundly without life like an empty door frame"; words are "just sounds" that people have "for what they never had and cannot have until they forget the words." In the narrative structure of Faulkner's novel, Addie is herself "just a shape to fill a lack."

The visual image of the coffin that appears in Tull's third monologue typographically disrupts, once again, the reader's expectations—for, although Faulkner has violated readers' expectations of linearity and wholeness in narrating *As I Lay Dying*, he at least uses words. With the visual image of the coffin, followed later by Addie's description of words, Faulkner creates a series of concentric visual images or shapes that serve both to contain his novel's meaning and to express the limits of narrative form. In Faulkner's thinking, each of the following is associatively synonymous: the visual figure of the coffin; the name "Addie"; the narrative form he has chosen for the book (it is spatial, a world laid out by compass and rule); and the book itself. *As I Lay Dying* effectively becomes Addie's coffin, a fiction in which she is silenced by the title; and, like her family in Jefferson cemetery, she might be listening to the other 58 monologues, but "[she'll] be hard to talk to."

As I Lay Dying has a profound effect on students who are themselves struggling to emerge from silence and to begin to explore the world's order and form, to discover whether it has any or whether they must join the human collective task of making form and meaning. Students may empathize with Addie's silence, and may find it reflected in Vardaman's obsession with his mother as a fish, or with Cash's inability to speak except to focus on the coffin's construction or need for balance. *As I Lay Dying* demonstrates the novelist's own struggle to emerge from silence, and students may believe that it is only partly successful, or that Faulkner is saying that it is possible to achieve only partial success.

In evaluating the relationship between the construction of form—as a coffin or a novel—and of meaning, ask students to think about Darl. Is he crazy? If so, what makes him crazy? Interestingly, Darl has by far the least difficulty with silence; he can speak for others as well as himself. Is he a mere scapegoat at the novel's end? Do the other members of his family believe he "knows too much"? Or has he failed in some basic way to create a form for what he knows? Darl is the only character who cannot make a connection between himself and some concrete object. He has no coffin, horse, fish, abortion, or reason to go to town. Students may find it difficult to believe that Darl "goes crazy" at the end of the novel, in part because, in many of his monologues, he closely resembles a traditional omniscient narrator, one whose own identity does not intrude. Who, then, is Darl? If he cannot express his connection in terms of an image, a form—coffin, novel—his knowledge and creativity become destructive. Darl simply cannot "be contained" in a form; therefore, as Cash realizes at novel's end, "this world is not his world; this life his life." In Darl's failure to achieve a form for human consciousness, Faulkner implies his own struggle for meaning. What to make of a diminished thing?—make something of it, find a word to fill the lack, write a novel that will reconcile human need for form with the formlessness of human consciousness. Cash's briefest monologue locates *As I Lay Dying* in the progression of Faulkner's career as a novelist: "It wasn't on a balance. I told them that if they wanted it to tote and ride on a balance, they would have to." *As I Lay Dying* rides precariously, a book about silent knowing necessarily told in words. Expecting to be told, students emerge from *As I Lay Dying* with the uneasy knowledge that words no longer—for the modernist—carry ultimate authority. As Addie expresses it, "the high dead words in time seemed to lose even the significance of their dead sound." Perhaps literary authority itself is at least a part of what "lies dying" in Faulkner's modern fictional universe.

LANGSTON HUGHES

Analyze Hughes's language in the lyrics included in the *NAAL*. What does his language tell us about his own theory or view of poetry? I read "Mother to Son" closely with students, focusing on the contrast between the mother's description of the stairway itself and the image she arrives at ("Life for me ain't been no crystal stair") as a controlling metaphor for her vision. The poem shows the mother arriving at modernist order in the chaos of "sometimes goin' in the dark" by making this particular image. What are its many connotations, and how does it raise the poem's level of diction? "Trumpet Player" shows the jazz musician arriving at his own "momentary stay against confusion" in the process of working through "smoldering memory" and "old desire": "But softly / As the tune comes from his throat / Trouble / Mellows to a golden note."

RICHARD WRIGHT

Discuss what "being a man" means to Dave Saunders. Why does the gun represent manhood to him? Does a black boy in the 1930s South automatically get "to be a man like any body else," or does he have to make that happen? Why does he want the power to "kill anybody, black or white"? How does Dave Saunders move beyond Booker T. Washington's views of black identity in *Up from Slavery*? Is Dave another heroic fugitive, like Frederick Douglass? Does he have a destination at the end of the story?

AMERICAN PROSE SINCE 1945

In the contemporary period, as William Pritchard observes in his general introduction, "even with the most exclusive standards, one can easily name fifty or so American novelists and story writers who are artists of real distinction." As teachers, our decisions to choose certain authors or stories over others in this period likely reflect our own personal reading taste or previous experience that certain authors and works are more successful than others in introducing students to the pleasure and power of contemporary American literature. In making my own selections, I am guided much more by my sense of what will please and move students than by current critical evaluations that might grant certain writers more importance than others. I want to leave students with a desire to read more contemporary literature, and I choose a few works that I know they will enjoy. The teaching notes that follow reflect those choices, as well as offer some guidelines for discussion of individual works.

Introducing Students to Contemporary American Drama

An introductory course in American literature, especially in twentieth-century or contemporary literature, offers students a unique opening into the experience and meaning of drama as an American literary form. American writers have certainly produced great plays prior to the contemporary period, and drama served a vital function for Americans as early as Royall Tyler's *The Contrast* (included in *NAAL*, Vol. 1), when delighted audiences flocked to view Jonathan's comic rendition of what an "American" in 1787 might look like. I suspect that very few of your students, however, will have thought much about the uses of drama in their own lives.

One way of beginning is simply to ask students to talk about drama in general. What do they associate with drama? Some may reply, "Shakespeare." Almost all of them will have read Shakespeare in high school; they may have learned, as a result, that drama belongs to an elitist category of literary forms. Are any students willing to challenge that impression? Others may recall acting in high school plays of mostly less seriousness—situation comedies, Hollywood musicals, plays written especially for high school acting. A few may have written and/or acted in original plays as children, or may have parents who participated in community theater groups. Others may associate a family trip to New York City to view a Broadway play as some initiation rite into adult life and culture. Some may associate drama with television situation comedies. Even with this limited range of responses to the experience of drama in their lives, you can begin to explore the variety of functions drama serves. What are some of the differences between literature that one reads, often alone in a room, and a play that may be "taking place" before the viewer's eyes, as that viewer sits in a group with others? Is a play "shown" or "told" when the performers stage it? What kinds of effects does the stage play make possible? And what does it mean to dramatize?

In initially asking students to describe their experience with drama, some may talk about movies as the form of drama with which they are most familiar. On the premise that Hollywood both reflects and creates American identity, the playwrights of the 1980s included in *NAAL* acknowledge cinema as integral to their own production. For Adrienne Kennedy's protagonist, the films she has seen seem to have replaced family experiences as the mold in which she finds her identity cast. For Sam Shepard (see more extensive discussion of *True West*), script writing becomes a version of self-creation, and the Hollywood producer an ironic stand-in for a father figure.

Contemporary drama may elicit students' ability to engage in the reading process more readily than contemporary American poetry, which often seems to deliberately distance the reader with its private meanings, idiosyncratic uses of language and imagery, and sense of barriers between speaking voice and reader of the text. Drama, however, seems to require a viewer; a play creates audience in the process of making character, situation, scene, and dramatic effect; the student, in the act of reading, becomes a collaborator in creating a visual image of the scene.

The plays included in *NAAL*, Volume 2, by their very choice of subject matter and realistic treatment, may particularly elicit the student's capacity to become engaged, to become created or recreated as audience. When Eugene O'Neill explored American family life in *Long Day's Journey into Night*, he did not exhaust our increasing fascination for the function and fate of the American family. Perhaps the crisis in family life for late twentieth-century Americans has brought on the crisis of consciousness that, earlier in the century, we associate with World War I and the question of the death or absence of God or design in the modern world. Family life continues to provide a central focus for Tennessee Williams, Arthur Miller, and Sam Shepard. If the American family is dead or absent, who or what "mothers" or "mirrors" an American identity that continues to evolve?

Exploring Intersections between Contemporary American Drama and Prose Fiction

In Kennedy and Shepard, contemporary drama offers a geographical as well as formal and thematic challenges to one dominant fictional form in contemporary American fiction, the *New Yorker* story. For earlier writers such as Fitzgerald and Faulkner, writing for Hollywood became a way to make money. In the "Prologue" to his 1952 novel *Invisible Man* (*NAAL* includes the "Prologue" and Chapter I), Ralph Ellison sets the tone for New York's view of the West

Coast when his nameless protagonist introduces himself by describing what he is not: "nor am I one of your Hollywood-movie ectoplasms." By the 1980s, as Kennedy and Shepard make clear, Hollywood becomes integral to American identity. Kennedy brings Hollywood directly onto the New York set, using the Columbia Pictures Lady and characters from Hollywood films as characters in her play; Shepard fully explores the meaning of the West and of Los Angeles for the contemporary American literary imagination.

Much of contemporary American fiction has been and continues to reflect East Coast and, particularly, New York life. Among the post-1945 prose writers included in *NAAL*, more than half have written important fiction set in New York City, and many have made their reputations by writing for the *New Yorker* magazine. Edmund Wilson, Vladimir Nabokov, John Cheever, James Baldwin, John Updike, Robert Stone, Bobbie Ann Mason, and Ann Beattie have all contributed to the *New Yorker*, and *New Yorker* fiction has established its own informal genre. Perhaps the moment at the end of Robert Stone's story "Helping," in which Elliot shoots a gun but no one gets killed, epitomizes one feature of the *New Yorker* story. In a word, the *New Yorker* story eschews the dramatic. The contrast between the anthologized *New Yorker* texts and Sam Shepard's *True West*—in which the anticipated violence between Lee and Austin does happen, and in which the relationship between characters motivates action as well as introspection—sets up related contrasts between contemporary prose and contemporary drama. By its very title, Shepard's play invites a geographical as well as a formal contrast with New York and *New Yorker* prose.

In the past decade, as the anthologized selections by Bobbie Ann Mason, Leslie Marmon Silko, Denise Chávez, and Louise Erdrich suggest, contemporary American literature has begun to rediscover the importance of the West—and to move the new literary frontier beyond the Hudson River. Kentucky, New Mexico, and North Dakota—in the works of these contemporary writers—have contributed both geographically and formally to revising the American identity. Setting up the geographic contrast between New York and non–New York may help your students to speculate on the evolving and defining role of contemporary writers.

EUDORA WELTY

Analyze the relationship between Leota and Mrs. Fletcher. Does Mrs. Pike exist? What function does Leota's fantasy life serve? Discuss the undercurrent of violence in "Petrified Man." How does Leota's story show her attempt to gain control over her life? Is she successful? Who is Billy Boy, why is she taking care of him, and where does he get his own power at the end of the story?

The loss of "Belle Reve" seems to establish the tarnished American Dream as one of Williams's central themes in *A Streetcar Named Desire*. Some students may see Blanche DuBois as a conventional symbol for the loss of that dream—as an unmarried, well-over-thirty southern belle, she worries about her clothes, her appearance, her ability to attract men, and finding alcohol to ease her loneliness. But is the loss of desirability, or desire itself, the play's subject? Does Blanche want to find an object for her desire, or to be a desired object?

Williams might have made desire itself a symbol; instead, throughout the play, he focuses our attention on explicit sexuality. What particular scenes define desire as sexual in the play? Ask students to discuss in particular the relationship between Stanley and Stella. Their attraction for each other is explicitly sexual, and most students will equate sexuality with heterosexuality—and, as it is presented in this play, with a hierarchy of physical dominance (the men in the play, especially Stanley, use physical abuse as part of sexual power; see Stanley's comment to Blanche, " 'Oh! So you want some roughhouse!' ").

But this play revolves around that moment in Blanche's past when she married a "young boy" who tried to find "help" in Blanche for his homosexuality. When she discovers him with "an older man who had been his friend for years," and that day tells him how much he disgusts her, he blows his head off. For most students, presuming that heterosexuality is "normal" and homosexuality "deviant," this moment will establish Blanche's tragedy as a conventional one—she has loved young and lost—and the moment in which homosexuality enters the play will quickly recede. Raise the possibility that from this moment on, Blanche's psychological core gender identity becomes ambiguous—despite the fact that Williams has made her a woman in the play; and suggest, as well, that although Stanley and Stella both seem secure in their gender identities, their very insistence on continuing to reaffirm their sexual relationship by means of violence—thereby asserting Stanley's "manhood" and Stella's "womanliness"— begins to raise the question of the origins of gender determination as well.

What would it mean to say that Blanche's sexual identity becomes ambiguous in the play? Near the end she tells Mitch, "'I don't want realism, I want magic! . . . I don't tell truth, I tell what *ought* to be truth.'" What are Blanche's props for her "magic"? Ask someone to study her array of furs, costumes, jewelry, and perfume in the play—she wears all of the trappings of gendered femininity, like the legendary Mae West (ironically, the statuette Mitch wins for Blanche at the amusement park). But her success in establishing her appearance depends on her avoiding the sun, and even electric light. Without the costumes, who would Blanche be? What would it mean to call her a "woman"? And who are her consistent objects of desire? Recall, with students, that she has been fired from her teaching job for having a relationship with a young boy; and she tells the paper boy, "'You make my mouth water.'" Whatever her sexual biology, Williams is not telling truth but "what *ought* to be truth." The play explores what women and homosexual men have in common; it does that (in my view) by focusing on gender construction in Blanche, not on biological sexual identity. Except for the fact that Williams makes her a woman, she might be a drag queen (she shares the queen's fascination with Mae West as a model to be imitated); and in exploring the psychology of the queen (Stanley asks Blanche, "'What queen do you think you are?'"), Williams is exploring the way female identity is made, not born.

Ask students to think about Stanley's response to Blanche. What motivates Stanley to rape her? What does she represent that makes him want to humiliate her? Blanche sees Stanley—with his phallic "genius"—as subhuman; Stanley sees Blanche as undermining his control over Stella ("'You remember the way that it was? Them nights we had together? God, honey, it's gonna be sweet when we can make noise in the night the way that we used to and get the colored lights going with nobody's sister behind the curtains to hear us!'"). But Stanley is also acting out of a variation on homophobia—or is homophobia a variation on misogyny? In the homosexual world, it takes courage for a man to become a drag queen, because in wearing women's clothes, the man sets himself up for the full violence of some men's hatred of women. Stanley hates Blanche because she insists on wearing women's costumes and yet refuses to define herself as degenerate or to excuse her sister for her submission to Stanley. In raping Blanche, he is raping the wearing of women's costumes, the flaunting of sexuality by women (or by men who refuse to be "phallic"). No wonder that Stella tells Eunice, "'I couldn't believe her story and go on living with Stanley.'" The sexual "stories" Blanche and Stanley tell totally contradict each other. Blanche exhibits desire without violence; Stanley achieves his through violence and humiliation. Ask students to talk about Stella's grief at the end of the play: "'What have I done to my sister?'" How has she betrayed Blanche? Has she also betrayed herself? In what version of sexual desire does the "truth" lie? The play ends with Stanley and Stella, having eliminated Blanche from their world, returning to their hierarchical heterosexual roles: Stella weeps in luxurious abandon, Stanley unbuttons her blouse. Is this desire? Or a more destructive lie than Blanche's "magic"?

BERNARD MALAMUD

"The Magic Barrel" works well to teach with *A Streetcar Named Desire*, because there are similarities between the works that help students formulate their questions. In "The Magic Barrel," Malamud creates Salzman the marriage broker as an Old Testament God figure who tries to keep love (and sex) out of the world. As a "commercial cupid" however, he is also someone others hire to re-fashion Paradise (clearly a "diminished thing" in the world Mala-mud's characters live in—like "Belle Reve"?). His idea of Paradise is to find a good woman for Leo, the rabbinical student, and to keep Leo away from his own daughter, Stella, a "fallen woman." (Is Williams's Stella also "fallen"?) When Leo falls in love with Stella's picture and arranges to meet her at the end of the story, Malamud depicts their meeting in "fallen" terms: Stella is dressed like a street-walker, Leo runs forward phallically "with flowers outthrust" (or as if he and Salzman have exchanged places, and Leo is now a cupid or the FTD florist's winged messenger, bearing flowers), and Salzman, convinced that there is no good man, chants prayers for the dead. But Leo pictures, in Stella, "his own redemption"; and Malamud sug-gests that although Leo becomes less than a rabbi by the end of the story, he becomes consequently more of a man, more of a human being. Simply loving, in this story, does recreate Paradise because it makes it possible, once again, for Leo to love God—and even to cre-ate God in a human image. In Malamud's terms, Leo's love for the fallen Stella makes him a good man, and, although Salzman mourns, the story has a happy ending. Less is more, for Leo. As he becomes the "diminished thing" in Salzman's eyes, he is more capable of hu-man love.

RALPH ELLISON

Compare Ellison's protagonist with Dave Saunders in Wright's "The Man Who Was Almost a Man." The two might seem incomparable in educational background and social possibilities; yet, how are they up against similar barriers? In the Prologue to *Invisible Man* the older protagonist writes, in retrospect, "Responsibility rests upon recognition, and recognition is a form of agreement." How is this observation relevant to his experiences as a young man in Chapter I? How is Blanche's statement in *A Streetcar Named Desire* ("I don't tell truth, I tell what *ought* to be truth") applicable to Elli-son's use of symbolic action in *Invisible Man*? Each of the major events of Chapter I—the fight with Tatlock, the electrified rug, the presence of the white woman, the boy's attempt to talk with blood in his mouth, his reference to "social equality," and the scholarship to the black college he receives at the end—can be read as symbolic.

And how does the boy's attempt to deliver the speech he himself has written comment on the literary tradition of American black writers? What are the symbolic as well as real obstacles he must overcome in trying to find his voice and to express his point of view? What might it take for the white men at the smoker to "recognize" and "accept" the invisible man? Is the white woman in a better position than the black boy? Does either have power in the world of the back room?

ARTHUR MILLER

Madness, confusion, desire, identity: these are the themes O'Neill, Williams, and Miller explore in their plays, and the family in each play becomes the place within which characters act out their roles. The family is also the place where we each develop a sense of individual identity and learn the social, emotional, and sexual roles we then choose to revolt against or to play out in our own lives. *Death of a Salesman* gives American family life itself the power to create character—almost as if the play is about the inability of any playwright to invent roles he or she has not already played or watched in the tragedy of family life. The family is both the play and the playwright. And in this play the family prescribes certain roles for each of the four main characters that they continue to reenact in the process of discovering what they are. Students, following Linda's cue, will focus on Willy Loman himself: "'Attention must be finally paid to such a person.'" Why doesn't Loman accomplish anything? Why does he have such trouble really talking to his sons? Neither of his sons is able to "catch on." How do they all get derailed? Unlike Mary Tyrone or Blanche DuBois, Linda Loman has no identity of her own. Is *Death of a Salesman* realistic in its portrait of Linda? What was her role in Loman's decline? Miller implies that Linda has kept her husband back from going to Alaska and "conquering the world"; is she to blame, or has she seen inadequacies in her husband that he was unable to recognize in himself? Does she never criticize Loman, or want to defend Biff against his father? Who raised these children, anyway? Is the role of American father as provider a myth without basis in fact? Who *does* "provide" in this play? And what is Miller indicting?—capitalism? family life in general? American fatherhood?

FLANNERY O'CONNOR

In "Good Country People" Mrs. Hopewell says, "'Everybody is different. . . . It takes all kinds to make the world,'" but she doesn't really mean it. She would prefer that all the world, and especially her daughter, be "good country people" like herself. What would it mean for Hulga to take her mother as her model? Contrast the two sets of mothers and daughters depicted in the story. What are Hulga's "crimes"? What makes her unforgivably "different" to her mother? What is Hulga looking for in Manley Pointer? What does she find? Look at the mother-child imagery of Pointer's "seduction." What do Manley and Mrs. Hopewell have in common? As unlikely as it might have seemed, Hulga has chosen as a love object a person who both infantilizes her and tries to idealize her—someone whose psychological connection with her resembles her mother's own. And what is the story's final betrayal? Is it possible for Hulga to escape being her mother's daughter?

ADRIENNE KENNEDY

The *NAAL* headnote focuses on two aspects of *A Movie Star Has to Star in Black and White*: Clara's relationship to her alter egos or movie fantasies, and Clara's feelings of not belonging. Students need help understanding the first, technical aspect of Kennedy's play before they can feel moved by her second, thematic statement.

Kennedy writes about Clara in one of her stage directions that Clara "lets her movie stars star in her life." For undergraduate students, allusions to black-and-white movies from the 1940s and 1950s that they likely have not seen may make Kennedy's play difficult to read, and you may not have access to tapes of the movies or time to show them to your students. However, the headnote helps explain Kennedy's specific allusions to the three movies in her play, and if you can help students visualize the stage setting, they will respond to her uses of "black and white" to make her point about Clara, the aspiring playwright. When Bette Davis recalls life in Savannah, Georgia, in 1929, and, as Scene I unfolds, becomes a transformation of Clara's mother, Kennedy manages to offer her reader/viewer a powerful experience of black and white perception. Black readers, projecting themselves into white actress Bette Davis, may find themselves mirrored by Davis's transformation, because she speaks out of black experience. White readers identify with the Bette Davis character only to find themselves seeing the world with a black character's eyes.

Ask students who have read O'Neill's *Long Day's Journey into Night* to contrast Kennedy's use of autobiography with O'Neill's. Once Kennedy convinces her reader/viewer that Bette Davis might be Clara, she frees Clara to have an existence of her own apart from her transformation of Kennedy herself. Clara becomes, by Scene III, an "actress" herself as she sits beside Shelley Winters in the boat. She speaks here not simply for Adrienne Kennedy, but for other black women who may aspire to write—and to take their own lives as seriously as they take their movie fantasies. By Scene III, Clara becomes a "floating" alter ego waiting for a viewer/reader to become attached to, just as Clara saw herself and her life in the movie roles Kennedy depicts in her play.

Ask students to focus on Kennedy's various uses of black and white throughout the play. Does *A Movie Star Has to Star in Black and White* end by underscoring issues of race or by transcending them? Or compare Kennedy's presentation of the black woman as survivor in Clara (who speaks at the end of the play while Shelley Winters drowns) with Peter Taylor's portrait of Aunt Munsie in "What You Hear from 'Em?." In Aunt Munsie's transformation, she becomes "not very reliable about dates and such things," and Taylor presents her as unable to tell her own story. Clara discovers her "history" in her movie fantasies and breaks through her own "bit part" to share the spotlight with the Columbia Pictures Lady who opens and closes the play.

ROBERT STONE

If drama externalizes feelings and relationships, then Robert Stone's story "Helping" creates its effect, in part, because it presents internalized violence and a tension that remain unresolved by the story's end, even if Elliot's missed shot at the pheasant provides Elliot himself with momentary relief. Many elements in the story contribute to building a sense that something violent is about to happen: Elliot's interaction with Blankenship; the content of Blankenship's dream and the memories of Viet Nam it evokes in Elliot; Grace's description of the Vopotik family and Vopotik's threats; Elliot's fantasy of cutting the necks of the Anderson family with barbed wire; Elliot's shotgun and his encounter with Professor Anderson on the ski trail. Some violence does occur: Elliot's rage at the psychiatrist, the sugar bowl Grace throws across the room, Elliot's shot at the pheasant. Does "enough" violence actually happen in the story to relieve the weight of suspense the reader carries by the end? Or has Stone managed to provide the antithesis of a cathartic experience for the reader? Are we left with an increasingly internalized sense of foreboding?

One line from "Helping" suggests that, for the contemporary reader, there will be no "help" at all. Elliot thinks, "The gods and I went mad together and made things as they are." If you have talked about modernism with your students in teaching material from the 1914–1945 section of *NAAL*, ask them how Elliot's thought takes modernism in a new direction. For my own students, I might suggest that, for the modernists, the emotional/psychological/metaphysical "solution" to the recognition of the death or absence of design in the universe was to find consolation in the writers' or poet's vision; it became the writer's job to order those "fragments I have shored against my ruins," as that earlier (T.S.) Eliot concludes at the end of "The Waste Land." For Robert Stone, post–Viet Nam, human beings cannot repair his sense of lost order; in fact, human beings seem to have collaborated with the gods to make things as they are. In the language of Alcoholics Anonymous, Stone seems to be suggesting that the human victims of the loss of order or design have themselves served as co-dependents; we resemble the Grace of "Helping" who tells Elliot, "'In my family we stay until the fella dies. That's the tradition. We stay and pour it for them and they die.'" Nothing "helps," especially not the professional helpers, in Stone's world; Elliot ends the story by expressing his need for, if not the helping hand, at least a "show" of hand, which might ease the post-modernist's despair with the modernist's consolation (might he then be free to interpret the hand as helping, much as the viewer in Wallace Stevens's world is free to interpret what the eye sees?). It seems more likely, as "Helping" ends without or before the show of hand, that Elliot will continue to look down the length of the gun and at some point "find himself down the sight."

Compare and contrast the ending of "Helping" with the ending of Malamud's "The Magic Barrel." How do the different protagonists differently interpret possibly divine signs?

JOYCE CAROL OATES

The "golden gloves" of Oates's story serve to protect the protagonist's hands, but, as the reader suspects at the end of "Helping," the power to make the world safe lies beyond the control of human hands for some contemporary writers. Ask students to compare "Golden Gloves" with "Helping." Has some external force undermined Stone's Elliot, or does his fear, anger, and sense of broken promise result from his own individual character or experience? Oates makes it clear that forces beyond her protagonist's control have altered the course of his life, beginning with his birth defect. She writes, "The blow you can't see coming is the blow that knocks you out—the blow out of nowhere. How can you protect yourself against a blow out of nowhere?" Ask students to differentiate between a benign but absent creator and a malignant external force. Does Oates's protagonist have any control over his life? What is the prognosis for the protagonist's relationship with his, as yet, unborn child? Several of the short stories included in the post-1945 section explore adult relationships between men and women. And for several of these relationships, Oates's description of what happens to her own protagonist may also apply: "It was his own death that had crashed into him—yet no more than he deserved. He was hit as one is hit only once in a lifetime. He was hit and time stopped." Comparing the protagonist's feelings about his wife at the end of "Golden

Gloves" with the male protagonist's feelings in Tom Wolfe's "The Master of the Universe," John Updike's "Separating," and Robert Stone's "Helping," assess the sense of arrested development that each of these authors conveys as time stops in some way for their characters. Has Oates managed to accurately convey the determinism of contemporary American life, or has she distorted what we have become? And is the protagonist's wife his new sparring partner, his double, his projected shadow self?

BOBBIE ANN MASON

The *NAAL* headnote gives Mason credit for resisting the temptation to present her characters "as caricatures to be ridiculed or pitied by a presumably more sensitive author and reader." Resisting this temptation marks a writer *of* rather than *about* region; and if the statement about Mason is accurate, suggests a new integration of *New Yorker* style with regionalist perception. In introducing Bobbie Ann Mason, I ask students to contrast her with Peter Taylor's "What You Hear from 'Em?," an earlier (1954) story by another author associated with the *New Yorker* who writes from Mason's neighbor state of Tennessee. Does the critical comment from Mason's headnote (above) also apply to Taylor's story, or does Taylor fall into caricature in his presentation of Aunt Munsie? I also ask students to read Mason in the context of recent Native American and Chicana writers (Silko, Erdrich, and Chávez, included in *NAAL*), all of whom explore lost family connections and the need to test out the power of storytelling to re-form or reclaim some sense of family, ethnic, or "antique" heritage. Contrast the absence of tension at the end of "Drawing Names" with the ending of *True West*. How does Mason's Carolyn retain her sense of possibility in human connection, even in family life, despite the images of failed connection and fractured family that pervade "Drawing Names"?

Ask students to consider the joke about the silent monks that Carolyn's father tells at Christmas dinner and to analyze her mother's response: "Can you imagine anybody not a-talking all year long?" Mason presents a family in which there is much talk and very little real conversation. Then look closely at the ending of the story. How do students interpret the gift left under the tree? One "gift" that remains "unopened" for Carolyn is conversation; she finds hope, as she imagines Jim and Laura Jean alone, in the "certainty that they would not be economical with words." One of the features readers have come to expect from *New Yorker* fiction is linguistic economy. Mason seems to be pushing the limits of economy at the end of this story, drawing out the visual image of the "old-fashioned scene," adding the (perhaps to some) unnecessary "Cheers" to Carolyn's vision of possibility in family as well as fictional forms. Is Mason arguing that in an era of lost family connections, it is time for writers to become more "wasteful" in their use of words?

SAM SHEPARD

Shepard's title, "True West," invites us to bring into the play our own associations, and I begin by asking students what the West means to them. For some, it may reflect historical possibility—connoting freedom, expansion, wide open spaces, a new beginning, the primacy of the individual and the individuating experience in family life. Others may associate the West with the loss or diminishing of these same possibilities, particularly students who live in or have visited Southern California, the geographical location of Shepard's play. But what possibilities seem lost, or in the process of constricting? Does the muted nostalgia for antiques in Bobbie Ann Mason's protagonist reflect changing times in Kentucky—once geographically west of the earliest English-settled regions of the country—and does Carolyn's disillusionment with her family's life reflect a loss of the "West"? How much do students associate the shrinking of the rural landscape in the Northeast with the loss of possibilities that may feel "Western"?

The Sunbelt expansion of the last two decades may have elicited "Western" associations for some Americans; how do Southern and Southwestern students view the increasing industrializing of their formerly rural or "frontier" landscapes? Where, geographically, is this country's current "West"? The Alaska pipeline boom of the 1970s may suggest that Americans still look for a goldrush quality in whatever region they associate with "West." What constitutes "West" for Dominican or Puerto Rican immigrants, or the sons and daughters of Cuban exiles? "West" of what? If America remains a land of possibility for persons South of our borders, then does "North" take on the associative features that American history, taught from a perspective of expansion that takes as its center an Eastern established culture, has taught us to associate with "West"? What does "West" mean for Native American writers from Eastern tribal genealogies, for whom resettlement meant the extinction of tribal culture? If there are many "Wests" in the American imagination, what do different students associate with their own "true" Wests as they begin reading Shepard's play, and what would the concept of a "false" West mean to them? And has Los Angeles itself now become the symbol of the "false" West?

Although students can easily read *True West* in preparation for a single class session, I allow 3, or even 4, classes for our discussion of the play, because it allows us to contemplate and begin to organize much of the post-1945 prose included in *NAAL*. From Lee's opening question in Scene 1, "So, Mom took off for Alaska, huh?,"

Shepard raises the question of where the "West" has shifted geographically and psychologically for late twentieth-century Americans. We examine the contrasts Shepard initially sets up between Austin and Lee in Scene 1. Which brother seems the most "Western" in terms of the Hollywood stereotype? Which represents the forces of stability? What different qualities of life does each brother initially value, and which seems more truly "Eastern" to your students? Some may argue that Austin is following the "true" path of expanded possibility by trying to write for Hollywood. For American writers, the prospect of selling a movie script or movie rights to a short story or novel is the imaginative literary equivalent of discovering a gold mine; is the process of defining oneself as a fiction writer, in 1980s America, equivalent to panning for gold, and has buying into the dream of writing the Great American novel (surely a "Western" fantasy) become the equivalent of purchasing a "salted" gold mine?

How does it affect the reader that *True West* opens by focusing on Austin, and Austin's point-of-view? Lee is the interloper, threatening disorder, trying to borrow Austin's car, undermining Austin's attempt to keep his mother's house and his own (life's) script in order. Lee seems to represent the cowboy, Austin a romantic traditionalist who reflects the endurance of small-town American values even in the Southern California suburb he calls home. Lee has primitive instincts, a raw hunger, a disregard for the social order, and a sense that "these days gas is gold"; Austin has an old-fashioned belief in security, contracts between people, love, the value of serious writing, and his ability to become reunited with his brother. Lee destabilizes Austin's structure; successfully competes for the attention of Austin's Hollywood producer Saul Kimmer; and, in the process, ironically restores Austin's own imaginative "West." Part of the wit of *True West* is the way Lee manages to revive even the jaded Hollywood producer's interest in the "West" and in making real "true-to-life" Westerns.

Scene 4 is a pivotal scene in the play and we discuss it at length. In this scene, students begin to associate Lee with the coyotes and Austin with the crickets, whose noises move in and out of the background. How has it happened that, by Scene 4, Austin is typing not his own screenplay but an outline for Lee's? Austin appears to have capitulated, in part, to retain some sense of control—at least over his own car keys. The scene reveals Austin as the "true" Western interloper, however; he fails to understand the terms Lee uses, such as "gooseneck" and "Tornado Country," suggesting that Austin's acquaintance with things Western has not emerged from actual experience. In this scene, despite Austin's avowed encouragement to Lee to try to sell his story, Lee increasingly becomes Austin's tutor, teaching him that "there aren't any mountains in the Panhandle" and that "family people" and brothers are the "kinda' people kill each other the most." Boundaries begin to dissolve between the two brothers, with Lee confessing, "I always wondered what'd be like to be you," and Austin reporting that "I always used to picture you somewhere." By the end of the scene, and the end of Act I, Lee's script has become their own, as well as a commentary on Shepard's script. We examine the concluding image of Lee's two "cowboys" chasing each other into the black prairie: "And the one who's chasin' doesn't know where the other one is taking him. And the one who's being chased doesn't know where he's going."

In Act II, Lee increasingly becomes Shepard's focus, as the two brothers exchange roles. They become partners—in crime and in scriptwriting. When Austin uses a Western cliché with Saul Kimmer in Scene 6 to describe his sense of broken contract—"Just trade horses in midstream?"—we begin to know how far Shepard has moved from the "true-to-life" Western of life in the suburbs of Southern California to the "true" Western of life-and-death struggle on a desert landscape, a landscape in which "changing horses in midstream" might actually have held meaning. Austin responds to his loss of control by mocking Saul's idea of what the "real West" looks like, and his criticism may reflect the attitudes of some of your students. There is much that is true in Austin's description of Westerns as stories in which grown men act like little boys, and in his assertion that "There's no such thing as the West anymore! It's a dead issue!"

Austin continues his attempt to define the terms of contemporary life, of drama, and of this particular play in Scene 7. In the distance he appears to achieve over his brother's triumph (as Lee becomes the screenwriter, not Austin), he offers an alternative title for *True West*—"between men, the coyotes and the crickets"—and identifies himself as the clairvoyant interpreter of the increasingly dislocated structure. As Lee asserts himself as a screenwriter and "legitimate" (has he gone straight? he's no longer a thief? has he become Saul Kimmer's "heir apparent"? has he discovered a birthright, an identity?), Austin continues to exchange roles and identities with Lee. Austin becomes the brother who drinks and who thereby resembles their biological father, whose story Austin proceeds to relate to Lee. Is *this*, at last, the "true" Western story? Are we all effectively adult children of alcoholics? Do the protagonists of Robert Stone's "Helping" and Bobbie Ann Mason's "Drawing Names," as they drink, begin to sound like Austin and Lee? Do we, indeed, "all sound alike when we're sloshed," as Austin claims? And from Nabokov to Cheever to Bellow to Kerouac to Mailer to Baldwin to Updike, does contemporary American prose provide the illusions of characters rather than the "real" thing, what Austin describes as "fantasies of a long lost boyhood"?

Scenes 8 and 9 present the full drama of the destabilization of the precarious identities Lee and Austin had achieved by choosing their contrasting occupations, values, and attitudes toward life, as we witness these early in Act I. Part of what Shepard seems to be dra-

matizing is precisely that precariousness; ask students if, in retrospect, Lee and Austin seem any less in intrapsychic conflict with each
other as the play opens than they become by Scenes 8 and 9, in
which that conflict becomes external and dramatized. Scene 8 de-
scends to the primitive level of human life, as Lee smashes the type-
writer with a golf club, the green world represented by the mother's
plants has been destroyed, and Austin has proven his skill at hunting
and gathering—toasters. Despite his increasing powerlessness to
ward off the seduction of the "true West"—his vision of life with his
brother in the desert—Austin continues to articulate the play's central theme. In Scene 8, the theme takes the image of coyotes "luring
innocent pets away from their homes." By the end of the scene, as
Lee crunches into one of Austin's many pieces of toast with a "huge
crushing bite," Shepard seems to be identifying Lee as the coyote
and Austin as the innocent household pet. Austin tells Lee that
"there's nothin' real down here," least of all himself, and he wants to
follow Lee into the desert in search of what is real. Does this become one meaning of the West, for Austin?—the place where the
late twentieth-century American goes in search of reality? Does
Austin thus reveal himself as the only brother who remains taken in
by the dream of the "true West"?

In the play's closing scene, the two brothers write a collaborative bit of dialogue for their screenplay that reflects their disjunc-
tive re-union. Ask students what is "wrong" with these sentences: "I
told ya' you were a fool to follow me in here. I'm on intimate terms
with this prairie." At first, Lee seems pleased with the word
"intimate." Reread aloud with students Mom's entrance into the
scene and the beginnings of the struggle between Lee and Austin.
What precipitates Lee's sudden reversal, his decision to abandon
Austin and their agreement? How does Austin respond? Does that
word "intimate" trigger Lee's panic? Throughout the play, Austin
seems to want more closeness than Lee does; Lee seems to flee connection, "intimacy," and his perception of Austin as increasingly dependent on him. What is the effect of Mom's entrance onto the
scene at this point in the play? What are the associations students
may see with the broken telephone cord Austin uses to subdue Lee?
Does Mom's presence transform the struggle between Austin and
Lee into a "womb" struggle?—the cord both symbolic of the broken
connection between them as well as the umbilical cord that unites
them as brothers?

As the play ends, Shepard presents a tableau of unresolved
tension between Lee and Austin, and a stage set that he describes as
a "desert junkyard at high noon." Have Lee and Austin already arrived at the desert, as Mom predicts? And is Austin also accurate
when he describes the desert he and Lee will end up on as a
"different desert"? And is the tension or conflict between Lee and
Austin unresolved at the end or simply fully "realized," fully drama-

tized? Austin states, near the end, "I don't know if I'm killing him. I'm stopping him. That's all. I'm just stopping him." Ask students to compare Austin's statement and the ending of *True West* with the moment in Oates's "Golden Gloves" in which the protagonist experiences the blow that "stops" him. Has Shepard dramatized a moment of arrested development in contemporary American society in his portrait of "grown men acting like little boys"? Do contemporary American prose writers resemble the two characters in Lee's screenplay, in which neither follower nor leader know where they are going? Consider Mom's statement: "This is worse than being homeless." Does *True West* suggest, by the end, that one of the reasons why we have lost the West as a mythic image of possibility is that there is no longer any home to flee from? The flight from domesticity of the early nineteenth-century white male writers only works if domesticity exists as a force to react against. But in *True West*, Mom has gone West to Alaska. Even Jack Kerouac's protagonist earns his sense of possibility as he hitches West because New York and New Jersey exist to return to. What happens if we also lose our myth of East? What happens when Mom returns home to find it transformed beyond her recognition? Without haven, what does flight mean? Where can Lee and Austin go if there is nothing to flee from? How can there be any "true" direction without a fixed point of origin?

ALICE WALKER

Walker's depiction of her mother-daughter bond differs considerably from O'Connor's. Where Mrs. Hopewell defines herself and her daughter by listening to the voices of conventional "good country people," the mother who narrates "Everyday Use" listens to her own inner voice and creates her own values. How are Dee and Maggie different? What explains Dee's decision to rename herself Wangero? How do the quilt's values change for her, and what do they mean to Maggie and the narrator? What does Walker mean by valuing "everyday use"—even though the quilts may be, as Dee claims, "priceless"?

ANN BEATTIE

Like the anthologized plays by Adrienne Kennedy and Sam Shepard, Ann Beattie also alludes to a movie from which she takes the title of the anthologized story. However, "Weekend," directed in France by Jean-Luc Godard, represents the antithesis of the Hollywood movies, and may recall for some students Saul Kimmer's distinction in *True West*, as Lee reports it in Scene 5, that "there's a big difference" between a film and a movie. Beattie's story "Weekend"

-186-

more closely resembles a film; what violence does take place in this *New Yorker* story takes place only in the language, and as disjunction.

Once again (as in Shepard's play) houseplants play a role (the contemporary writer's concession to the loss of the external green world?) and Lenore projects and simultaneously contains her own violent fantasies when Beattie writes about Lenore that she "will not offer to hack shoots off her plant for these girls." Otherwise "nothing happens" in this story; Lenore, the "simple" character, asks Beattie's quintessential contemporary question: "Why do I let *what* go on?" Ask students how they interpret Lenore's statement that she is "simple." What does it mean to be "simple" in contemporary life? "It is true; she likes simple things." Yet Lenore's life and Beattie's "Weekend" are more complex than that; is Lenore's love of the simple, Beattie's equivalent to Sam Shepard's evocation of the West? Does the word "simple" for Lenore allow her to defend against noticing the full extent of the lack of communication between her and George? "Weekend" presents a "simple" world of women, in which women are out of place; all of George's guests are "girls," and living with George without being married offers Lenore the illusion of choice.

George joins the list of contemporary characters who drink their way through their fictions. Ask students to recall Austin's statement, in *True West*, that we "all sound alike when we're sloshed." Does the statement apply to Beattie's portrait of George? As George drinks, Beattie shifts to passive voice: "another bottle has been opened." The point of the sentence seems to be that no one knows who has opened the bottle; agency unknown reflects the post-modern dysfunction.

How do students respond to Lenore's last action in the story, as she moves next to George on the couch? Beattie writes that Lenore leans her head on George's shoulder "as if he could protect her from the awful things he has wished into being." Lenore ends by giving George credit for "wishing" the existence of "awful things" in the world. Is this what Beattie means by "simple"? Does Lenore stay with George because she can attribute to him the agony of not being in touch? Because she can listen to him teach that "there can be too much communication between people," and therefore not have to look too closely at herself? Does "simple" mean attributing the state of the contemporary world to some other, human, agency, rather than focusing more clearly on the unknown agency of passive voice?

LESLIE MARMON SILKO

At that point early in "Lullaby" at which Ayah does not want to think about her dead son, she thinks instead "about the weaving and the way her mother had done it." Craft defends against sorrow, for Ayah, and for Silko, who weaves the loss of Native American tribal culture into Ayah's lullaby at the end of the story. Yet the promise passed down from generation to generation of Indian children from their mothers has been broken: "We are together always . . . There never was a time when this was not so." Ask students to explore thematic similarities between Silko's story and others in the post-1945 section. Like Stone, Mason, Shepard, Walker, and Beattie, Silko also portrays the family in dissolution; however, Ayah has lost her children to the Bureau of Indian Affairs and to cultural assimilation with white people. It is not possible for her to reclaim them or to restore her sense of family. The loss of the possibility of family affects the relationship between Ayah and Chato, as it does the relationship between Elliot and Grace in Stone's "Helping"; and, like Elliot, Chato and many other Native American men in "Lullaby" turn to alcohol to numb their despair. Ayah does not drink; her experience makes the men afraid of her and to look at her "like she was a spider crawling slowly across the room." Ask students to compare Ayah with the mother in Gertrude Simmons Bonnin's [Zitkala-Sä's] "Impressions of an Indian Childhood" (included in Vol. 2), and to compare Bonnin's portrait of the removal of Native American children from their reservations with Silko's, almost a hundred years later. Ask students to examine the problems in the mother-daughter relationship that Alice Walker portrays in "Everyday Use" when Dee also "emigrates" to another culture.

DENISE CHÁVEZ

Like her contemporaries included here, Chávez also writes about loss; but, unlike most others, she sees in loss some potential for growth, choice, and humor. Although references to Mexican and Chicano/Chicana culture pervade "The Last of the Menu Girls"—the "half lost melodies" of "Cielito Lindo," the illegal alien Juan Maria the Nose—Rocio Esquibel seems to see her own life as a menu, herself on the verge of making "that awesome leap into myself." When she does begin school and a new life, then has an accident that makes her a patient at Altavista Memorial, she experiences firsthand how rapidly things change: "No one took my menu order. I guess that system had finally died out . . . " Despite the humor of "The Last of the Menu Girls," Chávez also hints at some serious questions. Will it be Rocio's and Chávez's goal to expand the choices on the Chicana "menu"? Do "wetbacks and healthy college students" represent the two extremes of possibility for young Mexican-Americans, or are there other models? If Rocio refuses to nurse the dying, will she find a living Chicano/Chicana culture to nourish? When she returns to Altavista as a patient, Rocio's sister thinks she has lost part of her nose in the accident. What does link Rocio with Juan Maria the wetback? If Rocio emigrates beyond the world of Altavista Memorial, will she return to her childhood culture only as an alien? Is the Chicano/Chicana writer who chooses to write in English, and thus becomes accessible in the American literature classroom (and thus, teachable by English Departments instead of Spanish Departments), a kind of literary "wetback"? Or is she creating a model, a menu, of assimilation into biculturalism?

LOUISE ERDRICH

Like the two brothers in *True West*, the two Lamartine brothers in "Lulu's Boys," and indeed Lulu's boys themselves, become interconnected, their identities complementary and even interchangeable. Yet Erdrich works the complementarity to a different purpose than does Sam Shepard. Beverly Lamartine becomes a hero of contemporary Native American tribal culture in "Lulu's Boys," for he leaves behind Minneapolis, where "there were great relocation opportunities for Indians with a certain amount of natural stick-to-itiveness and pride," to return "westward," as Erdrich describes his trip, "over the state line and on across to the casual and lonely fields, the rich, dry violet hills of the reservation." For Beverly, the reservation represents home because Lulu's Henry Junior is a boy he considers his son. Is Erdrich suggesting here that contemporary urban Native Americans ironically associate "true west" with life on the reservation? Or is she writing a parable of lost paternity?

Certainly, parenthood is a problem for a decimated culture; recall Silko's "Lullaby" with your students. Bev's attempt to find a boy to father, however, expresses a hope of redemption for the American family that few characters in contemporary fiction share. Specifically compare the moments of Ayah's reunion with Ella, in "Lullaby," with Bev's reunion with Henry Junior. Bev encounters "a moment of confusion at the utter indifference in the boy's eyes," but unlike Ayah, Bev has a chance to make reparation for all the absent fathers, especially for the drunk Henry who commits suicide on the train tracks.

Ask students to look at Erdrich's implicit use of Native American imagery in her portraits of Bev and Henry. Specifically, Lulu remembers each brother by their tattoos, contemporary equivalents of Indian names: for example, might Bev, given his act of heroism in choosing to risk the return to domesticity and intimacy in Lulu's arms, in tribal culture have earned some kind of bird's name? Might he have been called Lone Swallow or Soaring Eagle? Despite Lulu's presence in the story's title, Erdrich's story tells Bev's tale, and it is a tale of flight. Even Bev's working class urban Indian customers, who buy his workbook sets, envision their children as "fledglings before they learn how to glide."

Compare and contrast Erdrich's Beverly Lamartine with Flannery O'Connor's Bible salesman, Manly Pointer, in "Good Country People." Recall Hawthorne's Wakefield, for students who have read that story. Erdrich tells a different tale in "Lulu's Boys." Or does she? Consider the portrait of Lulu as a woman who "seemed to fill pots with food by pointing at them and take things from the oven that she'd never put in." Has Erdrich given us the portrait of Bev's heroic return to domesticity, only to sacrifice the freedom of Lulu herself, or at least her realism? Lulu, like Ann Beattie's Lenore in "Weekend," inhabits "the sacred domain of her femininity." Is that the price Lulu must pay for easing the fragmented family?

AMERICAN POETRY SINCE 1945

You may find the general introduction to the "American Poetry Since 1945" period extremely useful for your own preparation in the classroom. After building the introduction on the work of three generations of post-war, 1960s and 1970s era, and contemporary 1980s poets, the editors comment on "the distinctive work of individual writers" who produce dazzling poems apart from major trends. They write, "the living world of contemporary poetry changes; new poets emerge, and existing poets, previously inaccessible or neglected, make themselves heard." In the interweaving of individual poems and groups of poets who wrote in the context of each other's work, of poetic influence that crosses generations and ethnic boundaries, and of shapes and sizes of poems, the introduction recalls for me the experience of wandering down the spiral ramp inside the Boston Aquarium, or watching the vertical tanks in the Monterey Bay Aquarium.

The anthology section becomes such an aquarium, poems and poets selected because they represent their kind, show how large and small can cohabit, resemble others and swim in schools, emerge remarkably to follow their own pursuits, and, above all, alter the viewer's perception of the depths, shapes, movement, and ecological balance of the microcosm of marine life. We associate some poets with "schools"—Vanderbilt, Black Mountain, Iowa; others, such as Niedecker, wrote without participating in any literary community. Some poets resemble their mentors; others deny their influence after incorporating the techniques of their predecessors. The possibilities of extending the metaphor may seem endless, but the point is somehow to provide a larger view for students that will give them a point of entry. No single class or course can teach undergraduate students all there is to know about American Poetry Since 1945, but with the help of the general introduction to the period, the anthologized selections, and your own personal preferences, you may at least facilitate for your students the experience of knowing certain poets are in the "tank" and watching some of them swim by.

Coincidentally, I like to introduce contemporary American poetry with Robert Lowell's "For the Union Dead," which opens with an image of the speaker pressing his nose against the glass of the old South Boston Aquarium. This poem first appeared in *Life Studies*, one of the collections that the editors credit with administering a "transforming shock" to post-war American poetry. The poem explores Lowell's autobiographical relationship to massive upheavals in American life and challenges readers not to be cowed, compliant, or servile. Other significant poems also reflect marine imagery: Lorine Niedecker's "Paean to Place," Elizabeth Bishop's "The Fish," James Wright's "With the Shell of a Hermit Crab," Anne Sexton's "Lobster," Adrienne Rich's "Diving into the Wreck," and Lorna Dee Cervantes's "Starfish." Together with "For the Union Dead," Rich's "Diving into the Wreck" can serve as a frame for your discussion of the material.

As the editors observe, "Many American poets do not want to think of their work as the fragments of modern literature." The general introduction to the period pulls the fragments together. In my own observations about the poetry, I have considered the general introduction as itself a "course guide," and in making the notes that follow, I hope merely to augment its usefulness as a way to organize your own classroom preparations or course outline. The editors describe their generalizations as provisional; the classroom can become, in part, a testing ground for what we can say about a body of literature that continues to change shape almost as we read it.

The individual headnotes will also help you manage your task of introducing students to the works. When in doubt about your own familiarity with a poet, work directly from the headnote, asking students to place the editors' statements against individual poems to see whether they make sense. In writing Exam Questions and Essay Topics for this section (see Chapter 7 of the Guide), I have worked from specific statements in the headnotes, and you may find these questions useful to organize classroom discussion.

As the period introduction observes, many of these writers learned their craft while majoring in English or studying with professors of English in colleges and universities. Contemporary poets have created their own industry and their own markets for their products by giving readings, teaching in writers' workshops, staffing Creative Writing programs, and working by means of writing book reviews and media commentary to promote the readership for their work. Both as students and consumers, then, we are all likely to encounter living poets; indeed, we may argue that our poets are made and not born, and that, for reasons we may not yet understand, our poets serve a socially and culturally useful function. Ask students to consider whether, as consumers and present or future taxpayers (who fund some of the grants that keep poets alive), they are getting anything that is useful to them. What are, or ought to be, the "uses" of poetry in contemporary American life? If you have read "Rip Van Winkle" with students a semester ago, ask them to consider whether the role of the American writer has changed since Washington Irving's time (see discussion of "Rip Van Winkle" in the Course Guide). Do we still need poet-chroniclers to tell us where we have been, where we are going? How much farther down the path—than we—are our poets? Do they truly see new directions we should follow? Can we trust them? What might we want our poets to do for us that they seem not to be doing at present?

In beginning to teach individual poets or poems, I choose the works I know and the writers I love. I also ask students to survey the Table of Contents for the "American Poetry Since 1945" section and to identify those poets and poems they recognize. Those works can become useful starting points for the rest of us, and I ask students to identify the points of contact they may have with the large body of texts included here. I may then work from their responses to the question concerning the "uses" of poetry to help match them up with unfamiliar poets or poems. If someone believes, for example, that poetry should make us aware of the fragility of our environment, I send them off to read Gary Snyder or Galway Kinnell. If students want to hear a strong woman's voice, I assign Adrienne Rich or Audre Lorde. Much as contemporary poets from all ethnic and regional backgrounds may be said to write for all of us, it can seem helpful to students interested in finding common ground to know what regions or ethnic groups individual poets represent.

Or they may identify with biographical details. Does it interest students to know that Robert Duncan never met his mother because she died at birth, that Richard Hugo's mother abandoned him, or that Elizabeth Bishop lost both parents by the time she was five and was raised by relatives? that Berryman, Plath, and Sexton committed suicide? that Levertov was born British? that Lowell and Roethke suffered nervous breakdowns? that Niedecker wrote "on the margins" of literary culture? that Robert Hayden was raised by foster parents? that Rich, Lorde, Duncan, Ginsberg, and Merrill made lesbian and gay choices in their personal lives? that Baraka changed his name from Leroi Jones? Assign students the task of choosing to read one new poet based on purely biographical, ethical, or regional information; then ask them to write briefly, even in class, about their reading experience. To what extent does familiarity or strangeness motivate their choice? To what extent does their choice become self-disclosing for them?

Consider, as well, your own training and predilections. What "works" for you? Having early been taught to "close read" individual poems, I pass the method along to students, balancing the need for coverage with luxurious class time on single poems. What kind of training did you have, and what would you like your students to have? Do you want them to be able to move beyond "close reading" to see larger intersections between poems and poets, between poetry and prose, between poetry and contemporary culture, between poetry and politics? Are any students willing to challenge your own approach with their own? Do any wish to read their own poems to the class?

EXAM QUESTIONS AND ESSAY TOPICS

The teaching notes in Chapter 5 contain many questions that you may easily adapt as topics for writing. In offering the following additional exam questions and essay topics, I have tried to suggest further directions for student thinking and research that may or may not emerge directly from class discussion. The first and most extensive set lists questions that address literary, historical, and genre connections between authors, followed in each period by questions related to the interpretation of some individual authors and texts. The second set includes problems and topics that emerge from examining authors within their own literary traditions or that focus on comparing authors across traditions.

I

VOLUME 1

1620–1820

HISTORICAL QUESTIONS

1. Define some of the basic concepts of Puritan ideology and illustrate their significance in specific works. Choose from among the following: (a) "new world" consciousness; (b) covenant theology; (c) typology; (d) innate depravity; and (e) irresistible grace. A few of the writers who address each of these concepts, and whom you will need to discuss, include: (a) Bradford and Bradstreet; (b) Bradford, Wigglesworth, and Edwards; (c) Bradstreet (in "Here Follows Some Verses upon the Burning of Our House"), Taylor, Winthrop, and Wigglesworth; (d) Taylor, Wigglesworth, and Edwards; and (e) Winthrop and Edwards.

2. Trace the connection between the Puritans' reliance on written covenant in Bradford's "The Mayflower Compact" and their emphasis on didactic to the exclusion of dramatic or personal vision in their literature.

3. Octavio Paz, among others, has called Puritan society a culture based on the principle of exclusion. Discuss, with particular

references to literary works, the evidence of this principle in Puritan life and culture.

4. Consider secular consequences of Puritan theology: the Puritans' attitudes toward Indians, ordinary life, witches, house servants, slavery, and infant damnation. Choose two of these topics and explore their treatment in literary works from the period.

5. Identify and discuss literary texts that reveal stresses on Puritanism or that illustrate schisms within Puritan and colonial consciousness.

6. Explore the contrast between personal and didactic voice in Puritan and early colonial literature.

7. Identify the literary forms available to colonial American writers. What limited their choice? How did they invent within these forms? What forms would survive for later writers to work within?

8. Cite several fundamental differences between Puritan thinking and deist thinking. Analyze specific literary works that illustrate these differences.

9. Describe the way the concepts of the self and of self-reliance develop and find expression in colonial and early American literature. Identify those specific figures or works that you see as significant and explain their contributions.

10. Trace the power of the written convenant in colonial and early American literature, beginning with "The Mayflower Compact."

11. Discuss the ways in which Benjamin Franklin and Thomas Jefferson alter the content of Puritan thinking without changing its form. How do their writings reflect earlier forms?

12. Slavery is an issue of conscience for some colonial and early American writers; for others it is fraught with ambivalence. Discuss the issue with references to several specific texts.

QUESTIONS ON INDIVIDUAL AUTHORS AND WORKS

Anne Bradstreet

1. Write a close analysis of a single lyric poem. Depending on how much analysis you have already done in class, choose from among the following: "The Prologue," "The Flesh and the Spirit," "The Author to Her Book," "Here Follows Some Verses upon the Burning of Our House," "As Weary Pilgrim."

2. Analyze a related series of stanzas from "Contemplations," and then discuss the relationship between these particular stanzas and the entire poem.

3. Compare and contrast the imagery of "To My Dear and Loving Husband" with Taylor's "Huswifery." How does the imagery characterize each poet's work?

4. Discuss the extent to which Bradstreet's poetry reflects Puritan thinking. Analyze in particular the way Bradstreet reflects her own spiritual and metaphysical fears in the process of describing an actual event in "Here Follows Some Verses upon the Burning of Our House."

5. Analyze the contrast between form and feeling in Bradstreet's work. In what ways does she use self-disclosure as a challenge to Puritan theology?

6. Trace imagery of nurturance and provision in Bradstreet's lyrics. Reread with particular attention to maternal and paternal imagery and references.

Edward Taylor

1. Write a close analysis of any of the poems from *Preparatory Meditations*. Identify the central metaphor or series of related metaphors, and describe the process by which Taylor converts the terms of each metaphor into an assurance of his own salvation.

2. Discuss the title of Taylor's group of poems, *Preparatory Meditations*. How does the title reflect his sense of the purpose of poetry?

3. Trace Taylor's use of objects from the natural world or of secular experience in "Upon Wedlock, and Death of Children," "Upon a Wasp Chilled with Cold," or "A Fig for Thee, Oh! Death," and examine the relationship in the poem between earthly life and spiritual salvation.

4. Discuss the extent to which Taylor's poetry reflects specific concepts of Puritan theology.

William Byrd

1. Write an essay in which you compare and contrast Byrd's "The Secret Diary of William Byrd of Westover 1709–1712" with a work by any of his New England contemporaries. Does Byrd reveal a colonial consciousness that transcends a specifically Puritan ideology?

Jonathan Edwards

1. Analyze the form and significance of "A Divine and Supernatural Light." (This topic works well if you have already analyzed "Sinners in the Hands of an Angry God" closely in class.)

2. Discuss Edwards's manipulation of biblical language in "Sinners in the Hands of an Angry God." What specific transforma-

tions does he perform? And how does his use of language in the "Application" section of the sermon differ from and comment on the earlier doctrinal section?

3. Discuss the fact that Jonathan Edwards and Benjamin Frankin were contemporaries. Explain, with specific references to their works and more general comments on their ideas, why this fact seems startling. (I expect students to consider scientific influences on Edwards and a Puritan heritage on Franklin.)

4. Write a brief comparative analysis of form and function in Edward Taylor's poems and Jonathan Edwards's sermons. (Students need to see the way each of these Puritans tried to demonstrate or even "prove," in Edwards's case, spiritual salvation, and the way each associates being saved with the authority of being able to find the right language.)

5. Discuss the following statement, from *The Nature of True Virtue*, in light of colonial American history: "Things are in natural regularity . . . when he whose heart opposes the general system, should have the hearts of that system, or the heart of the ruler of the system, against him . . . " Include in your discussion both the decision of the Puritans to settle in the New World and the later struggle of the colonists for independence.

Benjamin Franklin

1. Explain why the eighteenth century was called the Age of Experiment and consider the relevance of this term as a description of Franklin's writing.

2. Analyze the numerous metaphors Franklin uses in Poor Richard's maxims in "The Way to Wealth." Count and categorize the metaphors; summarize your findings. What are their origins, and how does he use them?

3. What is the "religion" Franklin "preaches" to his readers in Father Abraham's speech? How do you explain Franklin's use of religious metaphors in his writing?

4. Discuss several permanent contributions Franklin made to American life, ranging from the practical to the ideological.

5. Choose any single section or aspect of *The Autobiography* as the basis for analysis. *Or* contrast Franklin's choice of focus in its four parts; consider the significance of his choice to address the book to his son; read closely the letters that begin Part Two and comment on their significance to *The Autobiography* as a whole; discuss Franklin's various practical attempts to alter his moral character.

6. Following notes from class discussion, explain the various ways in which Franklin's *Autobiography* may be seen as "self-invention."

Elizabeth Ashbridge

1. Trace Elizabeth Ashbridge's search for voice in *Some Account of the Fore-Part of the Life of Elizabeth Ashbridge*. Incorporate in your discussion her response to the voices of others, especially spiritual voices.

2. Compare Elizabeth Ashbridge with Anne Bradstreet. How do their attitudes toward writing, motherhood, and God illuminate their similarities and their differences? How do their attitudes illuminate differences between Puritans and Quakers?

3. Trace Ashbridge's thought process in *Some Account of the Fore-Part of the Life of Elizabeth Ashbridge*. By what logical arguments does she reject what she terms "priestcraft" and come to accept herself as a Quaker? To what extent does Ashbridge rely on contextual experience in making decisions?

John Woolman

1. Compare the specific imagery of *The Journal of John Woolman* with that of Jonathan Edwards's "Personal Narrative," with the goal of demonstrating differences between Woolman's religious beliefs and world view and those of the Puritans.

2. Compare and contrast John Woolman's *Journal* with Elizabeth Ashbridge's *Some Account*. What can we infer about Quaker life in the colonies from these two writers? To what extent are differences in their narratives attributable to gender?

St. Jean de Crèvecoeur

1. For eighteenth-century writer St. Jean de Crèvecoeur, witnessing slavery firsthand leads him to lament the "strange order of things" in "Letter IX" from *Letters from an American Farmer*. Analyze the difficulty he has reconciling the existence of slavery and the great contrast between lives of plantation owners and slaves in Charles-Town with his own belief in a "sublime hand which guides the planets round the sun."

John and Abigail Adams

1. Compare and contrast one of Abigail Adams's letters to John with one of Anne Bradstreet's poems that serve as letters to her husband, absent upon public employment. How does Bradstreet's use of eighteenth-century poetic forms constrain feeling? How does feeling alter the potential for form in Adams's letters?

2. The letters that pass between John and Abigail Adams during the month of July, 1776, locate *The Declaration of Independence* within a context of private meaning. Examine the hopes these writers have for independence, and identify those that are not explicit within the document itself.

3. Debate the plausibility of the following statement: "The frequent intrusions of personal feeling into the letters of John and Abigail Adams reflect more than the intersection of personal and public life; they also suggest a change in values that would inspire other political and cultural revolutions at the turn of the nineteenth century."

Thomas Jefferson

1. Analyze specific ways in which *The Declaration of Independence* demonstrates the influence of eighteenth-century thought.

2. Based on class discussion, recapitulate the ways *The Declaration of Independence* uses literary devices to achieve its power.

3. Describe the evidence of Franklin's interests in "self-invention" in *The Autobiography*, and suggest ways in which Jefferson, with the assistance of Franklin, carries these interests into the political sphere of *The Declaration of Independence*.

4. Write a linguistic analysis of the antislavery grievance from "The Declaration of Independence" that the Continental Congress eliminated from its final version.

5. Edwin Gittelman has called *The Declaration of Independence* a slave narrative. In the colonial period, the only indigenous precedent for such a form was the Indian captivity narrative, represented in the *NAAL* by *Narrative of the Captivity and Restoration of Mrs. Mary Rowlandson*. Compare and contrast the form of Rowlandson's narrative with Jefferson's text, and explore the extent to which *The Declaration of Independence* may be considered a variant on the genre of Indian captivity narrative.

Olaudah Equiano

1. Examine those points of resemblance between Elizabeth Ashbridge's *Some Account* and Olaudah Equiano's *Narrative*. What does Ashbridge confirm about the horrors of servitude? What does Equiano tell us about the role the quakers played in the struggle for human freedom?

2. Reread the early chapters of Bradford's *Of Plymouth Plantation* and contrast the portrait of life aboard the *Mayflower* with Equiano's account of life aboard the slave ship. Consider the various meanings different colonial authors attribute to the word "removal."

Philip Freneau

1. Although Freneau's "To Sir Toby" is ostensibly about a sugar planter on the island of Jamaica, examine the poem for evidence that Freneau is also writing about Southern slavery. Locate references to slavery in his other anthologized poems, as well, and summarize the way slavery, for Freneau, contradicts eighteenth-century principles of reason and rights of man.

2. Evaluate the language of Freneau's historical poems against specific passages in Paine or Jefferson, and discuss the relative effectiveness of political and poetic voices within the context of American revolution.

Phillis Wheatley

1. Locate and discuss imagery in Wheatley's poems that directly or indirectly comments on her experience as a freed slave.

Royall Tyler

1. Explicate *The Contrast's* "Prologue" as Tyler's commentary on his own play.

2. Analyze references to style and fashion in *The Contrast*. Discuss ways in which Tyler uses these to convey the beginnings of American cultural identity.

1820–1865

HISTORICAL QUESTIONS

1. Discuss the following statement with reference and relevance to specific literary works: The Puritans were typological; the eighteenth-century writers were logical; but the early nineteenth-century writers were analogical in their way of knowing and expressing what it means to be an American.

2. Discuss changes in the concept of the American self in the early nineteenth century. Locate your discussion within specific works by Emerson, Thoreau, and Hawthorne.

3. Cite several fundamental differences between early nineteenth-century writers and their deist predecessors. Focus on the concept of self-invention, and, in specific literary works, discuss the early nineteenth-century evolution of this concept.

4. Research and explain the theory of romantic organicism in Bryant and Poe, at the same time exploring differences between these two poets.

5. Consider literary portraits of women engaged in heroic struggle or of escaping slaves portrayed as heroic fugitives. Compare and contrast portraits by Stowe, Fuller, and Douglass with Hester Prynne in *The Scarlet Letter* or Thoreau's autobiographical narrator in *Walden*.

6. Read some of Elizabeth Cady Stanton's lectures, addresses, and letters (not anthologized). Then compare and contrast "The Declaration of Sentiments" (1848, see Appendix) with its model, *The Declaration of Independence*. Analyze the nineteenth-century document with respect to style, imagery, concepts of nature and authority, and relative political effect.

7. Whether or not the earliest American realists wrote in a distinctive and innovative form, they make different choices of language and genre than their contemporaries. Choose to analyze a text by any of the following writers and explore elements of realism in the work: Longstreet, Stowe, Thorpe, Hooper, Stoddard, or Davis.

QUESTIONS ON INDIVIDUAL AUTHORS AND WORKS

Washington Irving

1. Compare and contrast Freneau's and Irving's uses of the historical situation as the subject of imaginative literature. What makes Irving more successful, and why is he more successful?

2. Discuss several different ways in which "Rip Van Winkle" addresses versions of the American dream.

3. Compare Rip Van Winkle with Franklin's Father Abraham in "The Way to Wealth." What do the two have in common?

4. "Rip Van Winkle" is an early work that casts the American woman as the cultural villain. Analyze the character of Dame Van Winkle in the story and discuss the significance Irving attributes to her death.

5. Although Irving's "Rip Van Winkle" and "The Legend of Sleepy Hollow" may make it appear that Irving wrote primarily fiction, a reading of the longer *Sketch-Book*, in which these stories first appeared, makes it clear that for Irving, himself, writing the literary sketch both preceded and made it possible for him to write works we now consider stories. For an out-of-class essay, read *The Sketch-Book* and write an essay in which you describe the various literary genres that Irving uses in the book. Then focus on either "Rip Van Winkle" or "The Legend of Sleepy Hollow" and explore both what the story's form shares with the other works in *The Sketch-Book* and

how it deviates from them. Speculate on what, in either story, makes it possible for Irving to cross over into fiction.

Augustus Baldwin Longstreet and the "Southwest Humorists"

1. Create a composite type of the Southwest humorist story-teller by analyzing the narrators in one tale by each of Longstreet, Thorpe, Hooper, and Harris.

2. Critics have noted the influence of Washington Irving's "The Legend of Sleepy Hollow" on the development of Southwest humor. Analyze Irving's character Brom Bones as a precursor of Sut Lovingood or another "ring-tailed roarer" from the humorist group.

3. Contrast the portrait of women in Longstreet's "A Sage Conversation" and Harris's "Mrs. Yardley's Quilting" with Stowe's portrait of Huldy in "The Minister's Housekeeper." Generalize, to comment on the divergence between "Southwest humor" and early regionalism.

4. Read Samuel Clemens's short essay, "How to Tell a Story" (*NAAL*, Vol. 2). Choose one of the tales by the Southwest humorists and evaluate the humor and the effectiveness of the narrator by Clemens's standards.

William Cullen Bryant

1. In his essays, Emerson repeatedly called for the emergence of an American poet. Focusing on Bryant's "The Prairies," argue that Bryant satisfied, in part, Emerson's demand. In what ways does Bryant move away from imitating British poetry? In what ways does the poem address American themes?

Ralph Waldo Emerson

1. Discuss one of the following statements from *Nature*:
   (a) "The use of natural history is to give us aid in super-natural history. The use of the outer creation, to give us language for the beings and changes of the inward creation."
   (b) "A man is a god in ruins. When men are innocent, life shall be longer, and shall pass into the immortal as gently as we awake from dreams."

2. Trace Emerson's thinking, image patterns, and particular forms of expression in one of the poems.

3. Explain why the poet is so important for Emerson, summarizing his argument in "The Poet."

4. Discuss the usefulness of analogy for Emerson. Choose several analogies he creates in *Nature* and explain their significance.

5. Explore any one of the following central concepts in Emerson's work in the context of your reading: the spiritual vision of unity with nature; the significance of language in achieving spiritual vision; basic differences between thinking and writing by means of analogy and by means of discursive logic; the theme of self-reliance; the significance of self-expression.

6. Explain how Emerson's philosophy, as he expresses it in *Nature*, represents the culmination of what it means to be an American in his time and place.

7. Explore what Emerson says, explicitly or implicitly, about race, class, or gender in American culture, and analyze Emerson's position in light of subsequent American history and political thought. If you choose to interpret Emerson from within an ideological position, define the terms of that position and analyze the way it distorts at the same time that it illuminates Emerson's work.

Nathaniel Hawthorne

1. Explicate character, theme, language patterns, style, use of point of view, setting, or design in any particular short story or in *The Scarlet Letter*. (The problem with assigning one of these topics, of course, is that you then have to deal with the standard interpretations students are likely to find if they go straight to the library. If I use a version of this question, I use it in in-class writing where the only book they may use is the *NAAL*.)

2. View the video adaptation (if you have one in your library) of "Young Goodman Brown." After examining the way the video interprets Brown's dream, argue that the adaptation is or is not a useful "reading" of the story.

3. Explain what Melville means by Hawthorne's "blackness" in his essay "Hawthorne and His Mosses" and discuss it with specific references to any two of the stories in the text (or any three, or with reference to specific characters in *The Scarlet Letter*).

4. Explore the moral ambiguity in any given Hawthorne character or work. What does reading "Rappaccini's Daughter" (or "The Minister's Black Veil" or "Young Goodman Brown") do to the reader's ability to discern "good" and "evil" characters?

5. Consider Hawthorne's presentation of women in his fiction. What attitudes inform his portraits of Beatrice Rappaccini, or of Hester Prynne?

6. Consider the relationship between "The Custom-House" and *The Scarlet Letter*. Where does the narrator stand in each work? In what ways might we consider "The Custom-House" an integral part of the longer fiction? Consider the particular use of "The Cus-

tom-House" as a way of "explaining" or delaying the fiction: might "The Custom-House" serve as Hawthorne's "black veil" in facing his readers?

7. Given the autobiographical references in "The Custom-House," consider the possibility that each of the major characters in *The Scarlet Letter* might also be aspects of the narrator's own persona. Discuss ways in which Hester Prynne, Arthur Dimmesdale, Roger Chillingworth, and Pearl complement each other thematically.

8. Given your earlier study of Puritan literature, trace elements of Puritanism in Hawthorne's stories or *The Scarlet Letter*, and discuss the extent to which Hawthorne himself embraces or critiques Puritan ideology. (Compare actual Puritans you have studied with Hawthorne's fictional characters: Anne Bradstreet with Hester Prynne; Edward Taylor with Arthur Dimmesdale; Jonathan Edwards with various ministers in Hawthorne, or with the narrator himself.)

9. Locate references to childhood in *The Scarlet Letter* and, focusing on Pearl, discuss Hawthorne's portrait of what it might have been like to be a Puritan child.

Edgar Allan Poe

1. Summarize Poe's theory of aesthetics as he expresses it in "The Philosophy of Composition" and discuss his application of that philosophy in "The Raven."

2. Explicate a short lyric ("The Lake," "Preface," or "To Helen") and discuss Poe's creation of the persona of the poet.

3. Discuss "The Sleeper," "The Raven," "Annabel Lee," and "Ligeia" in light of Poe's statement, in "The Philosophy of Composition," that "the death, then, of a beautiful woman is, unquestionably, the most poetical topic in the world—and equally is it beyond doubt that the lips best suited for such topic are those of a bereaved lover."

4. Explain what Poe means by his attempt to achieve "unity of effect," and trace the particular ways he manages this in "Fall of the House of Usher," "The Man of the Crowd," or "The Black Cat."

Margaret Fuller

1. Read the excerpt from Margaret Fuller's "The Great Lawsuit," published the year before Emerson published "The Poet." Focusing on comparison with Emerson, discuss Fuller's critique of the masculine assumptions of her generation of intellectuals.

2. At the end of the anthologized excerpt from "The Great Lawsuit," Fuller writes: "And will not she soon appear? The woman who shall vindicate their birthright for all women; who shall teach them what to claim, and how to use what they obtain?" Going be-

yond the boundaries of the *NAAL*, investigate the appearance of women speakers and political writers during the 1840s, when Fuller published her work. Research the work of Elizabeth Cady Stanton, in particular (see the Appendix to the Course Guide for the text of Stanton's "The Declaration of Sentiments," 1848), and argue that, just as Whitman fulfilled Emerson's prophecy at the end of "The Poet," Stanton "soon appeared" to provide the context of continuity for the developing voices of American women in the new Republic.

Harriet Beecher Stowe

1. From its origins in Harriet Beecher Stowe, regionalism as a genre took women characters and women's values seriously. Analyze Stowe's portraits of Eliza in the excerpt from *Uncle Tom's Cabin* and Huldy in "The Minister's Housekeeper," and discuss the values explicit in Stowe's work.

2. Stowe's regional sketch, "The Minister's Housekeeper," ends in comedy, with Huldy's marriage to the minister. Argue that the sketch does or does not belong to the literary tradition of early nineteenth-century American humor.

Henry David Thoreau

1. Discuss one of the following statements from *Walden*:
    (a) "Every morning . . . I got up early and bathed in the pond; that was a religious exercise, and one of the best things which I did."
    (b) "I fear chiefly lest my expression may not be *extra-vagant* enough, may not wander far enough beyond the narrow limits of my daily experience, so as to be adequate to the truth of which I have been convinced."

2. Cite several points of connection and divergence between Emerson's *Nature* and Thoreau's *Walden*.

3. Discuss in detail one point of significant comparison between Franklin's *Autobiography* and Thoreau's *Walden* and one point of significant contrast.

4 Explain specific ways in which Thoreau's *Walden* may be considered "practice" to Emerson's theory.

5. Emerson, whose philosophy influenced Thoreau, wrote that "words are also actions, and actions are a kind of words." Write an essay on *Walden* in which you demonstrate Thoreau's insistence on the truth of this statement or apply the same quotation from Emerson to "Resistance to Civil Government," paying particular attention to the relationship between self-expression and personal conscience.

6. Explore any of the following central concepts in Thoreau: the spiritual vision of unity with nature; the significance of language in achieving such a vision; the theme of self-reliance; the use of analogy as meditation (perhaps contrasting Thoreau with Edward Taylor); the significance of self-expression.

Frederick Douglass

1. Discuss the extent to which Douglass may be considered a transcendentalist.

2. Compare and contrast the way Douglass sets himself up as a model with the way Benjamin Franklin does it in *The Autobiography.*

3. Douglass writes his slave narrative as a series of incidents or adventures. Discuss the picaresque elements of the *Narrative of the Life of Frederick Douglass.*

4. Read Harriet Jacobs, *Incidents in the Life of a Slave Girl,* and compare it with Douglass's *Narrative.* Was the model of "heroic fugitive" possible for female slaves? Jacobs's *Incidents* depicts the network of relationships within the slave community and between black and white communities. Look for evidence of such a network in Douglass's *Narrative.* What explains Douglass's lack of attention to emotional connections?

5. In his prefatory letter to the *Narrative,* abolitionist Wendell Phillips compares Douglass to the signers of "The Declaration of Independence": "You, too, publish your declaration of freedom with danger compassing you around." Does the *Narrative* share formal similarities with "The Declaration of Independence" as well as rhetorical ones? Compare Jefferson's characterization of the British king and his itemizing of grievances with the design and structure of Douglass's *Narrative.*

6. Compare and contrast *A Narrative of the Captivity and Restoration of Mrs. Mary Rowlandson* with *Narrative of the Life of Frederick Douglass, an American Slave.* What formal, thematic, and historical continuities exist between these indigenous genres?

Walt Whitman

1. Write an essay in which you analyze "A Noiseless Patient Spider" (or "I Sit and Look Out," or any other short lyric poem) within the context of "Song of Myself."

2. Focusing on the following two quotations—from *Nature,* "I become a transparent eyeball. I am nothing. I see all," and from "Preface to *Leaves of Grass,*" "[the greatest poet] is a seer . . . is individual . . . he is complete in himself. . . . What the eyesight does to

the rest he does to the rest"—discuss thematic, philosophical, and technical connections between Emerson and Whitman.

3. Compare Emerson's "The Poet" with "Preface to *Leaves of Grass*." In what ways does Whitman claim to embody Emerson's idea of the American poet?

4. Choose one of the following quotations from "Song of Myself" and discuss it by suggesting several ways in which it describes what Whitman is attempting in the poem:

(a) "I know I am solid and sound, / To me the converging objects of the universe perpetually flow, / All are written to me, and I must get what the writing means."

(b) "I am an acme of things accomplish'd, and I am an encloser of things to be."

(c) "I know I have the best of time and space, and was never measured and never will be measured."

5. Discuss Whitman's poetry as a culmination point in the development of American identity. How does Whitman contribute to the ongoing evolution of self-reliance? of human freedom? of concepts of democracy?

6. Analyze the form of "The Sleepers." How does the speaker characterize himself? Is the poem a variation on an American dream?

7. Trace Whitman's various responses to the Civil War throughout the poems anthologized from *Drum-Taps*. Compare and contrast Whitman's war poems with the anthologized lyrics from Melville's *Battle-Pieces*.

8. Do a study of Whitman's use of the catalogue as a poetic device. Then illustrate, by means of close analysis, the effects Whitman achieves in a particular catalogue from "Song of Myself," or in the poems "There Was a Child Went Forth" or "The Sleepers."

9. Alternatively: Study and illustrate Whitman's use of parallel construction as a poetic device in the same poems.

10. Analyze Whitman's extensive use of ecstatic language in "Passage to India." How does it differ from the language of "Song of Myself"? How does "Passage to India" refine Whitman's vision?

Herman Melville

1. Argue that in describing Hawthorne's "power of blackness" in his review of *Mosses*, Melville was actually characterizing his own work. Focus on *Benito Cereno* in your analysis, and consider whether or not Melville focuses on black slaves as human beings.

2. Newton Arvin has written about *Benito Cereno* that "the story is an artistic miscarriage, with moments of undeniable power." Evaluate the fairness of this statement given your own reading of the story.

3. Imagine a retelling of *Benito Cereno* in which Babo becomes the hero. What particular inconsistencies within the story as it stands would the narrator have to resolve?

4. In "The Town-Ho's Story," Ishmael, the narrator of *Moby-Dick,* relates a tale of mutiny he once narrated—long before "telling" *Moby-Dick* itself—to a group of Spanish friends "smoking upon the thick-gilt tiled piazza of the Golden Inn." The story may appear to be as much a rehearsal for Melville's later stories as it was for *Moby-Dick* itself. Focusing either on *Benito Cereno* or on *Billy Budd, Sailor* in light of "The Town-Ho's Story," examine Melville's later explorations of mutiny or feared mutiny and the characters who develop or refine attributes Melville embodies in Steelkilt and Radney.

5. "The Encantadas" may appear to demonstrate Melville's powers of observation, and yet in these sketches, as in his other work, the narrator locates his fascination as much in the symbolic significance he attributes to nature as in the scene itself. Explore the particular symbolism of "The Encantadas" and link it to the symbolism of any other Melville work you have read in the course.

6. In "The Tartarus of Maids," Melville appears to identify with the maids; in *Billy Budd, Sailor*, he gives Billy feminine characteristics. Reconstruct, from these two works and from Sketch 8 of "The Encantadas," Melville's portrait of the feminine.

7. Part of what fascinates the reader (and possibly Melville himself) about Bartleby is his inscrutability. Describe the various "walls" Bartleby finds himself trapped behind and explore the ways in which the story's structure or design reinforces the reader's inability to penetrate the inscrutability of those walls.

8. Choose any one of the following moments of dialogue in Melville and use it as a prism through which to "read" the work in which it appears:

      (a) "Ah, Bartleby! Ah, humanity!'"

      (b) "Follow your leader.'"

      (c) "God bless Captain Vere!'"

9. Explore the two kinds of justice Melville sets in opposition in *Billy Budd, Sailor* and discuss the moral and thematic consequences of Billy's death.

Emily Dickinson

1. Compare and contrast Whitman's "A Noiseless Patient Spider" with Dickinson's 1138, "A Spider sewed at Night."

Study a group of poems with related themes. Then write an interpretation of one of the poems that includes your expanded understanding of the way Dickinson uses the theme in other poems in the group. Choose from among the following:

      (a) poems of loss and defeat: 49, 67, 305;

(b) poems about ecstasy or vision: 125, 185, 214, 249, 322, 465, 501, 632, 1400;

(c) poems about solitude: 280, 303, 441, 664;

(d) poems about death: 49, 67, 241, 258, 280, 341, 449, 510, 712, 1078, 1100, 1732;

(e) poems about madness and suffering: 315, 348, 435, 536;

(f) poems about entrapment: 187, 528, 640, 754, 1099;

(g) poems about craft: 441, 448, 505, 1129.

3. Poems 130, 328, 348, and 824 all contain images of birds. Trace and analyze the image from poem to poem. Or, study one of the following groups of poems and trace the related image pattern: (a) a bee or bees in 130, 214, 216, 348, 1405; (b) a fly or flies in 187 and 465; (c) butterflies in 214, 341, and 1099; (d) church imagery or biblical references in 130, 216, 258, 322, 640, 1545.

4. Compare and contrast the image of the snake in 986 with that of the worm in 1670.

5. Closely analyze the central image in one of the following poems: 754, "My Life had stood—a Loaded Gun—"; 1099, "My Cocoon tightens—Colors teaze—"; or 1575, "The Bat is dun, with wrinkled Wings—."

6. Locate images of size, particularly of smallness, in Dickinson's poetry. Working out from 185, "'Faith' is a fine invention," trace evidence that Dickinson perceived a relationship between size and literary authority. Alternatively, locate images of authority in the world (king, emperor, gentlemen) and contrast these with images Dickinson uses to create her own persona as poet.

7. Many Dickinson poems illustrate change in the consciousness of the poet or speaker. Choose a poem in which this happens and trace the process by which the poem reflects and creates the change.

Rebecca Harding Davis

1. Compare the relationships between Hester and Dimmesdale in *The Scarlet Letter* and between Hugh Wolfe and Deborah in "Life in the Iron-Mills."

2. Recall what Thoreau has to say in *Walden* about the "lives of quiet desperation" most men lead. Might Hugh Wolfe, like Thoreau, have chosen to simplify his life and retreat to a pond outside of town? Compare and contrast the conditions under which Wolfe makes his art with those Thoreau describes.

3. Study all of Davis's references to Deborah, who is generally depicted as being a "thwarted woman" who leads a "colorless life." Contrast her with the korl woman. Discuss the distance Davis creates between the real and the ideal woman in Wolfe's life.

HISTORICAL QUESTIONS

1. Compare and contrast uses of humor in Clemens, "The Notorious Jumping Frog of Calaveras County"; Harte, "The Outcasts of Poker Flat"; and Freeman, "The Revolt of 'Mother.'"

2. Writers following the Civil War introduced a new strain of pessimism and despair into American literature. Compare and contrast evidence of this mood in Bierce's "Chickamauga" and Stephen Crane's "An Episode of War."

3. Although frequently grouped together as "local color" writers, Bret Harte and Hamlin Garland reflect quite different concerns in their work than do Sarah Orne Jewett and Mary Wilkins Freeman. Examine the use of point of view in a male and a female writer from this group. Does the narrator look at or with the characters? What characters are excluded from sharing the point of view? What effect does this have on the fiction?

4. Choosing specific characters on which to base your analysis, discuss differences in the portrayal of women characters and women's experience in "local color" writers Harte and Garland and regionalist writers Jewett and Freeman.

5. In each of the following stories, the female character behaves in an unconventional way: Freeman's "A New England Nun," James's "Daisy Miller," and Dreiser's "Old Rogaum and His Theresa." Analyze the female characters in such a way as to explain some of the similarities and differences between regionalism, realism, and naturalism.

6. Unlike many of their early nineteenth-century predecessors, writers following the Civil War depicted people and places who might have been real by means of referential language. Others continued to use dream imagery in their work. Analyze Bierce's "Chickamauga," Jewett's "A White Heron," or Gilman's "The Yellow Wallpaper," focusing on how the use of dream, vision, or altered perception affects the realism of the fiction.

7. Many late nineteenth-century writers wrote in response to social conditions. Present a composite picture of their concerns by discussing the following group of texts: Clemens, "Letter IV"; Garland, "Under the Lion's Paw"; Washington, "The Atlanta Exposition Address"; Dreiser, "The Strike" from *Sister Carrie*.

8. Discuss one of the following groups of works, with the goal of explaining differences between regionalist, realist, and naturalist writers:

(a) James, "Daisy Miller"; Freeman, "A New England Nun"; Dreiser, "Old Rogaum and His Theresa";

(b) Jewett, "The Foreigner"; Wharton, *Ethan Frome*; Crane, "The Blue Hotel";

(c) Howells, "Editha"; Jewett, "A White Heron"; Crane, "The Bride Comes to Yellow Sky."

9. Reexamine the poems of Whitman or Dickinson in light of the focus on fiction by most post-1865 writers. Choose any single lyric poem and consider its patterns of language or symbolism in light of similar patterns in fiction by "local color," regionalist, or realist writers.

10. Research literary history of the post-1865 period and find other poets besides Whitman, Dickinson, and Crane. Write an essay analyzing individual poems and describing the larger context of work by a white woman such as Lydia Sigourney or a black woman writer such as Frances E. W. Harper.

11. Examine political writing by Washington and DuBois in the context of political writing in earlier periods of American literature. Does it share the same form? Does it innovate within the form? Does it combine forms? To what extent does it comment, implicitly or explicitly, on other literary genres of the late nineteenth or early twentieth centuries?

12. Read literary historians (Fred Lewis Pattee, V. L. Parrington, Robert Spillers) for their discussions of "local color" and regional writing. Analyze any story in the text by Jewett, Chopin, Freeman, Chesnutt, Harte, or Garland in light of the historical commentary.

13. Research a regional writer from your home state or region. Write an essay analyzing one of the sketches or stories by this writer.

14. Reread Howells's "Novel-Writing and Novel-Reading" and James's "The Art of Fiction," and construct the theory of realism that is possible using only these two texts.

15. Turn-of-the-century critics used the phrase "new realists" to describe the work of naturalists Crane, Dreiser, Norris, and London. Choose a work of fiction by any of these writers and consider the accuracy of the phrase. Based on your analysis, would you identify naturalism as a new genre or a derivative one (a "new" realism)? (Students interested in French literature may do a comparative essay on a novel by Zola and any of the American realist or naturalist texts, or might research some of Zola's own literary statements and evaluate those in light of statements and prefaces by Howells and James. Or read a novel by Flaubert and focus on connections between Flaubert and James.)

16. Whether in anticipation of, or in the general climate of Freud's 1900 *The Interpretation of Dreams,* sexuality concerns several writers of the 1865–1914 period. Analyze sexual imagery or attitudes

toward sexuality in several of the following works: Howells's "Editha," James's *The Turn of the Screw*, Jewett's "A White Heron," Chopin's *The Awakening*, Freeman's "A New England Nun," and Wharton's *Ethan Frome*.

QUESTIONS ON INDIVIDUAL AUTHORS AND WORKS

Samuel Clemens

1. Many readers of *Adventures of Huckleberry Finn* consider the ending flawed—Hemingway, for example, said that Twain "cheated"—while others have praised it. Write an essay in which you either defend or criticize the novel's ending, focusing on Huck's treatment of Jim.

2. The theme of pretending is one that unifies *Adventures of Huckleberry Finn*, although the word "pretending" takes on several different meanings and levels of significance as the novel unfolds. Describe three of these, and illustrate each by analyzing a specific character, scene, or incident from the novel.

3. If one were constructing a list of "classic" American books, *Adventures of Huckleberry Finn* would almost certainly appear on the list. Explore in detail why this is the case. In what ways does Clemens take American experience as his subject? What are the elements of Clemens's language and form that readers might consider particularly "American"?

4. Explore the relationship between the symbolism of the river and Clemens's narrative design or structure in the novel.

5. Analyze Clemens's portrait of Jim in light of your reading of Frederick Douglass. Is *Adventures of Huckleberry Finn* a slave narrative, or does Clemens use the discussion of slavery as a pretext to write about some other issue?

6. Consider Huckleberry Finn as an abused child. Explore the novel as a reflecton of late nineteenth-century attitudes toward child rearing.

7. Analyze Clemens's use of humor, focusing on "The Notorious Jumping Frog of Calaveras County" or "Letter IV" and one incident from *Adventures of Huckleberry Finn*.

8. Analyze Huck Finn's language in the opening passages of *Adventures of Huckleberry Finn*. Identify specific features of his syntax and discuss how Clemens uses Huck's style as a way to construct his character.

9. Analyze evidence of dialect in Huck Finn's speech and compare it with dialects spoken by several other characters in the novel. Compare Clemens's depiction of dialect in general with that of Bret Harte, Joel Chandler Harris, or Sarah Orne Jewett.

10. Identify and discuss features of the picaresque novel that Clemens uses in *Adventures of Huckleberry Finn.*

11. Analyze Clemens's portrait of Tom Sawyer. Is he model, rival, alter ego, or mirror for Huck? Does he develop in the novel?

12. Analyze Clemens's portrait of Jim. Does he have an independent existence in the novel or does he merely reflect the way others see him? Compare his portrait with portraits of black characters in the Joel Chandler Harris tales or in Charles Chesnutt's "The Goophered Grapevine."

13. Study the female characters in the novel. What stereotypes does Clemens use? Do any of his female characters transcend stereotype?

14. Death is a frequent motif in the novel. Comment on its various thematic and symbolic uses, and analyze in particular Huck's symbolic death in Chapter VI.

15. Analyze the character of Jack Halliday in "The Man That Corrupted Hadleyburg" and compare and contrast him with Rip Van Winkle in Irving's tale and Sam Lawson in Stowe's "The Minister's Housekeeper."

16. At the end of "The Man That Corrupted Hadleyburg," Clemens writes, "the man will have to rise early that catches [the town] napping again." Such an image of rising and waking from a nap recalls other dreamers in American fiction. Write an essay on the motif of sleep and dream in "The Man That Corrupted Hadleyburg," and evaluate Clemens's commentary on the American dream as a literary theme.

17. Analyze Clemens's use of the con man or the mysterious stranger in "The Man That Corrupted Hadleyburg," Howard L. Stephenson, and compare Stephenson with his analogues in *Adventures of Huckleberry Finn*, the King and the Duke.

18. Write an essay on elements of theater in Clemens's work (as anthologized in the *NAAL*), commenting on the relationship between the art and act of oral storytelling and the narrative form Clemens devises for written stories.

W. D. Howells

1. Analyze Howells's "Editha" in terms of his assertions, in "Novel-Writing and Novel-Reading," that "the truth which is the only beauty, is truth to human experience," and that "the imagination . . . can absolutely create nothing; it can only compose."

2. Study "Novel-Writing and Novel-Reading" for what it tells us about Howells's attitudes toward gender and class. Consider whether the character Editha reflects those attitudes or the referential experience of late nineteenth-century women. Contrast Editha with Freeman's character Louisa Ellis in "A New England Nun."

Henry James

1. Examine Howells's "Novel-Writing and Novel-Reading" and James's "The Art of Fiction" and discuss points of convergence and divergence.

2. In "The Art of Fiction," James writes, "A novel is in its broadest definition a personal, a direct impression of life." With this quotation as your point of reference, analyze the particular "impression" James is trying to create in "Daisy Miller," "The Real Thing," or "The Beast in the Jungle."

3. James has often been called a psychological realist, more interested in the development of consciousness than in portraying character types and social reality. Discuss the extent to which this observation holds true in "Daisy Miller" or "The Beast in the Jungle."

4. Analyze "The Real Thing" as a story in which James explicitly chooses to define the word "real," and show how James's characterization of the Monarchs evolves a theory of fiction.

5. Although "Daisy Miller" appears to focus on the portrait of Daisy herself, a reader might argue that James's real interest is in Winterbourne. Rethink the events of the story as Daisy herself might have viewed them, and suggest ways in which the author of "A White Heron" or of "A New England Nun" might have differently handled both the story and the portrait of Daisy.

6. Bring together evidence of James's interest in convention and social forms from all four anthologized stories, and analyze a particular scene from one of them that illustrates James's analysis of social reality.

7. James perfected the use of point of view as a narrative device. Choose one incident from "The Beast in the Jungle" and analyze his use of point of view in that story. What does it reveal? What does it conceal? How does it achieve its effectiveness? What is its significance in terms of the story's themes?

8. Compare "The Man That Corrupted Hadleyburg" and *The Turn of the Screw* as experiments in how to tell a story.

9. In Chapter XXII of *The Turn of the Screw*, the governess writes: "I could only get on at all by taking 'nature' into my confidence and my account, by treating my monstrous ordeal as a push in a direction unusual, of course, and unpleasant, but demanding, after all, for a fair front, only another turn of the screw of ordinary human virtue." Explore James's use of the term "nature" for the governess and evaluate how it motivates her "turn of the screw of ordinary human virtue."

10. Choose an interpretation of *The Turn of the Screw* that you find particularly compelling and defend it with a close reading of the text.

Sarah Orne Jewett

1. Compare and contrast Jewett's Sylvy in "A White Heron" with May Bartram of James's "The Beast in the Jungle."

2. The tree, the hunter, the cow, and the heron all seem to possess mythical significance in "A White Heron." Choose to discuss one of them in relationship to Sylvy, and explore the way Jewett combines elements of folk or fairy tale and literary realism.

3. Compare and contrast the relationship between James's governess/narrator and Mrs. Grose in *The Turn of the Screw* with the relationship between the narrator and Mrs. Todd in Jewett's "The Foreigner."

4. Read T. B. Thorpe's "The Big Bear of Arkansas" (*NAAL*, Vol. 1). Viewing the Southwest humorists as precursors of the late nineteenth-century "local-color" writers, contrast Thorpe's attitude toward the bear hunt with Jewett's attitude toward Sylvy's search for the bird in "A White Heron." Or, imagine "A White Heron" told from the point of view of the young ornithologist, and explain why this other story might have been accepted for publication in the sporting magazine of the Southwest humorists, *The Spirit of the Times*.

5. Unlike Clemens, Howells, and James, Sarah Orne Jewett did not write essays about writing or reading. Fill in the gap in literary history, using the two anthologized stories as a foundation, and write the essay that wasn't: "How to Tell a Story," by Sarah Orne Jewett. You may also choose to title the essay, "Fiction-Writing and Fiction-Reading" or "The Art of Fiction."

6. In an attempt to differentiate between regionalism and realism, compare and contrast Jewett's "The Foreigner" and James's *The Turn of the Screw* as "ghost stories."

7. Research other writers in the regionalist tradition and write about work by Alice Cary, Rose Terry Cooke, Harriet Beecher Stowe (*The Pearl of Orr's Island*), or Mary Austin, all of whom are available in paperback texts.

Kate Chopin

1. Kate Chopin writes in *The Awakening*, "The children appeared before her like antagonists who had overcome her; who had over-powered and sought to drag her into the soul's slavery for the rest of her days." Using this quotation as a springboard, discuss it with respect to Aunt Sally from *Adventures of Huckleberry Finn*.

2. Consider alternative titles for Clemens's and Chopin's novels: "The Awakening of Huckleberry Finn" and "The Adventures of Edna Pontellier." Comment on the incongruity of each of these al-

ternative titles in terms of the novels' designs, themes, and development of the central character.

3. Analyze the character of Mlle. Reisz in *The Awakening* and compare her with Louisa Ellis in Freeman's "A New England Nun." How does Chopin limit Mlle. Reisz's possibilities and influence on Edna in her novel?

4. Edna Pontellier is caught in the contradictions between the way others see her and the way she sees herself. Identify several moments in which this becomes apparent, and show Edna's growing awareness of the contradiction.

5. Count, characterize, and analyze the numerous women of color in *The Awakening*. What does their presence and their treatment in the novel suggest about Edna's (and Chopin's) attitudes toward human development for nonwhite and poor women?

6. Find and read Elizabeth Cady Stanton's 1896 essay "The Solitude of Self" and analyze the character of Edna Pontellier in light of the essay by Chopin's feminist contemporary.

7. Some readers have described Edna's death in *The Awakening* as suicide; others view it as her attempt at self-realization. Argue the relative truth of both interpretations.

8. *The Awakening* contains elements of regionalism, realism, and naturalism. Identify these by choosing exemplary characters or scenes from the novel and basing your distinctions on close analysis.

9. Compare the relationship between Edna Pontellier and Mlle. Reisz in *The Awakening* with the relationship between the narrator and Mrs. Todd in Jewett's "The Foreigner."

Mary E. Wilkins Freeman

1. Identify the common theme (or themes) that link "A New England Nun" and Chopin's *The Awakening* and briefly discuss the way each work develops its theme.

2. One central theme in nineteenth-century American literature portrays the individual in conflict with the community. Discuss the specific ways in which Louisa Ellis enacts this conflict.

3. Both "The Revolt of 'Mother'" and "A New England Nun" portray women who triumph over the material conditions of their existence. Describe the nature of that triumph and the process by which they achieve it.

4. Examine the use of the window and the barn doors as framing devices in the two anthologized stories. As an option, read other stories in which Freeman uses framing devices (see "An Honest Soul," "A Mistaken Charity," "A Village Singer," or "A Church Mouse" from the Norton edition, *Selected Stories of Mary E. Wilkins Freeman*, edited by Marjorie Pryse). Compare form in Freeman's fiction with form in Howells, James, or Jewett.

5. Compare and contrast Oakhurst in Harte's "The Outcasts of Poker Flat" and Freeman's Adoniram Penn. Do they triumph, or are they defeated men?

Charles W. Chesnutt

1. Explore the way in which Chesnutt manipulates point of view in "The Goophered Grapevine" and the effect this has on the story's ending.

2. Read the anthologized "Uncle Remus" stories by Joel Chandler Harris. Compare and contrast Chesnutt's use of the folk tale and the folk narrator with that of Harris.

3. Compare and contrast Irving's use of folk materials early in the nineteenth century with Chesnutt's use of folk materials in "The Goophered Grapevine."

4. While almost all of the writers in the genre of regionalism were women, Charles Chesnutt uses elements of regionalism in "The Goophered Grapevine." With references to anthologized works by Stowe (Vol. 1), Jewett, Chopin, and Freeman, analyze Chesnutt as a regionalist writer.

Hamlin Garland

1. Compare and contrast Garland's portrait of the women in "Under the Lion's Paw" with Freeman's in "The Revolt of 'Mother.'" How does each author present women's ability to confront poverty?

2. Garland's narrator views his characters from the outside. Analyze specific scenes in the story to show how this outsider's view predetermines the reader's understanding of the characters' actions.

3. Are the characters in "Under the Lion's Paw" individuals or types? Compare the story with Howells's "Editha." Does the use of types or stereotypes limit the effect of realism?

Charlotte Perkins Gilman

1. How does Gilman's realism differ from the realism of W. D. Howells? Does the narrator of "The Yellow Wallpaper" recognize any correspondence between her own perception and external reality? In what ways does Gilman violate Howells's proscriptions in "Novel-Writing and Novel-Reading"?

2. Consider "The Yellow Wallpaper" as Gilman's portrait of the American woman as writer. What does the story suggest about the literary authority of the woman writer? What obstacles stand in the way of her creation? What is her ultimate work of art?

3. Compare and contrast Gilman's narrator of "The Yellow Wallpaper" with James's governess in *The Turn of the Screw*. Are both women mad? If you argue that they are, evaluate James's and Gilman's differing perspectives on women's madness.

Jane Addams

1. Explain what Addams means by her chapter's title, "The Snare of Preparation," from *Twenty Years at Hull-House*.

2. Consider James's Daisy Miller from the perspective Addams presents in the excerpts from *Twenty Years at Hull-House*. To what extent is James's novella a critique of women's education? To what extent is Addams's portrait of the "sheltered, educated girl" an explanation of Daisy Miller's vulnerability?

3. The social problems that result from the corruption of Hadleyburg in Clemens's novella are by no means as severe as those Addams documents in *Twenty Years at Hull-House*—child neglect, wife abuse, prejudice, intoxication, social isolation. Yet Addams responds differently to her perception of these problems. Compare and contrast "The Man That Corrupted Hadleyburg" and the excerpts from *Twenty Years at Hull-House* (a) as visions of human nature, and (b) as responses to that vision.

Edith Wharton

1. Compare and contrast James's Daisy Miller with Wharton's Mattie Silver in such a way as to illustrate differences between Wharton's realism and that of Henry James.

2. Consider the relationship to landscape that Jewett's Mrs. Todd in "The Foreigner" or Freeman's Louisa Ellis in "A New England Nun" appear to have. How does Wharton's use of landscape contrast with that of Jewett and Freeman?

3. Compare Ethan Frome with Irving's Rip Van Winkle, Melville's Bartleby, or Hawthorne's Wakefield. Argue that, for all her interest in the narrative technique of the late nineteenth-century, Wharton's thematic interests more closely resemble her male predecessors and those of romantic American fiction.

4. In her critical biography of Edith Wharton, *A Feast of Words*, Cynthia Griffin Wolff identifies the motif of the threshold in *Ethan Frome* and associates it with the novel's central theme. Examine references to thresholds throughout the novel, consider their thematic significance, and write an essay based on the implications for character and theme.

5. Compare and contrast the marital relationship between Wharton's Zeena and Ethan Frome in *Ethan Frome*, and Freeman's Sarah and Adoniram Penn in "The Revolt of 'Mother.'"

W. E. B. DuBois

1. Explore the points of conflict between DuBois and Booker T. Washington, as illustrated in the anthologized selections from both writers. What reality do black people face, according to DuBois? Do they inherit it? Can they change it? And in what way is their identity contingent on that reality?

Frank Norris

1. Locate Norris's allusions to animals and animal-like behavior in the excerpt from *Vandover and the Brute*. Analyze what he is trying to say about human motivation and character.

2. Although critics do not generally consider Samuel Clemens a naturalist, "The Man That Corrupted Hadleyburg" has certain affinities with Norris's *Vandover*. Compare and contrast elements of realism and naturalism in each work.

3. Compare and contrast the correspondent from Stephen Crane's "The Open Boat" with Norris's Vandover. Analyze the prose style, thematic content, use of narrative point of view, and portrait of human nature that these works convey.

Stephen Crane

1. Analyze the natural "forces" that the characters struggle against in "The Open Boat." How do they deal with their lack of control over those forces?

2. "An Experiment in Misery" suggests that society is made up of forces beyond an individual's control. Trace the protagonist's encounter with these forces, and analyze the language by which Crane personifies the malicious intent of the city's misery.

3. Despite the apparent irrationality of its characters, "The Blue Hotel" moves logically and inexorably toward its conclusion. Study the evidence of irrationality in the story's portraits of human behavior; then describe the linear progression by which the Swede's initial comment—"'I suppose there have been a good many men killed in this room'"—comes to control events.

4. In "The Bride Comes to Yellow Sky," Jack Potter's marriage appears to alter forever Scratchy Wilson's perception of reality. Argue that, for Crane, marriage itself becomes an external force. Does the story's humor mitigate the oppressiveness of this force?

5. Explore the relationship between Crane's poems and his fiction. Does Crane's choice of the lyric poem allow him to develop aspects of his major themes that his fiction does not fully explore?

Theodore Dreiser

1. Analyze the social forces that serve as Dreiser's theory of reality in "The Strike" from *Sister Carrie*. How does his involvement in the strike affect Hurstwood's identity, his sense of self?

2. Examine the portrait of family life Dreiser presents in "Old Rogaum and His Theresa." What forces make it, like the city in Crane's story, such "an experiment in misery"?

Henry Adams

1. Henry Adams writes in his *Education* that "From earliest childhood the boy was accustomed to feel that, for him, life was double." Explain the significance of Adams's particular kind of "double vision." Compare it with the internal contradiction Edna Pontellier feels in *The Awakening* and the "double consciousness" of DuBoisean black identity.

2. What happens to Adams's perception of design and order in the universe over the course of his *Education*? How does it happen that "he found himself lying in the Gallery of Machines at the Great Exposition of 1900, with his historical neck broken by the sudden irruption of forces totally new"?

3. Explain and comment on the following statement from the *Education*: "Adams began to ponder, asking himself whether he knew of any American artist who had ever insisted on the power of sex, as every classic had always done; but he could think only of Walt Whitman; Bret Harte, as far as the magazines would let him venture; and one or two painters, for the flesh-tones. . . . American art, like the American language and American education, was as far as possible sexless."

4. The anthologized chapters from *The Education* contain much evidence that Adams viewed himself as a transitional figure. Identify several points at which he "broke his life in halves again," and trace his progress from his early sense that the eighteenth century was his companion to his entrance into the twentieth century at the close of Chapter XXV.

5. Compare William Bradford's *Of Plymouth Plantation* and *The Education of Henry Adams*. Do the two works belong to the same genre?

HISTORICAL QUESTIONS

1. At the end of Frost's poem "The Oven Bird," we find the following lines: "The question that he frames in all but words / Is what to make of a diminished thing." Making specific references to several works by other poets and prose writers, explain how this statement expresses a common theme in twentieth-century American writing.

2. Choosing several different works, discuss changes in American writers' attitudes toward God or religion in the twentieth century.

3. Compare an early nineteenth-century poem (such as Bryant's "Thanatopsis," *NAAL*, Vol. 1) with an early twentieth-century poem (Frost's "Directive"). Discuss the way both poems reflect dramatic radical shifts in paradigm or perspective in their time.

4. Choose any three twentieth-century works and show how they respond to the following quotation from Wallace Stevens, "Of Modern Poetry":

> The poem of the mind in the act of finding
> What will suffice. It has not always had
> To find: the scene was set; it repeated what
> Was in the script.

5. Explain the parallel concerns in the following statements: (a) "The poem is a momentary stay against confusion" (Frost, "The Figure a Poem Makes"); (b) "These fragments I have shored against my ruins" (Eliot, "The Waste Land"); (c) "Poetry is the supreme fiction, madame" (Stevens, "A High-toned Old Christian Woman").

6. Examine traditional twentieth-century lyric poems by Robinson, Wylie, and Millay. How does each of these poets turn traditional form to the service of twentieth-century themes?

7. Read a short story by a British modernist writer, such as Lawrence, Woolf, or Joyce. Compare and contrast it with a story by an American modernist.

8. Many modernist lyric poems are about poetic form itself. Analyze one of the following poems (or any other poems by Frost, Stevens, or Williams) with particular attention to the poet's awareness of form: "The Wood-Pile," "A Quiet Normal Life," or "To Elsie."

9. Analyze the use of poetic forms by modernist poets. Examine the following: Frost's sonnets, "Mowing," "The Oven Bird," "Once by the Pacific," "Design," or "The Gift Outright" (or find and read all of Frost's sonnets in his complete poems and write about his use of the form); Stevens's use of the ballad stanza in "Anecdote of the Jar" or his use of tercet stanza form in "The Snow Man" and "A Quiet Normal Life"; Williams's near-sonnet "The Dance"; Pound's sonnet, "A Virginal," or the poem he calls a villanelle although it is

not, "Villanelle: The Psychological Hour"; or Bishop's nearly perfect villanelle, "One Art."

10. Examine modernist poets' use of traditional metric forms. Analyze what Frost does to and with iambic pentameter in "Desert Places" or how Stevens uses it in "The Idea of Order at Key West."

11. In the introduction to Marianne Moore in the *NAAL*, Nina Baym writes, "Pound worked with the clause, Williams with the line, H. D. with the image, and Stevens and Stein with the word; Moore, unlike these modernist contemporaries, used the entire stanza as the unit of her poetry." In an out-of-class essay, choose poems by each of these writers that will allow you to further explain the distinctions Baym creates in this statement.

12. In British poetry, Robert Browning developed and perfected the dramatic monologue. Find and discuss dramatic monologues by several American modernists. Evaluate their uses of, or variations on, Browning's form.

13. Although American poets have not yet—according to critical consensus—produced an epic poem, several twentieth-century poets have made the attempt. Research features of classical epic poetry and identify epic characteristics in Williams's *Paterson*, Pound's *The Cantos*, H. D.'s *The Walls Do Not Fall*, Eliot's *Four Quartets,* and Crane's *The Bridge.*

14. Locate and read one of the following modernist poetic statements, and then analyze one of the author's anthologized poems in light of what he has written about craft: Frost, "The Figure a Poem Makes" (included in the *NAAL*); Stevens, from *The Necessary Angel*; Williams, "Edgar Allan Poe"; Pound, "A Treatise on Metre," or another essay from *The ABC of Reading*; Crane, "General Aims and Theories."

15. Compare and contrast the realism of a twentieth-century story with the realism of Clemens, Howells, James, or Wharton. Analyze Sherwood Anderson, "The Egg"; William Faulkner, "Barn Burning"; or Ernest Hemingway, "The Snows of Kilimanjaro," paying particular attention to the twentieth-century writer's innovations in point of view or use of symbolism.

QUESTIONS ON INDIVIDUAL AUTHORS AND WORKS

Black Elk

1. Why does Black Elk seem to think it important that his story be told? Why does John Neihardt think it is important? Do they both have the same reasons? Analyze "Heyoka Ceremony" as Black Elk's attempt at making a connection with an audience, and comment on how the chapter offers a working definition of the very process of "raising consciousness."

2. Arnold Krupat ("The Indian Autobiography: Origins, Type, and Function," *American Literature*, 53 [1981], 22–42) has written that "to see the Indian autobiography as a ground on which two cultures meet is to see it as the textual equivalent of the 'frontier.'" Write an essay in which you comment on this statement and its significance for understanding *Black Elk Speaks*.

3. In the second (1961) edition of *Black Elk Speaks*, John Neihardt changed the title page of the text from "as told to John Neihardt" to "as told through John Neihardt." Explain the significance of this change, and interpret the relationship it suggests between Neihardt and Black Elk, and between Neihardt and *Black Elk Speaks*.

4. Compare and contrast *Black Elk Speaks* with two other American texts, Benjamin Franklin's *The Autobiography*, and *Narrative of the Life of Frederick Douglass, an American Slave* (both from *NAAL*, Vol 1). Focus on the relationship between central narrator and autobiographical text. How does each text reflect different choices by the speaker in terms of self-presentation, connection to history, choice of significant events, and literary form?

5. Compare and contrast Gertrude Simmons Bonnin [Zitkala-Šá]'s autobiographical writing ("Impressions of an Indian Childhood," "The School Days of an Indian Girl," "An Indian Teacher among Indians") and narrative voice with that of Black Elk in the excerpts from *Black Elk Speaks*. Both writers were Sioux; evaluate their respective roles as "holy man" and "teacher," comment on their different experiences with biculturalism, and compare the points at which they break off their autobiographical accounts.

6. Mary Hunter Austin was a white woman who spent a lot of time with Indians in New Mexico and wrote about connections between Indian oral poetry and the imagist movement among early twentieth-century American poets. In her many books about Indians she established herself as an expert, and one of our earliest theoreticians about Native American poetry. Read Mary Austin's "Shoshone Land" and "The Basket Maker" from *The Land of Little Rain* (available in Marjorie Pryse, ed., Mary Austin, *Stories from the Country of Lost Borders* [New Brunswick, N.J.: Rutgers University Press, 1987]) and evaluate Austin's biculturalism in light of Neihardt's description of collaborating with Black Elk.

Ellen Glasgow

1. Analyze what makes "the difference" for Margaret. Demonstrate the connection Glasgow creates between change in self-concept and change in world view.

2. Compare Margaret with earlier portraits of wives in American fiction, specifically with Edna Pontellier in Chopin's *The*

Awakening and Gilman's narrator in "The Yellow Wallpaper." How does Margaret's husband control and define her reality for her?

Willa Cather

1. Compare *My Mortal Enemy* with Glasgow's "The Difference." How do both stories portray the relationship between changes in perception and changes in reality?

2. Cather writes as an early twentieth-century regionalist in "Neighbour Rosicky." How does this story reflect the themes and point of view of earlier regionalist writers Jewett and Freeman?

3. Like Garland's "Under the Lion's Paw," "Neighbour Rosicky" is set in the West. Compare and contrast the influence of place in these stories. What mitigating vision does Cather offer, and how does it contrast with Garland's forces of economic despair?

Gertrude Stein

1. In characterizing her "description of the loving of repetition" in *The Making of Americans*, Stein writes: "Then there will be realised the complete history of every one, the fundamental character of every one, the bottom nature in them, the mixtures in them, the strength and weakness of everything they have inside them, the flavor of them, the meaning in them, the being in them, and then you have a whole history then of each one. Everything then they do in living is clear to the completed understanding, their living, loving, eating, pleasing, smoking, thinking, scolding, drinking, working, dancing, walking, talking, laughing, sleeping, everything in them." Apply the statement specifically as a description of what she attempts in *The Good Anna*.

2. Some twentieth-century critics have identified Walt Whitman as a modernist poet. Reread "Song of Myself" (*NAAL*, Vol. 1) and examine the uses of the expansive first-person narrator in Whitman and in the excerpt from Stein's *The Making of Americans*. Based on what you find in Stein's experimental prose, argue that Whitman, as well, experiments in modernist writing.

3. Analyze the linguistic transformations Stein performs on individual sentences in the excerpt from *The Making of Americans*. Locate similar sentences; identify points of transition in the prose; compile a lexicon and note the appearance of new and startling words.

4. *The Good Anna* depicts a series of hierarchical relationships between women. Explore the theme of power and influence in friendship, as Stein explicitly writes about it in Part II of the novel, and comment on Stein's view of women in general, as it emerges

from the text. In our own contemporary terms, to what extent does Anna identify with traditionally male attitudes toward women?

5. Sarah Orne Jewett, like Gertrude Stein, also lived for many years with a woman (Annie Adams Fields, the widow of Hawthorne's publisher James T. Fields) and also wrote much about relationships between women in her fiction. Reread Jewett's "The Foreigner" (*NAAL*, Vol. 2) and compare and contrast Jewett and Stein in terms of their treatment of relationships between women, their respective conception of mothers, and the extent to which their work expresses differences between regionalism and modernism.

6. Analyze closely the relationship Stein's Anna has with Jane and Edgar Wadsmith in *The Good Anna*. Compare and contrast Anna and Stein's portrait of Anna with the governess and her narrative portrait in James's *The Turn of the Screw*. Comment on the relationship between realism and modernism that the two works express. What happens if you imagine interchanging the characters in the two works?

7. Examine Stein's use of humor in *The Good Anna*. Reread Stowe's "The Minister's Housekeeper" (*NAAL*, Vol 1), analyze Anna's relationship with Doctor Shonjen, and consider differences between Stowe and Stein as humorists.

Robert Frost

1. Analyze the narrator's attitude toward death in "After Apple-Picking" and in "An Old Man's Winter Night." How does each poem serve as a buffer against mortality and meaninglessness?

2. Analyze one of the following poems to show how Frost's poetic technique itself serves as his own "momentary stay against confusion": "Once by the Pacific," "Desert Places," or "Design."

3. Illustrate how Frost applies the following statement from "The Figure a Poem Makes" to his use of iambic pentameter in "Home Burial": "The possibilities for tune from the dramatic tones of meaning struck across the rigidity of a limited meter are endless."

4. Analyze Frost's use of the sonnet form in the following poems: "Mowing," "The Oven Bird," "Once by the Pacific," and "Design."

5. One of the most striking characteristics of Frost's poetry is his creation of a speaking voice. Examine the following poems and analyze the relationship between speaker and hearer: "The Pasture," "The Tuft of Flowers," "A Servant to Servants."

6. Examine the image of loss of Paradise or the "fall" in "Fire and Ice," "The Oven Bird," and "After Apple-Picking."

7. Analyze "'Out, Out—'" in light of the last two lines of "The Oven Bird."

8. Choose one of the following poems not anthologized in the *NAAL* for further close analysis: "A Minor Bird," "The Investment," "The Hill Wife," "The Cow in Apple-Time."

9. In "The Gift Outright," Frost has written a small history of American literature. In the poem, he personifies the American land as female. Trace the imagery of sexual conquest in the poem and explore what it reveals about Frost's conception of the American poet.

10. "Directive" advises its readers to get lost in order to find themselves. How does this poem reflect Frost's twentieth-century world view? What are the relative values of disorientation and reorientation? How does "Directive" offer a modern version of the American dream?

Sherwood Anderson

1. At the end of "The Egg," Anderson's narrator writes, "I wondered why eggs had to be and why from the egg came the hen who again laid the egg." Analyze the multiple symbolism of the egg, what it comes to represent by the end of the story, and how Anderson uses it to unify his narrative.

2. Paraphrase the above quotation from "The Egg" as follows: "I wondered why stories had to be and why from the story came the storyteller who again produced the story." Each of the anthologized stories from *Winesburg, Ohio* bears some relation to George Willard. Discuss the significance of this relation, using the paraphrased quotation, if helpful.

3. Anderson and Cather were contemporaries and each chose to write about regional life. Compare and contrast the narrators of "The Egg" and *My Mortal Enemy*. What significance does the story each narrator tells have for the narrator's own developing consciousness? What role does region play in that developing consciousness?

Wallace Stevens

1. Apply Stevens's statement, "Poetry is the supreme fiction, madame," from "A High-toned Old Christian Woman," in close analysis of "A Quiet Normal Life." What does Stevens mean by the concept of a "supreme fiction," and how does the man in "A Quiet Normal Life" live by it?

2. One of the most famous lines from Stevens, and one of the most enigmatic, appears in "Sunday Morning": "Death is the mother of beauty." Summarize the major points in the argument by which the speaker in this poem transforms Sunday morning from a day of religious observance for the dead into a celebratory day of the sun.

3. Closely analyze the sun imagery in stanza VII of "Sunday Morning." Then write an interpretation of "Gubbinal" that builds on what you have observed.

4. Both "Anecdote of the Jar" and "Study of Two Pears" take as their central focus some inanimate object. Analyze the meaning these two poems share and the syntactic and semantic techniques Stevens uses to create that meaning.

5. Discuss the particular kind of technical experiment Stevens uses in "Thirteen Ways of Looking at a Blackbird." How does this poem convey meaning?

6. "The Idea of Order at Key West" contains two poems or singers: the woman who sings and the poem's speaker. Analyze the relationship that exists between the two of them.

7. Compare and contrast the poems of Robert Frost and Wallace Stevens, focusing on one of the following pairs: Frost's "An Old Man's Winter Night" and Stevens's "A Quiet Normal Life"; Frost's "Desert Places" and Stevens's "The Snow Man"; Frost's "Directive" and Stevens's "A Postcard from the Volcano." In what ways do Frost and Stevens each contribute to the modernist's ways of knowing the world? (Alternatively, assign Richard Poirier's book on the two poets, *The Way of Knowing*, and ask students to critique his argument with reference to specific anthologized poems.)

8. Examine the poems in which repeated activities of (1) looking at things, or (2) playing musical instruments or singing appear (see discussion of Stevens in Chapter 6 for the groupings of these poems), and explore the significance of the activity for the writing of poetry in Stevens.

9. Explicate, with references to other poems by Wallace Stevens, Professor Eucalyptus's statement in "An Ordinary Evening in New Haven": "The search / For reality is as momentous as / The search for god."

William Carlos Williams

1. At the end of "To Elsie" Williams writes, "No one / to witness / and adjust, no one to drive the car." Analyze the poem to show how he arrives at this image; then comment on how this image addresses Frost's concerns in "The Oven Bird" or "Desert Places" and Stevens's in "A High-toned Old Christian Woman" or "Of Modern Poetry."

2. In "A Sort of a Song," Williams writes, "No ideas / but in things." Analyze the anthologized poems that appear to be about things rather than ideas: "The Red Wheelbarrow," "Death," "Classic Scene."

3. Some of William's poems directly or indirectly address the writing of poetry. Discuss what the following poems tell us about his poetic theory: "Portrait of a Lady," "Spring and All," "The Wind Increases," "The Term."

4. Analyze the specific features of Williams's use of language in "To Elsie" or in the excerpts from *Paterson*.

5. Describe the form Williams invents in "The Ivy Crown." Discuss the effects this form has on the reader. How does the form contribute to a reader's understanding of the poem?

6. Compare the two Williams poems that derive from paintings by Brueghel, "The Dance" and "Landscape with the Fall of Icarus." Locate and study these paintings in the library. What relationship does Williams achieve between the visual and the verbal experience? Is it necessary to see the paintings in order to "see" the poems?

Robinson Jeffers

1. Compare and contrast Jeffers's use of nature in his poems with Frost's. Choose one of the following pairs: "Once by the Pacific" and "Shine, Perishing Republic"; "Birches" and "Hurt Hawks."

2. In several poems Jeffers takes birds as his central symbol. Closely analyze "Vulture" in the context of his other bird poems, "Hurt Hawks" and "Birds and Fishes."

3. Unlike most of his contemporaries, Jeffers locates his poems in an actual place—the central California coastline. Study his references to Pt. Lobos, Carmel, and Monterey in the anthologized poems. Then, closely analyze either "Boats in a Fog" or "Carmel Point," paying particular attention to the significance of a place.

Marianne Moore

1. Moore's work resembles that of Wallace Stevens in its interest in ideas. Choose one of the following pairs of poems, focusing on your analysis of Moore, and discuss the resemblance: "The Idea of Order at Key West" and "A Grave"; "Of Modern Poetry" and "Poetry."

2. Moore experiments with form and line lengths in "The Fish" and "The Mind Is an Enchanting Thing." Analyze one of these poems, playing close attention to the relationship between form and meaning.

3. Like Jeffers, Moore also writes poems about birds. Compare and contrast "Bird-Witted" with "Hurt Hawks."

4. Study Moore's work for explicit statements about what po-

etry is and does. Analyze these statements in light of class discussion, and construct a prose version of her poetic theory.

5. Analyze one of the following poems by Marianne Moore with the aim of describing the poem's form and demonstrating the relationship between form and meaning in the poem: "To a Snail," "Poetry," "The Fish," or "Nevertheless."

T. S. Eliot

1. Eliot writes, in "Tradition and the Individual Talent," that the individual personality and emotions of the poet recede in importance and his meaning emerges from his place in cultural tradition. He writes that "No poet . . . has his complete meaning alone." Examine his use of classical allusions in "Sweeney among the Nightingales." What does a modern reader need to know in order to understand the allusions, and how does that understanding enhance our meaning of the poem?

2. Describe the progression of images and themes in "The Waste Land," locating the central image in each of the five sections of the poem.

3. Eliot himself considered "The Waste Land" to be "a poem in fragments." Explain why this is an appropriate description of the poem, how it addresses Eliot's twentieth-century world view, and how he attempts to resolve the fragmentation at the end of the poem.

4. Analyze the persona of the speaker in "The Love Song of J. Alfred Prufrock" by examining the way he sees the world.

5. Like Williams, Eliot tried to achieve exactness and compression in creating his visual image. Find "Preludes" in the library and analyze Eliot's use of the image in that poem.

6. Eliot dedicates "The Waste Land" to Ezra Pound, who offered suggestions for revision. Read Pound's "Hugh Selwyn Mauberley," published just before "The Waste Land," and locate similarities between the two poems.

Eugene O'Neill

1. Discuss what O'Neill's character Edmund calls "faithful realism" in *Long Day's Journey into Night*. Is this play a work of realism in the Howellsian or Jamesian sense? In what way does it extend the concerns of the earlier realists to include twentieth-century concerns?

2. O'Neill suggests that modern life is more difficult for women than for men—if morphine addiction becomes a more extreme response to the modern condition than the alcoholism of

Mary Tyrone's husband James. Discuss continuities between Edna Pontellier in Chopin's *The Awakening* and Mary Tyrone in *Long Day's Journey into Night*.

3. If you have studied early nineteenth-century American literature, locate *Long Day's Journey into Night* as the culmination of themes and concerns that have set a direction in American fiction from "Rip Van Winkle" on. What does the play have to say about versions of the American dream; about individual identity; about self-reliance; about social exclusion; and about the development of consciousness?

Katherine Anne Porter

1. Trace the evolution of Miranda's expanding consciousness in *Old Mortality*. Analyze how Porter uses time to dramatize that evolution.

2. Amy makes the following statement about family: "'The whole hideous institution should be wiped from the face of the earth. It is the root of all human wrongs.'" Discuss homelessness as a condition for the twentieth-century writer. Include in your discussion Anderson, from *Winesburg, Ohio*, and O'Neill, *Long Day's Journey into Night*.

3. Consider Porter's characterization of Miranda in the context of other portraits of American women: Chopin's Edna Pontellier and O'Neill's Mary Tyrone.

Zora Neale Hurston

1. Compare and contrast Hurston's Janie with Jean Toomer's Fern. Consider especially the development of "conscious life" for each character.

2. Finish reading *Their Eyes Were Watching God*. Analyze Janie's development as an independent person in light of class discussion of Chapter 2. Comment further on the relationship between Janie and her listening friend, Pheoby. Or trace Hurston's use of folklore through the novel and comment on its significance.

3. One of the commonplaces about American slavery is that slaveholders often separated members of slave families from each other. Analyze the excerpt from *Their Eyes Were Watching God* as Hurston's attempt to heal the lingering impact of separation imposed by slavery and sexism.

F. Scott Fitzgerald

1. In Hemingway's "The Snows of Kilimanjaro," the narrator/protagonist recalls his friend Julian, a pseudonym for Fitzgerald, and his friend's fascination with the rich. Hemingway writes, "He thought they were a special glamourous race and when he found they weren't it wrecked him just as much as any other thing that wrecked him." Consider Hemingway's description of Fitzgerald as an interpretation of what happens to Dexter Green in "Winter Dreams." What gets "wrecked" for Dexter?

2. Many protagonists in modern American fiction strive to achieve individual goals that express their lives' meaning. Explore the diversity among these goals and meanings by analyzing what motivates the following fictional characters and comparing them with the "winter dreams" of Dexter Green: Gertrude Stein's Anna of *The Good Anna*; Zora Neale Hurston's Janie from *Their Eyes Were Watching God*; Hemingway's Harry from "The Snows of Kilimanjaro.

3. Analyze Dexter Green as a paradigmatic twentieth-century "modern." Discuss him in context with Anderson's Elmer Cowley in "Queer," Pound's Hugh Selwyn Mauberley, Eliot's J. Alfred Prufrock, or O'Neill's Edmund.

William Faulkner

1. Keep a journal of your thoughts, frustrations, and insights as you read *As I Lay Dying*. In particular, note your use of visual reading skills. Does the novel allow you to develop visualization as a reading technique, and if so, how? Pay close attention to Faulkner's effects on your actual reading process, and comment.

2. Often the use of the journey as a plot device in a novel implies character development. Which character(s) develop in *As I Lay Dying*? Analyze the evidence of character development or lack of it, and discuss how Faulkner's use of character affects interpretation in *As I Lay Dying*.

3. Faulkner once stated that he wrote *As I Lay Dying* from start to finish in six weeks, and that he didn't change a word. While Faulkner was known to exaggerate, he conveys an essential fact about this novel, that he wrote it easily, quickly, and as if it were the product of a single action. Explore the ironies inherent in such a description of the novel's creation. Compare Faulkner's description of how he wrote *As I Lay Dying* with Addie's statement, "I would think how words go straight up in a thin line, quick and harmless, and how terribly doing goes along the earth, clinging to it, so that after a while the two lines are too far apart for the same person to straddle from one to the other . . . "

4. Throughout *As I Lay Dying*, Faulkner's characters use mea-

surement and geometry as a way to depict the world, and Faulkner himself created a map of Jefferson County which "located" the Bundrens' journey within the larger world of his fiction. Find the map on the flyleaf of an edition of *Absalom, Absalom!* Consider Faulkner's use of spatial form and spatial relations as a unifying element in *As I Lay Dying.*

5. In class we have discussed *As I Lay Dying* as epistemology, a set of ways of knowing the world. Explore the idea of the novelist as a carpenter, and *As I Lay Dying* as one of the tools—rather than one of the products—of Faulkner's trade.

6. Critics have often commented on Faulkner's use of comedy in *As I Lay Dying.* Think about the various meanings of comedy, and evaluate the extent to which *As I Lay Dying* may be considered a comic novel.

7. Examine *As I Lay Dying* from the point of view of family dynamics or social process. Is "Bundren" an identity these family members all share? What is the ontology, the way of being a Bundren? To what extent is Faulkner commenting on the American, especially the Southern, family? Evaluate the perspectives with which the outsiders in the novel view the Bundrens. Which is reality? How does Faulkner demonstrate his characters constructing it?

8. Critics often associate Faulkner's portrait of the Snopeses with his perception that the "new South" following Reconstruction had lost its agrarian values. Analyze the particular "Snopesism" in "Barn Burning."

Langston Hughes

1. Analyze the linguistic devices Hughes uses in "Dear Dr. Butts." Compare his use of language in the short story with that in poems such as "Mulatto" or "Morning After."

2. Discuss what Hughes's poetry tells a reader about his own poetic theory. Closely analyze "Trumpet Player," in which he creates the musician as a type of the poet.

3. Place Hughes's work in the context of black musical forms invented in Harlem in the early twentieth century. Is black poetry the way Hughes writes it, like jazz, a new genre? If so, is it invented or derivative? What are its characteristics? If "black poetry" is a genre, does Countee Cullen write in it?

AMERICAN PROSE SINCE 1945

The teaching notes on this period in Chapter 6 include questions that will work either to stimulate discussion or as exam questions or essay topics. In addition, in assigning writing on contemporary literature, I often ask students to place a story, play, or poem within the context of literary tradition, genre, or theme (see the lists in Chapter 5). Occasionally I ask students to write an interpretation of a short story or a line-by-line analysis of the dialogue in a scene or a lyric poem in an out-of-class essay. On examinations I try to ask questions that will lead them to look at works in new ways.

1. In the opening passages of "Life-Story," John Barth's narrator writes, "He being by vocation an author of novels and stories it was perhaps inevitable that one afternoon the possibility would occur to the writer of these lines that his own life might be a fiction, in which he was the leading or an accessory character." Explore the variety of themes and techniques by which late twentieth-century writers depict their life stories. Include the following works in your discussion: Edmund Wilson, "The Old Stone House"; Ralph Ellison, from *Invisible Man*; Norman Mailer, from *The Armies of the Night*; James Baldwin, from *The Fire Next Time*; and Barth, "Life-Story."

2. Is heroism possible in contemporary society as it is portrayed by our fiction writers? Discuss the possibilities for heroism in the following heroes or anti-heroes: Vladimir Nabokov's Pnin; Saul Bellow's Tommy Wilhelm; Arthur Miller's Willy Loman; Norman Mailer's "Mailer"; Philip Roth's Sheldon Grossbart; and Robert Stone's Chas Elliot.

3. In their efforts to record and understand the mystery of life, many contemporary writers reflect a fascination with the grotesque, the inexplicable, or the fantastic. Compare and contrast evidence of this fascination in the following works: Eudora Welty, "Petrified Man"; Bernard Malamud, "The Magic Barrel"; Flannery O'Connor, "The Life You Save May Be Your Own" or "Good Country People"; and Thomas Pynchon, from *The Crying of Lot 49*.

4. White middle-class urban life and marriage become a central subject for several contemporary writers. Discuss the different treatment of this subject in the following works: John Cheever, "The Country Husband"; Norman Mailer, "The Man Who Studied Yoga"; John Barth, "Life-Story"; Tom Wolfe, "The Master of the Universe"; John Updike, "The Happiest I've Been" and "Separating"; and Robert Stone, "Helping."

5. While contemporary writers no longer take upon themselves the responsibility for "defining" what it means to be an American, many continue to reflect on what Norman Mailer describes as "the forces now mounting in America" and "the intensely peculiar American aspect" of contemporary life. Discuss current criticisms or assessments of American life in the following works: Edmund Wilson, from *Upstate*; Ralph Ellison, from *Invisible Man*; Arthur Miller, *Death of a Salesman*; Norman Mailer, from *The Armies of the Night*; James Baldwin, from *The Fire Next Time*; and Thomas Pynchon, from *The Crying of Lot 49*.

6. Betrayal by mothers—or by sisters—is one variation of the

exploration of the influence of family on contemporary life. Stella, at the end of *A Streetcar Named Desire*, cries, "Oh God, what have I done to my sister?" Explore relationships between women in Eudora Welty, "Petrified Man"; Williams's *Streetcar*; Flannery O'Connor, "The Life You Save May Be Your Own" and "Good Country People"; Bobbie Ann Mason, "Drawing Names"; and Alice Walker, "Everyday Use."

7. Examine as a group the anthologized stories by twentieth-century southern women regionalists Porter, Welty, and O'Connor. Do these writers alter the nineteenth-century concept of regionalism, and if so, how? if not, how do they extend the genre? Are twentieth-century regional writers also modernist writers?

8. Read Thomas Wolfe, "The Lost Boy," and the anthologized fiction by William Faulkner, focusing in particular on their use of southern material. Do they present that material differently than the southern women writers Porter, Welty, Mason, Walker, and O'Connor, or than playwright Tennessee Williams?

9. Only dramatists, among contemporary writers, appear to perceive the possibility for genuine tragedy in American character and American life. The anti-heroes of fiction disappear in Tennessee Williams and Arthur Miller. Despite the pathos of their lives, Blanche Dubois and Willy Loman are tragic. Analyze one of these characters as a tragic hero, paying particular attention to the way the dramatic form precludes the experimentation of Mailer, Barth, or Pynchon. Alternatively, compare and contrast Blanche DuBois and Willy Loman with Saul Bellow's Tommy Wilhelm in *Seize the Day*.

10. Comment on the way the American plays included in the *NAAL* use formal divisions: O'Neill's acts in *Long Day's Journey into Night*; Williams's series of scenes in *A Streetcar Named Desire*; Miller's free movements from scene to scene in *Death of a Salesman*; and use of scene divisions in Adrienne Kennedy or Sam Shepard.

11. Compare and contrast the way Williams constructs Blanche DuBois's southern speech with the way Faulkner, Welty, or O'Connor do for their southern characters in the anthologized stories.

12. "The family has always been a subject in western drama; in modern drama, however, beginning with the plays of the Norwegian Henrik Ibsen and the Russian Anton Chekhov, family becomes the central concern" (from the Arthur Miller headnote). Consider the accuracy of this statement in comparing the dramatic families in *Long Day's Journey into Night*, *Death of a Salesman*, and *True West*.

13. Read a play by Lillian Hellman (*Little Foxes, The Children's Hour*), Lorraine Hansberry (*A Raisin in the Sun*), Ntozake Shange (*For Colored Girls Who Have Considered Suicide* . . .), or Marsha Norman (*'Night, Mother*) and compare it with one of the plays in the *NAAL*.

14. Locate and read one of O'Neill's earlier "expressionistic"

plays written during the twenties and compare it with *Long Day's Journey into Night*.

15. Note that the three major plays included in the *NAAL* were written and produced during the 1940s. Read an essay on theater history in that period and try to find out what made that decade such a productive one for drama.

16. Find a play, verse drama, or adaptation by a twentieth-century poet or fiction writer and compare it with one of the plays included in the *NAAL* and with the poet's or novelist's other work.

17. Read anthologized selections by John Cheever, John Updike, Robert Stone, Bobbie Ann Mason, and Ann Beattie. Based on these stories, identify formal and thematic features of the *New Yorker* story. Then read a short story published in the *New Yorker* during the past year and evaluate it as an example of the "genre" of *New Yorker* fiction you have described.

18. Choose one of the following statements from contemporary American fiction or drama and argue that it articulates a central theme for post-modernist or contemporary writers. Use references to several additional writers or works in supporting your argument.

(a) "The gods and I went mad together and made things as they are." (Robert Stone, "Helping")

(b) "The blow you can't see coming is the blow that knocks you out—the blow out of nowhere. How can you protect yourself against a blow out of nowhere?" (Joyce Carol Oates, "Golden Gloves")

(c) "We all sound alike when we're sloshed." (Sam Shepard, *True West*)

(d) "This is worse than being homeless." (Sam Shepard, *True West*)

(e) "There can be too much communication between people." (Ann Beattie, "Weekend")

(f) "We are together always . . . There never was a time when this was not so." (Leslie Marmon Silko, "Lullaby")

19. One of the central questions for readers of *Black Elk Speaks* involves understanding the meaning of biculturalism. Explore the concept of biculturalism for contemporary Native American writers Leslie Marmon Silko and Louise Erdrich. Alternatively, consider the meaning of cultural assimilation for members of minority groups in America and examine the following works and their treatment of assimilation: Ralph Ellison, from *Invisible Man*; Alice Walker, "Everyday Use"; Leslie Marmon Silko, "Lullaby"; and Denise Chávez, "The Last of the Menu Girls."

20. American playwrights have often used siblings within a family to stand for divisions within the self or for two opposing forces. Consider the relationships between James, Jr., and Edmund in *Long Day's Journey into Night*; Blanche and Stella in *A Streetcar*

Named Desire; Biff and Happy in *Death of a Salesman*; and Austin and Lee in *True West*.

21. At the end of his headnote on Louise Erdrich, William Pritchard writes: "She is a strongly regional and ethnic writer, yet in reading her one feels those qualities not as limitations but as rooted solidities out of which ranging, even universal values and situations may be experienced." Implicit in Pritchard's statement is the assertion that the terms "regional" and "universal" are opposites, and that regional and ethnic fiction may have limitations. In exploring the validity of this assertion, choose two works of short fiction included in the post-1945 section, one which you consider "regional" and one "universal" in theme or appeal. Compare and contrast the two works, in an attempt to explore the meaning of these two apparently contradictory terms.

AMERICAN POETRY SINCE 1945

1. Test the accuracy of the following statements from the poets' headnotes by evaluating them in the context of your own reading of the poet's work.

(a) Lorine Niedecker: "Like other experimental American poets, she uses the space of the page to suggest the movement of the eye and mind across a field of experience."

(b) Robert Penn Warren: "What poetry most significantly celebrates is the capacity of man to face the deep, dark inwardness of his nature and fate."

(c) Randall Jarrell: "He is master of the heartbreak of everyday, and identifies with ordinary forms of loneliness."

(d) Richard Wilbur: " . . . the most adequate and convincing poetry is that which accommodates mixed feelings, clashing ideas, and incongruous images."

(e) A. R. Ammons: "Ammons has been driven to many kinds of poetic experiments in his effort to make his verse responsive to the engaging but evasive particularity of natural process, and each new book continues this formal invention."

(f) Denise Levertov: " . . . her explicitly political poems are not often among her best however; their very explicitness restricts her distinctive strengths as a poet, which include a feeling for the inexplicable, a language lyrical enough to express wish and desire, and a capacity for playfulness."

(g) Gary Snyder: "Throughout his life Snyder has sought alternatives to a contemporary Western world which, for him, is profoundly out-of-balance."

(h) Sylvia Plath: "Seizing a mythic power, the Plath of the

poems transmutes the domestic and the ordinary into the hallucinatory, the utterly strange."

(i) Michael Harper: "Harper writes poems to remember and to witness, but at times the urgency of the content overpowers his form and his language can't sustain the urgency the poem asserts."

2. Lorine Niedecker and Richard Hugo both wrote poetry about significant landscapes. Compare and contrast the technical or formal features of their attempts to create a spirit of place in their work.

3. Research Charles Olson's theory of poetics; read his manifesto, "Projective Verse," from *Human Universe*. Extend your reading of Olson's poetry beyond the anthologized selections, then test the accuracy of the following statement from the Olson headnote: "Like certain techniques of meditation and yoga, Olson's theory seems an effort to bring mental activity (here writing) in touch with its instinctive physical origins."

4. Many of Elizabeth Bishop's poems concern themselves with loss and exile. Examine the relationship between biography and specific poems in which these themes dominate. Then test the following statement from the Bishop headnote: " . . . her remarkable formal gifts allowed her to create ordered and lucid structures which hold strong feelings in place."

5. Both Robert Hayden and Gwendolyn Brooks wrote sequences of poems based on life in black communities. Compare and contrast Hayden's sequence "Elegies for Paradise Valley" and Brooks's anthologized poems from *A Street in Bronzeville*. How do both poets make use of the technique of collage? What are their technical and thematic differences?

6. Write an essay about contemporary American poetry based on Randall Jarrell's observation, "the gods who had taken away the poet's audience had given him students."

7. The Robert Lowell headnote describes Lowell's poetry as moving between poles: of repetition and revision, of the random event and history, of New England and "elsewhere." Choose one of the anthologized poems and explore the presence of poles or tensions.

8. Almost as if they are poetic "siblings," Denise Levertov, Robert Duncan, and Robert Creeley trace their formative influences to W. C. Williams and H. D. Choosing representative poems by each of these three, related by their choice of literary models, explore "family" influence. You may choose to trace the influence of Williams or H.D.; or you may focus instead on the "sibling" qualities of Levertov, Duncan, and Creeley.

9. Working out from the headnote's comment on Robert Creeley that "he may be the most self-conscious passionate poet we have," focus on several specific poems and explore the tensions in

Creeley between "the self-conscious mind and the instincts of the body."

10. Allen Ginsberg's use of long lines was a deliberate experiment for him, the "long clanky statement" that permits "not the way you would *say* it, a thought, but the way you would think it—i.e., we think rapidly in visual images as well as words, and if each successive thought were transcribed in its confusion . . . you get a slightly different prosody than if you were talking slowly." Read "Howl" and other anthologized poems, paying particular attention to Ginsberg's use of the "long line."

11. Frank O'Hara has written about his work, "The poem is at last between two persons instead of two pages." Explore your own sense of audience and connection with O'Hara's poems; then consider whether his statement also applies to other contemporary American poets.

12. Galway Kinnell and Philip Levine have written of Walt Whitman's influence on their work, as well as their influence on each other. Choosing specific poems as the basis for your commentary, examine thematic and formal connections between Kinnell, Levine, and Whitman.

13. The John Ashbery headnote identifies Ashbery with a group of "Language" poets, Charles Bernstein, Lyn Hejinian, and Michael Palmer. Locate the work of one of these poets and read representative poems, in light of Ashbery's own work. Or trace the claims the headnote makes for Ashbery, that "his poems show an awareness of the various linguistic codes (including clichés and conventional public speech) in which we live and through which we define ourselves."

14. The following quotation from W. S. Merwin, which appears in the headnote, describes the way one of his own prose works in progress brings together "almost all of my interests—interests in nonliterate peoples, in their and our relation to the earth, to the primal sources of things, our relation to the natural world, . . . the destruction of the earth for abstract and greedy reasons." Working with this statement of Merwin's thematic interests, identify their presence in the poems included in the anthology.

15. The headnote on James Wright identifies one of this poet's strengths as "a reliance on the power of a poetic image to evoke association deep within the unconscious." Yet, in many of Wright's poems, he also depicts a real, external landscape. Close-read one of Wright's poems and examine the relationship between internal and external "landscape" in his work.

16. In one of the poetry seminars that Robert Lowell taught at Boston University, both Sylvia Plath and Anne Sexton were students in the class. Imagine that they went out for coffee one night after class, and reconstruct a discussion they might have had. What might they have had to say to each other about their work?

17. More than any other contemporary American poet, Adrienne Rich has located and explicated women's lives and their relationships to each other, to their communities, to history. Her poems also reflect her "understanding of change as the expression of will and desire." Write an essay in which you trace the continuum of women's relationships to each other that appear in Rich's poetry, and in which you also locate the poems along the timeline of composition dates that Rich provides, examining evidence of what she has termed, in an essay by the same title, "When We Dead Awaken: Writing as Re-Vision."

18. Consider the appropriateness of Audre Lorde's own phrase to describe her poetry: "a war against the tyrannies of silence."

19. Locate Simon Ortiz within the Native American tradition of literature, as represented in *NAAL* by Gertrude Simmons Bonnin [Zitkala-Sä], Black Elk, Leslie Marmon Silko, and Louise Erdrich. What themes and forms cross genres for these writers?

20. Explore the themes of Simon Ortiz's poetry: traveling a journey, the power of storytelling, dislocations of Indian identity, exploitation of the American land.

21. Explore the connections Rita Dove draws between individual moments of her personal history and larger historical forces. Compare and contrast her use of black history with that of other anthologized black women poets, Gwendolyn Brooks and Audre Lorde.

22. All three Chicano and Chicana writers included in *NAAL* intermix Spanish phrases and lines in their work. Choose one or more of the three (Alberto Ríos, Lorna Dee Cervantes, and Denise Chávez), and analyze the effects and effectiveness of the inclusion of Spanish in the work.

23. Like other contemporary American women poets— Adrienne Rich and Rita Dove—Cathy Song writes about family ties and ancestors. Explore the power of family in Song' work.

24. Find examples of the use of traditional poetic or metric forms by post-1945 poets and analyze the relationship between form and meaning. Choose, for example, among the following sonnets or near-sonnets: Jarrell, "Well Water"; Brooks, "Kitchenette Building"; or any of Rich's "Twenty-One Love Poems."

25. The following poems all reflect the autobiography of the poet: Elizabeth Bishop, "In the Waiting Room"; Robert Lowell, "My Last Afternoon with Uncle Devereux Winslow"; Allen Ginsberg, "To Aunt Rose"; James Merrill, "The Broken Home"; Frank O'Hara, "In Memory of My Feelings"; and Sylvia Plath, "Lady Lazarus." Choose one of these poems for close analysis, locating it in the context of autobiographical poems by other writers.

26. Poems that are addressed to or are about family members tell us a great deal about differences between contemporary poets,

as well as family relationships in the twentieth century. Explore one of the following groups of poems:

(a) mothers: Gwendolyn Brooks, "The Mother" and Adrienne Rich, "Snapshots of a Daughter-in-Law";

(b) fathers: Theodore Roethke, "My Papa's Waltz"; John Berryman, "Dream Song #384"; James Merrill, "The Broken Home"; James Wright, "Autumn Begins in Martins Ferry, Ohio"; and Sylvia Plath, "Daddy";

(c) sisters: Denise Levertov, from *Olga Poems*; and Cathy Song, "Lost Sister"; and brothers: W. S. Merwin, "To My Brother Hanson."

27. Poems addressed to other contemporary poets, living or dead, tell us a great deal about the poet writing the poem and the poet honored by the dedication. Choose any of the following poems for close analysis, working within the context of the anthologized work by the poet to whom the poem is dedicated or addressed:

(a) Elizabeth Bishop, "The Armadillo," for Robert Lowell;

(b) Robert Lowell, "Skunk Hour," for Elizabeth Bishop;

(c) Anne Sexton, "Sylvia's Death," for Sylvia Plath.

28. Contemporary poets have written about nature in many different ways. Explore some of the variations: does nature become the object of perception and the reason for precision in language? does it serve as the symbolic projection of human emotions and fears? does it provide an alternative world within which the poet can locate a coherent vision? Choose several poems from the following list: Elizabeth Bishop, "The Moose"; James Dickey, "The Heaven of Animals"; Richard Hugo, "The Lady in Kicking Horse Reservoir"; A. R. Ammons, "Corson's Inlet"; James Wright, "A Blessing"; and Sylvia Plath, "Blackberrying."

29. Locate and read statements on poetry by post-1945 poets; then analyze particular poems in light of the poets' statements. Choose, for example, Levertov, "Some Notes on Organic Form," from *Poet in the World*; Baraka, "Expressive Language" and other excerpts from *Home: Social Essays*; Snyder, "Poetry and the Primitive," from *Earth House Hold*; Rich, "When We Dead Awaken," from *On Lies, Secrets, and Silence*.

30. Poets often first publish their poems in small books or collections. Find and read one of the following titles, study the order of poems in the collection, and then analyze the poem included in the *NAAL* within the context of the other poems with which it was originally published. The title of the anthologized poem appears in parentheses.

(a) Elizabeth Bishop, *Geography III* ("In the Waiting Room," "The Moose," or "One Art")

(b) Robert Lowell, *Life Studies* ("Memories of West Street and Lepke")

    (c) Gwendolyn Brooks, *A Street in Bronzeville* ("Kitchenette Building," "A Song in the Front Yard," or "The Vacant Lot")

    (d) James Wright, *The Branch Will Not Break* ("A Blessing")

    (e) Adrienne Rich, *The Dream of a Common Language* ("Twenty-One Love Poems")

31. Read the anthologized poems from one of the following connected poem sequences and describe the intertextual connections within the sequences: Gwendolyn Brooks, *A Street in Bronzeville*; John Berryman, *Dream Songs*; Adrienne Rich, *Twenty-One Love Poems*; and Rita Dove, *Thomas and Beulah*. Or extend your reading to include all of the poems in the Brooks, Rich, or Dove sequences and consider them as a single connected work.

32. What do contemporary poets have to say about some of the traditional themes of poetry—love, death, loss, or the passing of time? Choose to analyze two or three poems from one of the following groups:

    (a) love—Lorine Niedecker, "[Well, Spring Overflows the Land]"; Robert Lowell, "Skunk Hour"; Robert Creeley, "For Love"; Adrienne Rich, from *Twenty-One Love Poems*; Gary Snyder, "Beneath My Hand and Eye the Distant Hills. Your Body"

    (b) death—Randall Jarrell, "The Death of the Ball Turret Gunner"; John Berryman, "Dream Song #384" ("The maker slants, flowerless, day's almost done"); Frank O'Hara, "The Day Lady Died"; W. S. Merwin, "For the Anniversary of My Death"; Anne Sexton, "The Truth the Dead Know" or "Sylvia's Death"; Michael Harper, "Death Watch"

    (c) loss—Theodore Roethke, "The Lost Son"; Elizabeth Bishop, "One Art"; Randall Jarrell, "Thinking of the Lost World"; James Merrill, "Lost in Translation"; W. S. Merwin, "Losing a Language"; Philip Levine, "Animals Are Passing from Our Lives"; Audre Lorde, "Separation"; Cathy Song, "Lost Sister"

    (d) the passing of time—Lorine Niedecker, "[He Lived—Childhood Summers]"; Elizabeth Bishop, "In the Waiting Room"; Robert Hayden, "Middle Passage"; Robert Lowell, "Memories of West Street and Lepke"

II

QUESTIONS AND TOPICS THAT EMERGE FROM EXAMINING LITERARY TRADITIONS

1. In *Of Plymouth Plantation*, William Bradford writes, "But here I cannot but stay and make a pause, and stand half amazed at this poor people's present condition; and so I think will the reader,

too, when he well considers the same." With this quotation in mind, examine *Narrative of the Life of Frederick Douglass.* Look for patterns in the two prose texts: how does each construct an audience? on what terms does each writer convey a sense of beginning, of "new world," both in historical and literary terms? what specific material and ideological circumstances oppress the writers of these texts? In what way does each text establish questions that later writers will address? how do the texts differently deal with the problem of literary authority? what are the didactic purposes of the narratives?

2. Taylor and Bradstreet were contemporary Puritan poets, and yet their poems record radical contrasts in their construction of lyric voice, use of form and imagery, and attention to the Puritan context within which they wrote. Explore these contrasts in specific poems.

3. Bradstreet and Wheatley were the first white and black American women to publish poetry. Examine Wheatley's poems in light of Bradstreet's "The Prologue." Can you find any evidence of conscious encoding in Wheatley's poems? Is she aware, as Bradstreet was, that as a woman or a black her poems might be "obnoxious" to "each carping tongue"? Compare in particular the formal elements of Wheatley's poems with some of Bradstreet's, especially stanzas from "Contemplations," "The Flesh and the Spirit," and "As Weary Pilgrim."

4. Consider the extent of Bradstreet's and Wheatley's acceptance of received theology by examining one of the following pairs of poems: "Contemplations" and "Thoughts on the Works of Providence"; "The Flesh and the Spirit" and "To the University of Cambridge, in New England"; or "As Weary Pilgrim" and "On the Death of the Rev. Mr. George Whitefield, 1770."

5. Polemical writers in each literary tradition use rhetorical language to move their audiences. Choose works from the following writers as the basis for cross-traditional analysis: Edwards, Jefferson, Sojourner Truth (in the NALW), Fuller, Stanton (in the NALW), Washington, and DuBois. In particular, examine Stanton's "The Declaration of Sentiments" (place on reserve) in the context of Jefferson's The Declaration of Independence; consider ideological similarities between Edwards's "Great Revival" thinking in "Sinners in the Hands of an Angry God" and the "Atlanta Compromise" of Washington's "The Atlanta Exposition Address"; or discuss the radicalism (for their contemporaries) of Jefferson, Fuller or Stanton, and DuBois.

6. Show how the lyric poem develops across historical periods in the works of each of the following groups of writers: Taylor, Emerson, and Whitman; Wheatley, Harper (in the *NALW*), Brooks, and Lorde.

7. Demonstrate how concepts of black identity determine

prose forms in works by the following writers: Douglass, Chesnutt, Toomer, and Ellison.

8. The genre of autobiography reveals many differences between writers from separate literary traditions. Examine segments of some of the following autobiographical narratives, choosing figures from each tradition, and outline contrasts in social position and economic class, educational background, audience, or didactic purpose: Edwards, "Personal Narrative," Franklin, *The Autobiography*, or Hawthorne, "The Custom-House"; Harriet Jacobs ("Linda Brent"), from *Incidents in the Life of a Slave Girl* (in the *NALW*) or Hurston, "How It Feels to Be Colored Me"; and Douglass, *Narrative*, or Baldwin, from *The Fire Next Time*.

9. Some writers, while not choosing the genre of autobiography, still include enough autobiographical allusions in their poetry or fiction to tantalize the reader or critic. Consider the use of autobiographical material in literature outside the genre of autobiography from each of the four traditions, perhaps choosing from among the following lists: Taylor, Thoreau, Whitman, Melville, or Lowell; Bradstreet, Dickinson, Gilman, Porter, Levertov, or Rich; Wheatley or Brooks; Hughes or Ellison.

10. In an out-of-class essay, consider points of connection, useful contrasts, or central themes in each of three works that may be considered focal points for black and white male and white female literary traditions: Douglass's *Narrative*, Clemens's *Adventures of Huckleberry Finn*, and Chopin's *The Awakening*. Read one of the following works by a black woman writer and include it in your analysis of works from the *NAAL*: Toni Morrison, *The Bluest Eye* (in the *NALW*) or *Sula*, or Alice Walker, *The Color Purple*.

11. Examine plays by Susan Glaspell (*Trifles*, in the *NALW*) and Baraka (*Dutchman*, to be placed on reserve in the library) in the context of class discussion of O'Neill's *Long Day's Journey into Night*. Or research other black and female playwrights and write an essay on Lillian Hellman (*The Children's Hour* or *Little Foxes*), Lorraine Hansberry (*A Raisin in the Sun*), or August Wilson (*Fences, Joe Turner's Come and Gone*).

12. Choose a pivotal writer in a tradition other than white male. Write an essay in which you compare the perspective a reader achieves in examining a particular text within the context of the writer's literary tradition with the perspective he or she might have in placing the text within the context of the writer's white male contemporaries. Useful writers for this assignment include: Jewett, Cather, Rich, or Welty; Hurston, Brooks, or Walker, and Chesnutt, Hughes, and Wright.

13. Analyze the following four lyric poems, one from each literary tradition: Frost, "The Gift Outright"; Brooks, "Kitchenette Building"; Hughes, "Dream Variations"; and Rich, from "Twenty-

One Love Poems." Focus on the disparate voices and perspectives the poems reveal.

14. Examine cross-gender characters. Choose to compare a male protagonist created by a women writer, such as Rosicky in Cather's "Neighbour Rosicky" or Mr. Shiftlet in O'Connor's "The Life You Save May Be Your Own," with a female protagonist in a male writer's fiction—such as Hawthorne's Beatrice Rappaccini, James's Daisy Miller, or O'Neill's Mary Tyrone.

15. Compare black characters created by white writers with black characters created by black writers, in pairings such as Melville's Babo and the autobiographical persona in Douglass's *Narrative*; Stowe's Eliza and "Linda Brent" in *Incidents in the Life of a Slave Girl* (in the *NALW*); Clemens's Jim and Chesnutt's Uncle Julius.

16. Compare women characters created by male writers, such as Irving's Dame Van Winkle, Hawthorne's Hester Prynne, James's Daisy Miller or May Bartram, O'Neill's Mary Tyrone, Toomer's Fern, Faulkner's Addie Bundren or Dewey Dell, or Williams's Blanche DuBois, with women characters created by female writers, such as Stowe's Eliza, Jewett's Sylvy ("A White Heron"), the narrator of Gilman's "The Yellow Wallpaper," Edna Pontellier in Chopin's *The Awakening*, Porter's Miranda, or Walker's Mama ("Everyday Use").

17. Read works by writers outside the list of major authors in the four major traditions that illuminate questions of cross-gender or cross-racial interest or that increase our understanding of the development of literary traditions, and explain how and why they are significant. Choose from the following list: Mary Rowlandson, *A Narrative of the Captivity and Restoration* (to examine a white woman's view of Indian men); Edgar Allan Poe, poems and stories about women; Rebecca Harding Davis, "Life in the Iron-Mills" (to raise issues of class and working conditions in pre–Civil War industrialism); W. D. Howells, "Editha" (to examine another realist's portrait of a woman character); Joel Chandler Harris (for a white man's transcription of black folk life); Henry Adams, "The Dynamo and the Virgin" from *The Education* (for a white male writer's sense of woman as a source of symbolism); Sherwood Anderson, "Mother" from *Winesburg, Ohio* (to compare a woman character by a writer who deeply influenced Faulkner with one of Faulkner's own female characters); William Carlos Williams's "Portrait of a Lady" (a poem that raises questions of literary convention); H. D.'s "Leda" or "Helen" (a woman poet's sense of woman as a source of mythology); Dorothy Parker, sketches (for an example of humor in the white women's tradition); Thomas Wolfe, "The Lost Boy" (another example of a writer using autobiographical material in a genre other than autobiography); Hart Crane, "At Melville's Tomb," John Berryman, "Homage to Mistress Bradstreet," Allen Ginsberg, "On Burroughs'

Work," Anne Sexton, "Sylvia's Death" (for questions of literary influence).

18. Examine the southern tradition as represented in the *NAAL*. Focus in particular on those writers who do not figure as major authors in any literary tradition, such as Smith, Byrd, Longstreet, Thorpe, Harris, Glasgow, Wolfe, Warren, or Dickey. What generic or thematic concerns link some of these writers? Can you describe the development of southern literature in a chronological reading of the representative figures in the *NAAL*? In examining writers from the four major traditions, to what extent are their works informed by southern history or identity? Consider minority writers in the context of their chronological contemporaries. Are Douglass, Hurston, or Wright anomalous in their respective literary periods when we consider them as southern, rather than as black or women writers? Consider writers in different genres, such as Byrd and Jefferson; Poe and Douglass; Faulkner or Wolfe; Dickey or Warren and Welty or Walker. Are these writers so diverse in form and theme that their southern ties become negligible, or does that southern heritage link them significantly, in spite of their differences?

19. Define a literary tradition on your own according to genre or theme. Defend your list of writers and works, and choose for class analysis a particular work that both represents your larger list and illustrates its central concerns. (Some possibilities include the writers interested in protest, populist, or activist themes—Gilman, Ginsberg, Kerouac, and possibly Mailer; or women who wrote works with feminist themes or characters, such as Bradstreet, Fuller, Stowe, Stoddard, Dickinson, Davis, Jewett, Chopin, Freeman, Gilman, Wharton, Cather, Stein, H. D., Porter, Parker, Hurston, Welty, Walker, Sexton, Rich, and Plath—you may break down this list into feminist writers by century, or by genre, or by region; writers interested in animals; lesbian and gay writers or writers interested in lesbian or gay themes.)

20. Study the Jewish writers represented in the *NAAL*—Odets, Malamud, Miller, Bellow, Roth, Ginsberg—and the *NALW*—Yezierska, Rukeyser, Olden, and Paley. Choose a representative text for close analysis and view it either within the context of other works in the tradition, with works by the writer's contemporaries from a variety of traditions, or paired with a significant work from another tradition.

21. Study the relationship between marginality and vision or social stigma and literary authority in works by white male writers.

(a) The colonial period appears to be unique in American literature, in that it did not produce white male writers who considered themselves marginal (with the exception of Roger Williams and John Woolman, who were not part of the Puritan community). Speculate concerning some of the reasons why this is the case. Might the absence of men who wrote against the established ideology have somehow made it easier for Anne Bradstreet to write at all? (None of her contemporaries chose to establish themselves as marginal, perhaps leaving the possibility open to a woman; and in Puritan culture, where marginality might lead a man to predict his own damnation, a woman—a flawed version of an already flawed creation—might have less to lose by embracing marginality.)

(b) Many white male writers in the early nineteenth century wrote as if they were marginal. Choose representative texts (by Irving, Hawthorne, Thoreau, Whitman, or Melville) and consider what the marginal characters in these fictions have to say about the relationship between white male authors and marginality.

(c) Examine Clemens's Huck Finn or James's John Marcher ("The Beast in the Jungle") as representative of lonely, isolated, and marginalized characters.

(d) Twentieth-century white male authors frequently explore the theme of social difference. Some created their most powerful fictions based on this theme. Examine the theme in Anderson, Jeffers, O'Neill, Faulkner, Bellow, or Williams, and speculate on the white male writer's fascination with marginality.

APPENDIX: "THE DECLARATION OF SENTIMENTS"

SENECA FALLS WOMAN'S RIGHTS CONVENTION,

JULY 19–20, 1848

In July 1848, Elizabeth Cady Stanton and Lucretia Mott gathered together a group of women to plan the first women's rights convention to be held in Seneca Falls, New York. They modeled their agenda on antislavery and temperance conventions, and Stanton modeled her draft of "The Declaration of Sentiments" on the 1776 *The Declaration of Independence*. After discussion and amendments, the document received a hundred signatures from both women and men. Following the convention, the proceedings were ridiculed by clergy and in the press, and many of the women who had signed the declaration subsequently removed their names and their influence. In her autobiography, *Eighty Years and More* (1898), Stanton wrote, "If I had had the slightest premonition of all that was to follow that convention, I fear I should not have had the courage to risk it . . . " "The Declaration of Sentiments" initiated Stanton's writing career on behalf of women's lives and women's rights, a career that would extend until her death in 1902.

—M.P.

DECLARATION OF SENTIMENTS

When, in the course of human events, it becomes necessary for one portion of the family of man to assume among the people of the earth a position different from that which they have hitherto occupied, but one to which the laws of nature and of nature's God entitle them, a decent respect to the opinions of mankind requires that they should declare the causes that impel them to such a course.

We hold these truths to be self-evident: that all men and women are created equal; that they are endowed by their Creator with certain inalienable rights; that among these are life, liberty, and the pursuit of happiness; that to secure these rights governments are instituted, deriving their just powers from the consent of the governed. Whenever any form of government becomes destructive of these ends, it is the right of those who suffer from it to refuse allegiance to it, and to insist upon the institution of a new government, laying its foundation on such principles, and organizing its powers in such form, as to them shall seem most likely to effect their safety and happiness. Prudence, indeed, will dictate that governments long established should not be changed for light and transient causes; and accordingly all experience hath shown that mankind are more disposed to suffer, while evils are sufferable, than to right themselves by abolishing the forms to which they were accustomed. But when a long train of abuses and usurpations, pursuing invariably the same object, evinces a design to reduce them under absolute despotism, it is their duty to throw off such government, and to provide new guards for their future security. Such has been the patient sufferance of the women under this government, and such is now the necessity which constrains them to demand the equal station to which they are entitled.

The history of mankind is a history of repeated injuries and usurpations on the part of man toward woman, having in direct object the establishment of an absolute tyranny over her. To prove this, let facts be submitted to a candid world.

He has never permitted her to exercise her inalienable right to the elective franchise.

He has compelled her to submit to laws, in the formation of which she had no voice.

He has withheld from her rights which are given to the most ignorant and degraded men—both natives and foreigners.

Having deprived her of this first right of a citizen, the elective franchise, thereby leaving her without representation in the halls of legislation, he has oppressed her on all sides.

He has made her, if married, in the eye of the law, civilly dead.

He has taken from her all right in property, even to the wages she earns.

He has made her, morally, an irresponsible being, as she can commit many crimes with impunity, provided they be done in the presence of her husband. In the covenant of marriage, she is compelled to promise obedience to her husband, he becoming, to all intents and purposes, her master—the law giving him power to deprive her of her liberty, and to administer chastisement.

He has so framed the laws of divorce, as to what shall be the proper causes, and in case of separation, to whom the guardianship of the children shall be given, as to be wholly regardless of the happiness of women—the law, in all cases, going upon the false supposition of the supremacy of man, and giving all power into his hands.

After depriving her of all rights as a married woman, if single, and the owner of property, he has taxed her to support a government which recognizes her only when her property can be made profitable to it.

He has monopolized nearly all the profitable employments and from those she is permitted to follow, she receives but a scanty remuneration. He closes against her all the avenues to wealth and distinction which he considers most honorable to himself. As a teacher of theology, medicine, or law, she is not known.

He has denied her the facilities for obtaining a thorough education, all colleges being closed against her.

He allows her in Church, as well as State, but a subordinate position, claiming Apostolic authority for her exclusion from the ministry, and, with some exceptions, from any public participation in the affairs of the Church.

He has created a false public sentiment by giving to the world a different code of morals for men and women, by which moral delinquencies which exclude women from society, are not only tolerated, but deemed of little account in man.

He has usurped the prerogative of Jehovah himself, claiming it as his right to assign for her a sphere of action, when that belongs to her conscience and to her God.

He has endeavored, in every way that he could, to destroy her confidence in her own powers, to lessen her self-respect, and to make her willing to lead a dependent and abject life.

Now, in view of this entire disfranchisement of one-half the people of this country, their social and religious degradation—in view of the unjust laws above mentioned, and because women do feel themselves aggrieved, oppressed, and fraudulently deprived of their most sacred rights, we insist that they have immediate admission to all the rights and privileges which belong to them as citizens of the United States.

In entering upon the great work before us, we anticipate no small amount of misconception, misrepresentation, and ridicule; but we shall use every instrumentality within our power to effect our object. We shall employ agents, circulate tracts, petition the State and National legislatures, and endeavor to enlist the pulpit and the press in our behalf. We hope this Convention will be followed by a series of Conventions embracing every part of the country.

Resolutions: Whereas, The great precept of nature is conceded to be, that "man shall pursue his own true and substantial happiness." Blackstone in his Commentaries remarks, that this law of Nature being coeval with mankind, and dictated by God himself, is of course superior in obligation to any other. It is binding over all the globe, in all countries and at all times; no human laws are of any validity if contrary to this, and such of them as are valid, derive all their force, and all their validity, and all their authority, mediately and immediately, from this original; therefore,

Resolved, That such laws as conflict, in any way, with the true and substantial happiness of woman, are contrary to the great precept of nature and of no validity, for this is "superior in obligation to any other."

Resolved, That all laws which prevent woman from occupying such a state in society as her conscience shall dictate, or which place her in a position inferior to that of man, are contrary to the great precept of nature, and therefore of no force or authority.

Resolved, That woman is man's equal—was intended to be so by the Creator, and the highest good of the race demands that she should be recognized as such.

Resolved, That the women of this country ought to be enlightened in regard to the laws under which they live, that they may no longer publish their degradation by declaring themselves satisfied with their present position, nor their ignorance, by asserting that they have all the rights they want.

Resolved, That inasmuch as man, while claiming for himself intellectual superiority, does accord to woman moral superiority, it is pre-eminently his duty to encourage her to speak and teach, as she has an opportunity, in all religious assemblies.

Resolved, That the same amount of virtue, delicacy, and refinement of behavior that is required of woman in the social state, should also be required of man, and the same transgressions should be visited with equal severity on both man and woman.

Resolved, That the objection of indelicacy and impropriety, which is so often brought against woman when she addresses a public audience, comes with a very ill-grace from those who encourage, by their attendance, her appearance on the stage, in the concert, or in feats of the circus.

Resolved, That woman has too long rested satisfied in the circumscribed limits which corrupt customs and a perverted application of the Scriptures have marked out for her, and that it is time she should move in the enlarged sphere which her great Creator has assigned her.

Resolved, That it is the duty of the women of this country to secure to themselves their sacred right to the elective franchise.

Resolved, That the equality of human rights results necessarily from the fact of the identity of the race in capabilities and responsibilities.

Resolved, therefore, That, being invested by the Creator with the same capabilities, and the same consciousness of responsibility for their exercise, it is demonstrably the right and duty of woman, equally with man, to promote every righteous cause by every righteous means; and especially in regard to the great subjects of morals and religion, it is self-evidently her right to participate with her brother in teaching them, both in private and in public, by writing and by speaking, by any instrumentalities proper to be used, and in any assemblies proper to be held; and this being a self-evident truth growing out of the divinely implanted principles of human nature, any custom or authority adverse to it, whether modern or wearing the hoary sanction of antiquity, is to be regarded as a self-evident falsehood, and at war with mankind.

Resolved, That the speedy success of our cause depends upon the zealous and untiring efforts of both men and women, for the overthrow of the monopoly of the pulpit, and for the securing to woman an equal participation with men in the various trades, professions, and commerce.